Developing exhibitions

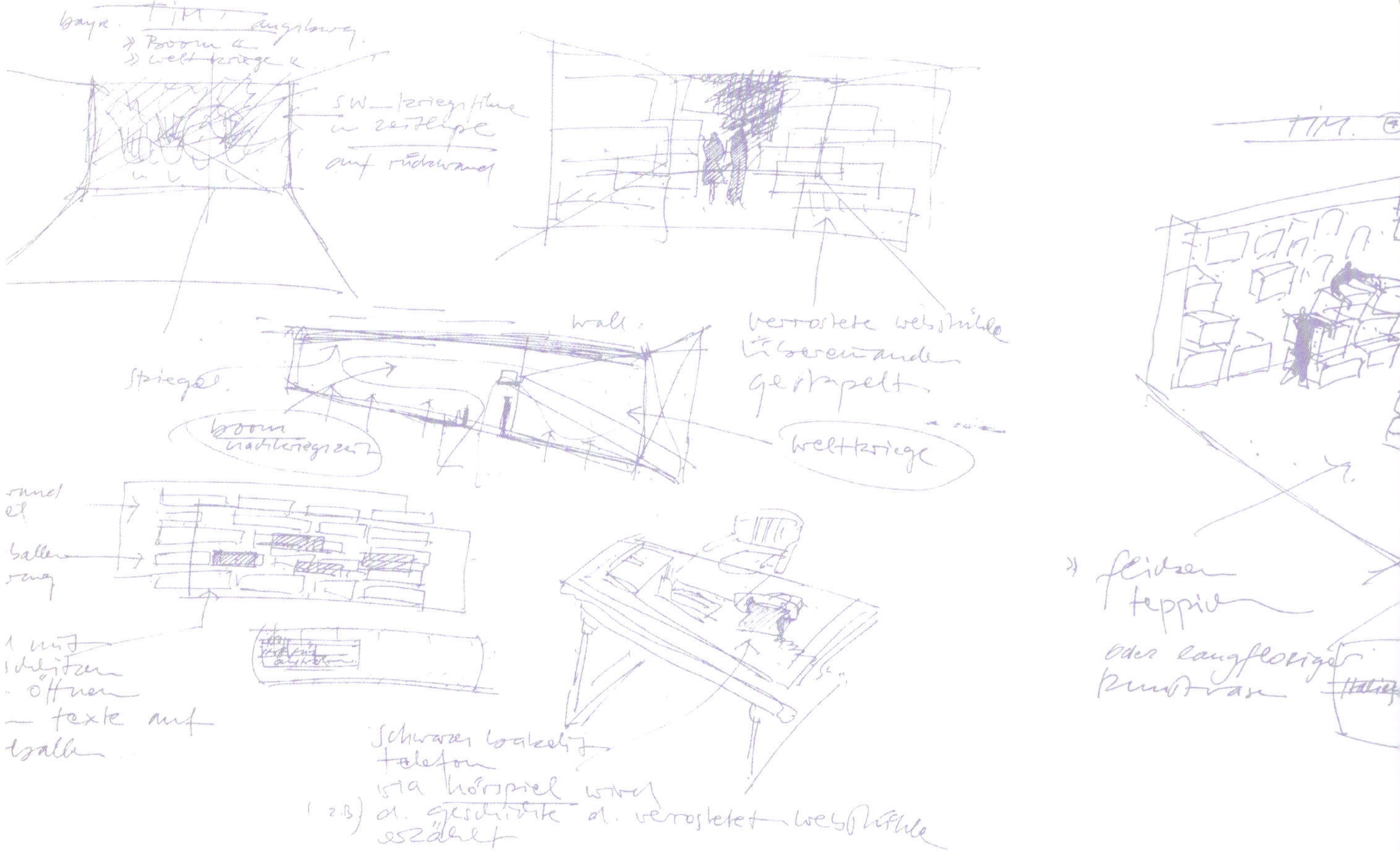

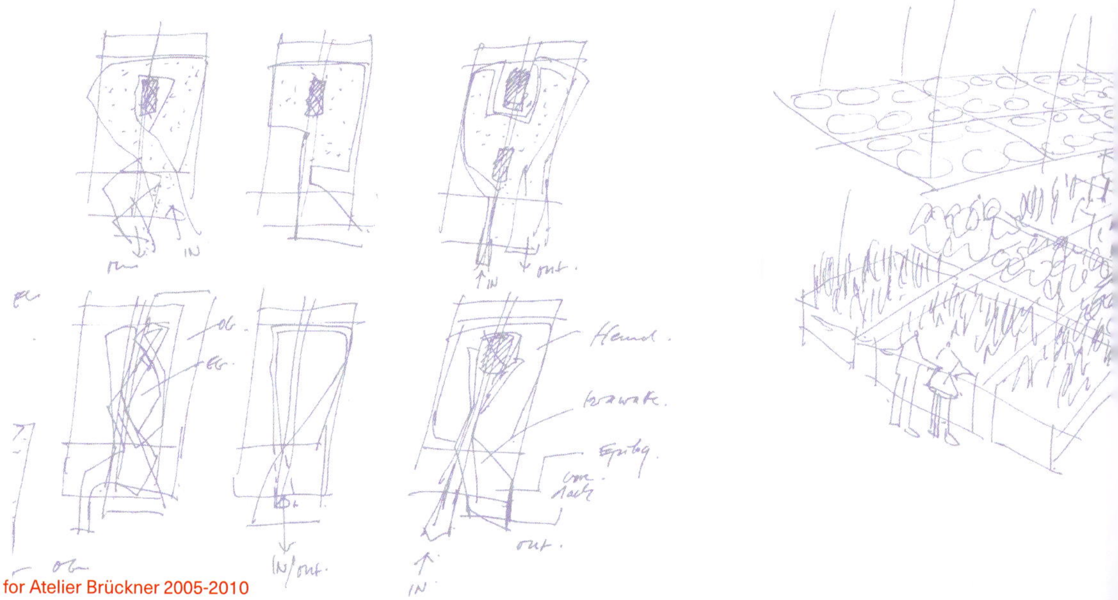

Developing exhibitions

There is a method in this madness

Dirk Houtgraaf

Massimo Negri

European Museum Academy

Contents

Section 3 Some process elements in more detail 103

Appendix

Addendum

1. There is a method in this madness

1.1. The scope of this publication and its audience

Why on earth would you want to make an exhibition?

Developing exhibitions, and to actually build and exploit them, requires a kind of madness. For one thing, there is no doubt that an exhibition is one of the most complicated media to get a story across. When finished and open for visitors, the participating audience wanders freely around, without even bothering to read your storyline. Then secondly, it is an expensive medium. To develop and build a storyline in three dimensions, with the diversity of media and expertise involved, is a stressful, intense and costly process. And thirdly, you hardly can call it a modern medium. Its essence might not have changed in a hundred years. In addition, they are strongly linked with museums, an institution which hardly can be seen as a forerunner in modern times.

However, exhibitions are still very popular and do attract even growing audiences. It is clear some aspects of museums have proved to be very competitive as attractions. Also, department stores, hotels, restaurants, airports and other locations are increasingly adopting the language of exhibitions and sceneries as a tool for involving their audience.
The real, the physical and the authentic might be the (a) explanation, the key to the success of museums. Experiencing 'the real thing'. That is at least what we, the authors, think and what we hope for.
An interesting sideline: the growing popularity of events, festivals, events and festivals and the like fits into the thinking that experiencing and the authentic are more and more important. We do believe so, even after the pandemic COVID-19 lock-down we all experienced.

A methodology for building these successful but complicated storytelling constructs

You would expect a full-grown, proven and tested methodology ready with so many exhibitions a year during the long years of museums. This is not the case, however. Yes, there are some descriptive, basic methodologies in some books or website[1] and some good guidelines too. But there seems hardly anything in-depth on the planning process, in such a way that a developer can immediately use it. Copy-paste ready so to say. And easy.

An easy-to-use, ready-made methodology would save time, energy and money, as there is no easy-to-use methodology yet. Many of us do re-invent it during the development process, which is a waste of time. Moreover, there often is too much ambiguity in the process, as each and every new exhibition development frequently starts with a new aggregation of people, with different experiences and different ways of doing things. Frustrating complications therefore are almost innate in the process.

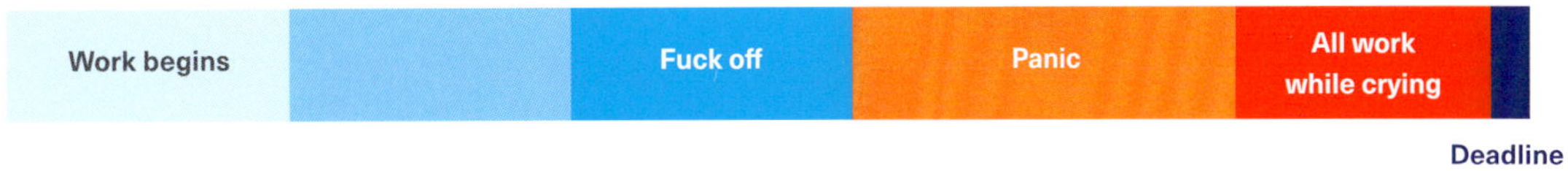

Process of exhibition development as it is perceived too often. By courtesy of the Astra Museum

The European Museum Academy therefore thinks it wise to deliver an extensive methodology, a roadmap, based on the expertise earlier described in books, articles, the expertise of its members and its museological courses. This EMA methodology is a detailed descriptive structuring on how the institution might best organize or structure its overall knowledge, its resources, and several key aspects of the planning process.

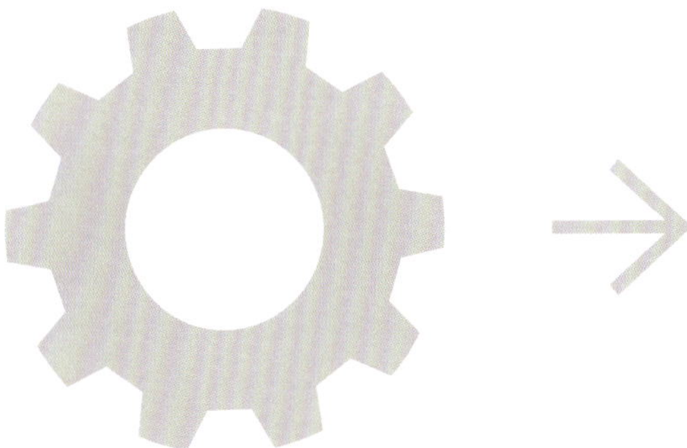

The process of developing an exhibition is a fine-tuned teamwork work process.

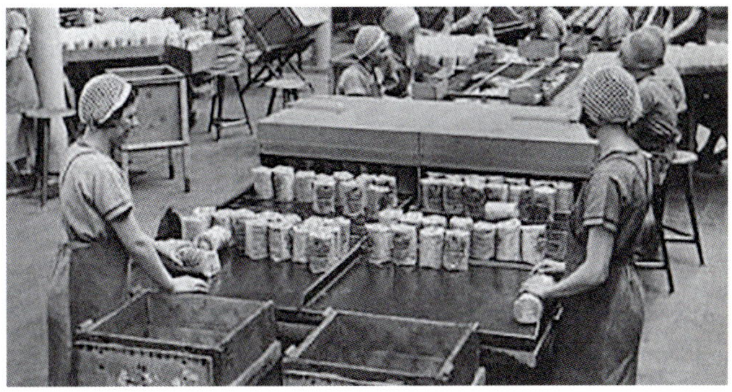

Verkade factory, 1931. Collection Zaans Museum

Mainly focused on getting it done, i.e. the operational side

Museums might have an aura of 'high culture', even a kind of 'holiness'. The production of exhibitions however is a very earthly business. Our mindset – that is: in this book - is not unlike a factory. We discuss the methodology in producing an exhibition with the input of collections, content expertise, design skills, visitor psychology and so on.

We have a focus on the producing side, on the processes, and on the development of content and storylines. This means we skip most of the subjects you'll find in other museum books. We do not go into success factors with audiences. We do not reflect on collections, on the essence of museums, and such. Our focus is on what to do in what order and how to manage the processes.

However, as we are deeply engaged with the museum, it will be impossible to be consistent all the time.

The methodology has a much broader applicability

Writing a book or a set of brochures, developing stories in zoos, developing an online exhibition, designing a store: any product with a strong content and storyline component can benefit from the methodology described. We know it does, although we wil pay no attention to it. But if you read descriptions of toolsets, keep a wider use in mind.

In addition, we would argue to use a little more space to talk about the content outline and the storyline than you might understand from this book. Somehow that is where it all starts and also at the end the central element of the presentation or exhibition. The content and storyline are important for the choice of medium.

1.2. For whom

This book is primarily for museum professionals developing an exhibition. A physical one, in space. Simple as that. It is not bedside literature. It is a manual, with schemes, and systems should be spelled out to everyone. It is meant to set the process straight, right at the start. We would like to have it upon the table, with personal notes, marked passages and coffee stains. A book well used during the day. Some figures enlarged and filled, hanging on the wall. As some tools are easily printable and copied, we will have printable parts on the internet too. The book has, of course, a wider use too. We know it will be useful for trainers and (university) teachers who are in need of a complete toolset.

Established museum practice

This process we describe, in general, is established museum practice. We are not pretending to have invented a new methodology. What is new, however, in the descriptions to follow, is the detailed structuring and strict sequence of phases. What is new too, is the inclusion of dedicated tools within each of these stages.

1.3. Sections in this book and reading priority

This book in essence is on the methodology for developing and producing an exhibition – and takes into account what steps need to be taken, delivers some tools and gives ideas on how to organize the people and teams. This will be the major part of the book – section 1, 2 and 3. Section 1 discusses the building blocks and the general outline, while section 2 addresses specifically the team and how to deal with expectations.
Section 3 discusses some of the phases and ideas in more detail.

Section 4 is an addendum, aimed to help choosing your topics way ahead in a multi-annual plan. We include this part as you have to make choices before actually starting. Which topics? How do they fit within the multi-annual planning and the list of activities?

Section 5 is on the European Museum Academy and the authors and supporters of this book. Then, there is an appendix describing the storyline development in a series of sites: the Limes..

Do read section 1

For many, section 1 will be a good enough read. At least as a start, that is. Especially when you are part of a small museum, with few staff, you might concentrate on the basics. Then you could take your pick of the topics discussed in chapter 3. We think especially the content and storyline development – not an easy read though - will be of value.

1.4. Visuals first

We started compiling the book the traditional way by explaining the ideas and tools in words, ending each part and chapter with the accompanying visuals, schemas, building blocks. The tools annex building blocks were in a way embedded in explanations. We re-arranged, however. Given our aim for a reference work, we did put the tooling, the visuals, upfront, followed by the explanations. Thus, there is no slow introduction, perhaps making it less a readable, but more concise, direct, to the point. At least that is what we hope. And, it was not meant to be a bedtime lecture anyway.

2. The methodology introduced

Museums are commentators. Storytellers. They reflect on society, its history and its 'Umwelt'. Their essential 'language' is primarily visual and organized in what is called exhibitions, a three-dimensional story with objects, with their individual settings and overall scenography; moving and still images; labels and text panels; media presentations; and so on. All these elements, and their overall effect, are vital visual components. They come together in a gallery space to engage visitors in a particular story, a concept, or extended information on a particular subject. The space might be more or less focused on transmitting content or on an unforgettable experience. The audience however almost never follows a strictly prescribed path. It 'reads' the narrative by walking and wandering through the space, picking up the clues as they come along.

Organizing the visual and spatial language

The challenge, then, is to get the museum's message or intentions across, to translate them into a visual and spatial language that will engage the audience and communicate effectively. To translate its knowledge and resources into a display, a museum will usually follow a plan, which may be highly developed or more informal. In all likelihood, a team composed of museum professionals from inside and outside the institution will be involved, along with certain work protocols or procedures. That process, and the intended message to be shared with the museums audience, will ultimately reflect the museums core body of information and holdings, and how it is organized, as well as how other critical components of the planning process, such as installation design and teamwork, have been realized.

But before: (re)positioning, setting your key parameters, and picking your choice

In the end it is the result that counts. But what is it that counts? What should you regard as convening results? What actually is it that the museum wants to establish? What does the museum want to be or to become? For which audiences?
A word of reassurance. You probably know the answers. It will be a great help though if they are written down – 'on the table' – as an acknowledged guide in decision-making processes.

2.1. On the exhibition process methodology itself

The major part of the book – its core – is the methodology itself. It describes the process of developing a (physical) exhibition. There are three different groupings of toolsets.

Phasing: the process scheme itself and its (sub)divisions

As has already been said, this book is about making the most of exhibition planning by mastering essential parts of the process. It focuses on certain critical factors in the process of conceiving, defining, organizing, and realizing long- or short-term installations. The process is divided into many modular units, phases and subphases, each with its own deliveries, and consequently delivering to the next units. Each (sub)phase is described and shown in its context.

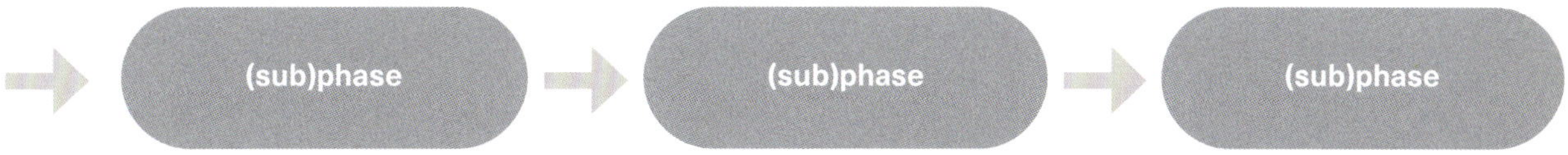

There is essentially no difference in developing a temporary exhibition or a permanent one. There is a difference of scale and 'lasting quality', but the process steps do work for both.

Additional structuring tools

It is maddening how many things need to be done. Structuring content, text writing, keeping finances, and so on. There are however methods to help actually doing it. These additional structuring methods 'fit' into the general process scheme. They are additional tools, of which we propose some.

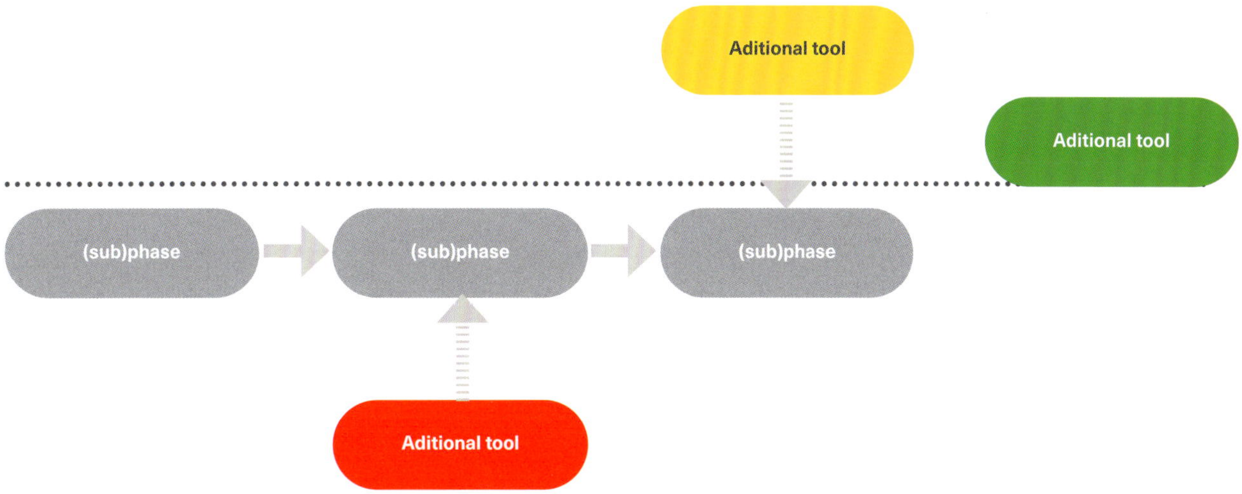

Some of these methods will be discussed at the relevant phase. Others, which are more generic to the process, do have their own chapter.

Organizing people and teams

Developing an exhibition is a team effort, with many expertises and crafts involved. Which ones? How to organize them along the road? Which cooperative teams are to be organized and which line of command is needed? We do have some guidelines you could use. And they are needed as not all your stakeholders or team members have the same familiarity with the museum world and the creation of an exhibition. It is consequently vital you share a common language. Even basic terms might have different connotations. And you certainly need to share the tasks, roles and responsibilities in a very clear and commonly understood way.

2.2. Not one single truth

Of course, there is no single one 'true' methodology. There are more ways to do the job, as is proven each year in many thousands of cases. As board members of the European Museum Academy we are very aware of this. We are also aware there are strong national and cultural 'flavours' in how we do things. However, we do believe this general structure is an excellent tool, and one which can easily 'adopt' the additional structuring methods and team-organizational ideas we propose or the alternative ones which are preferred by a museum. So, our methodology is very strict and structured, but also very open to include your own loved ways of doing things within the general grid.

2.3. Expectations translated into a list of relevant parameters

The process of developing is one thing. But it is up to the exhibition to deliver results. What are these results? To have all implicit and explicit expectations clear, it would be wise to have a list of parameters set beforehand. A warning though. This could easily turn into a less realistic wishlist. Therefore it would be helpful to stick to the really important matters. Also, you have to monitor the parameters you really care for.

There might be some obvious parameters, such as the visitor review, the average or median time spent, the attracting power, i.e. the amount of visitors attending and in congruence the public relations attractiveness. And as the judgement of competitors, collegues and experts is often valued, you could take this into account too.

Naturally it is wise to identify your key audiences and describe them in recognizable parameters and possibly as real-life type of persons (personas). The difficulty is to do it in such a way that it can actually be identified, measured, classified. Any divisions of your audience in target groups which cannot be identified and targeted is useless.

More business-based parameters would be the budget use (did it stay within budget, is 5 to 10 % saved for alterations and repairs), the time pressure (easy done or fairly stressed), or the cost-benefit ratio. The ratio of sponsoring involved might be another one.

Then there are the more strategic perspectives, often harder to put into concrete numbers. Did it strenghten the strategic positioning and reputation of the museum? Does it 'fit' with what the museum stands for? Is the museum's current positioning – its reputation and position with civil groups, funding agencies and so on – as it should be? Should there be a repositioned mission and strategic perspective?
For measuring the more strategic perspectives, you might need to go into visitor reviews, whether quantitative (surveys) or qualitative (focus groups).

Parameters	Minimum	Satisfied	Great
Amount of visitors			
Score given / target group	7.4	7.8	8.1
....			
Cost-benefit (financial)		Break-even	
.... etcetera			

2.4. Timeslots in a multi-year planning

What exhibitions are there to be developed? How many, parallel, in what sequence? When?

We strongly propose an 'empty' multi-year planning, including all holidays, school seasonality special days and so forth, before choosing the topics of the forthcoming exhibitions. The topics then can be 'fitted in'. Every museum has – or should have – a scheduled overview ready for the forthcoming 2-3 years. A multi-year planning like this would serve as a rolling 'forecast' on what to develop and when. It would take temporary exhibitions and events as well.

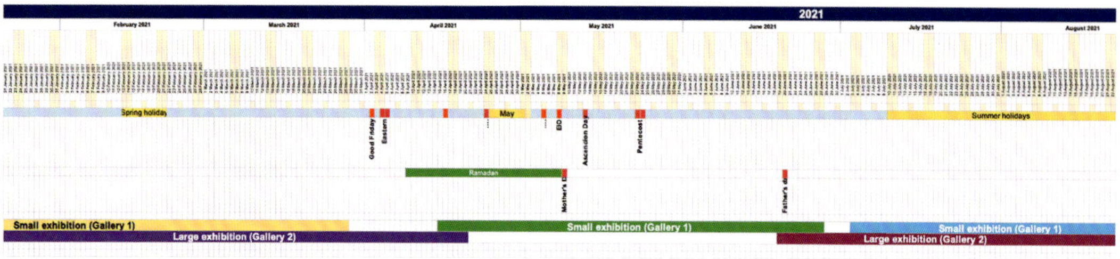

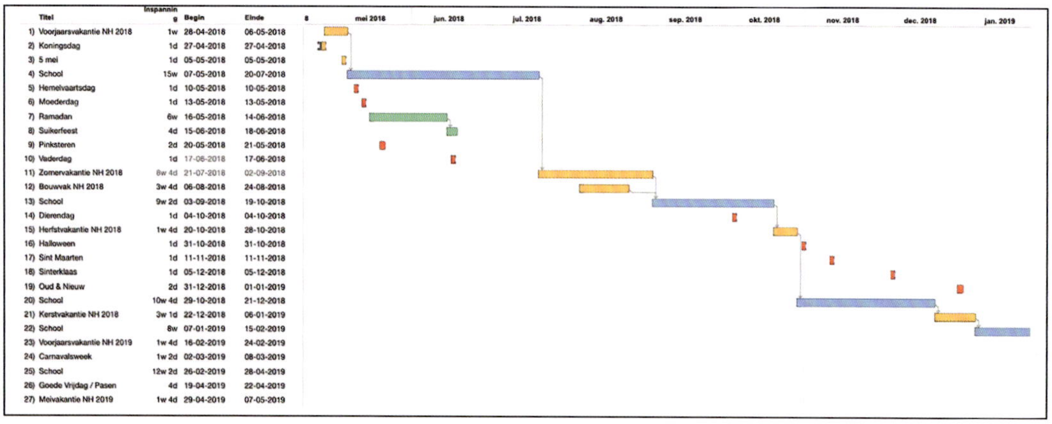

2.5. Choosing the exhibition topics / themes

Choosing exhibition themes, with an attractive core-story and appropriate title, is key. It is a branding process, a key strategic issue for your museum. It often is a very subjective process as well.

We have some tooling which might help in 'objectifying' it by asking different stakeholders in and outside the museum to score the different proposals on for example its attractiveness, its 'fit' with the museum and its potential costs.

The result should then be visualized in a positioning matrix, as is explained in the section on planning ahead.

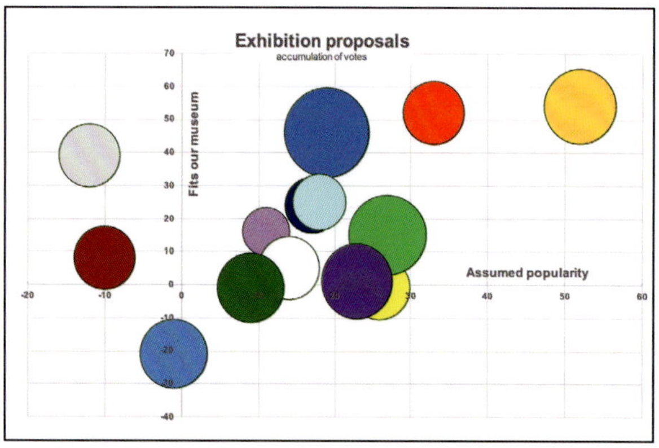

Main Gallery - proposals	Accumulated points: Assumed popularity	Accumulated points: Fits our museum	Estimated material costs	Sponsoring & funding changes
Proposal 1	52	54	€ 350.000	18
Proposal 2	19	46	€ 500.000	21
Proposal 3	17	24	€ 200.000	1
Proposal 4	11	16	€ 150.000	1
Proposal 5	26	-1	€ 250.000	6
Proposal 6	33	52	€ 250.000	-6
Proposal 7	-12	39	€ 250.000	-14
Proposal 8	27	15	€ 400.000	-2
Proposal 9	14	5	€ 250.000	8
Proposal 10	-10	8	€ 250.000	5
Proposal 11	9	-1	€ 300.000	16
Proposal 12	23	1	€ 350.000	15
Proposal 13	-1	-21	€ 300.000	27
Proposal 14	18	25	€ 200.000	4

3. In the context of a functional plan

A museum is more than an agglomerate of exhibitions of course. Many functions have to fit in. In recent years the accent of museums has been moving to 'visitors first' - with a critical social role in the public debate and an emphasis on entrepreneurial thinking. It thus becomes crucial to answer the following question: what are the activities that you and your financiers consider essential to fulfil the goals considered most important?

If one has a look at the plan of newly established museums, it can be clearly perceived that there is a progressive enlargement of the space devoted to the 'other spaces', such as the entrance, 'front desk' services, commercial spaces (shop, café), meeting rooms, library, auditorium, rooms for classes, etc.

When there is a functional plan ready and established – as in most museums – this paragraph can be ignored. However, when the exhibition development is part of a major transition or of a new museum, you might give some attention to a functional plan ready before starting the exhibition developments.

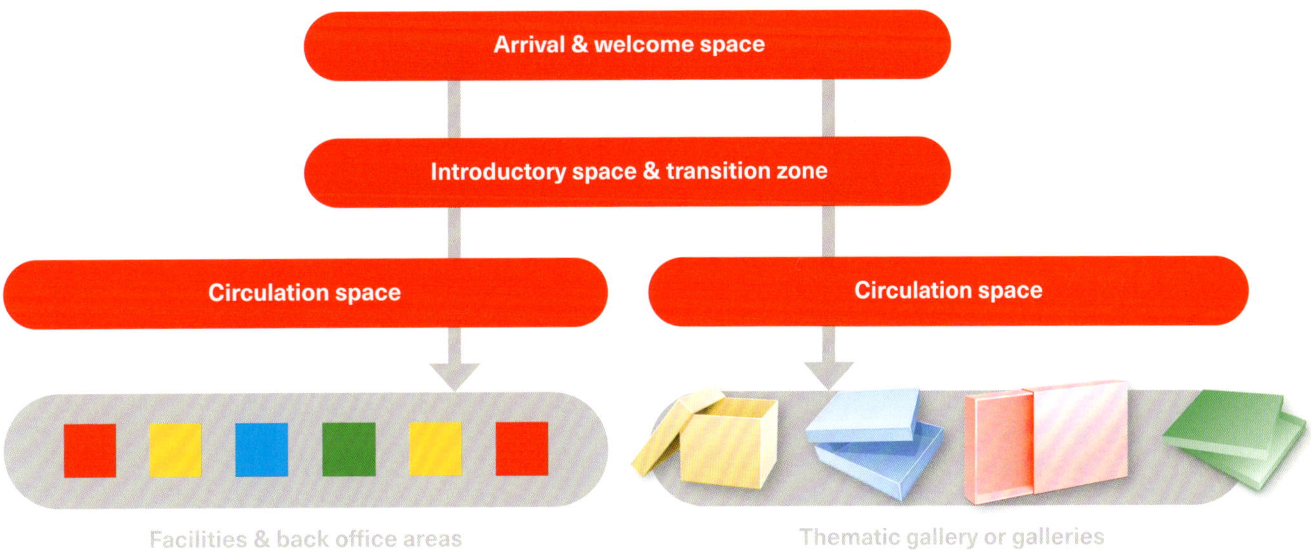

3.1. Museum functions

This trend towards a more prominent role and a rethinking of its business model reflects a new look at the functions to be housed in a museum. It is thus necessary to have a detailed description of the functions which are vital and indispensable and their hierarchy in the whole context of the project.

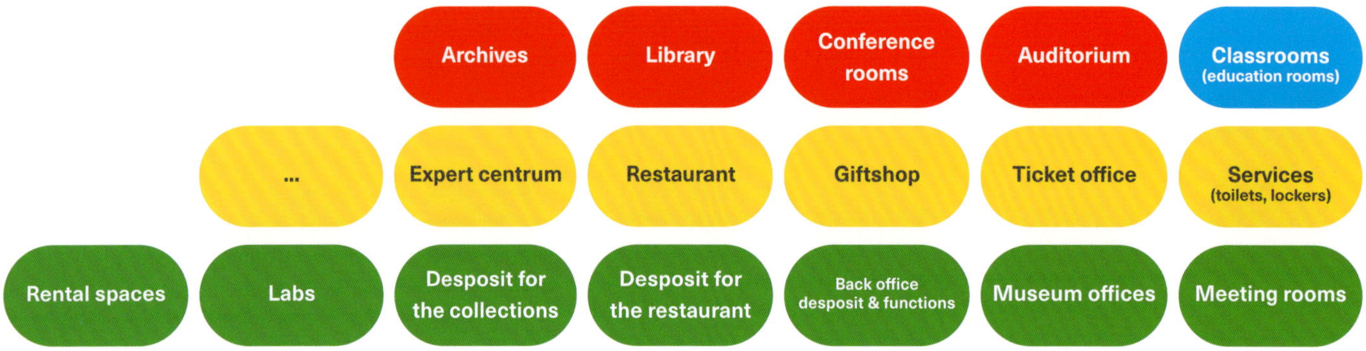

Much can be said about a museum and its functions and functioning, but we confine ourselves to a functional plan. On the basis of the priorities there is a possible list including spaces for meeting and socializing for each category of users, including a children's museum for families and a space of narrative and memory for the third and fourth ages. There will be entertainment and recreation: restaurant, café, outdoor relaxation spaces, shopping and suchlike. There might be offices for co-workers and sometimes 'fluid spaces' for students and young people engaged in creative projects and new forms of cultural entrepreneurships. There might be residence areas for researchers, artists, or visitors selected on the basis of agreements with cultural and voluntary associations, universities, research and study centres, and spaces available for future project developments not yet foreseeable.

Of course, there is a minimal need, such as an entrance, permanent exhibition and galleries for temporary exhibitions, a conference hall, laboratories for restoration, formal learning spaces as classrooms for training at different levels, an archive, staff and collection management functions and such.

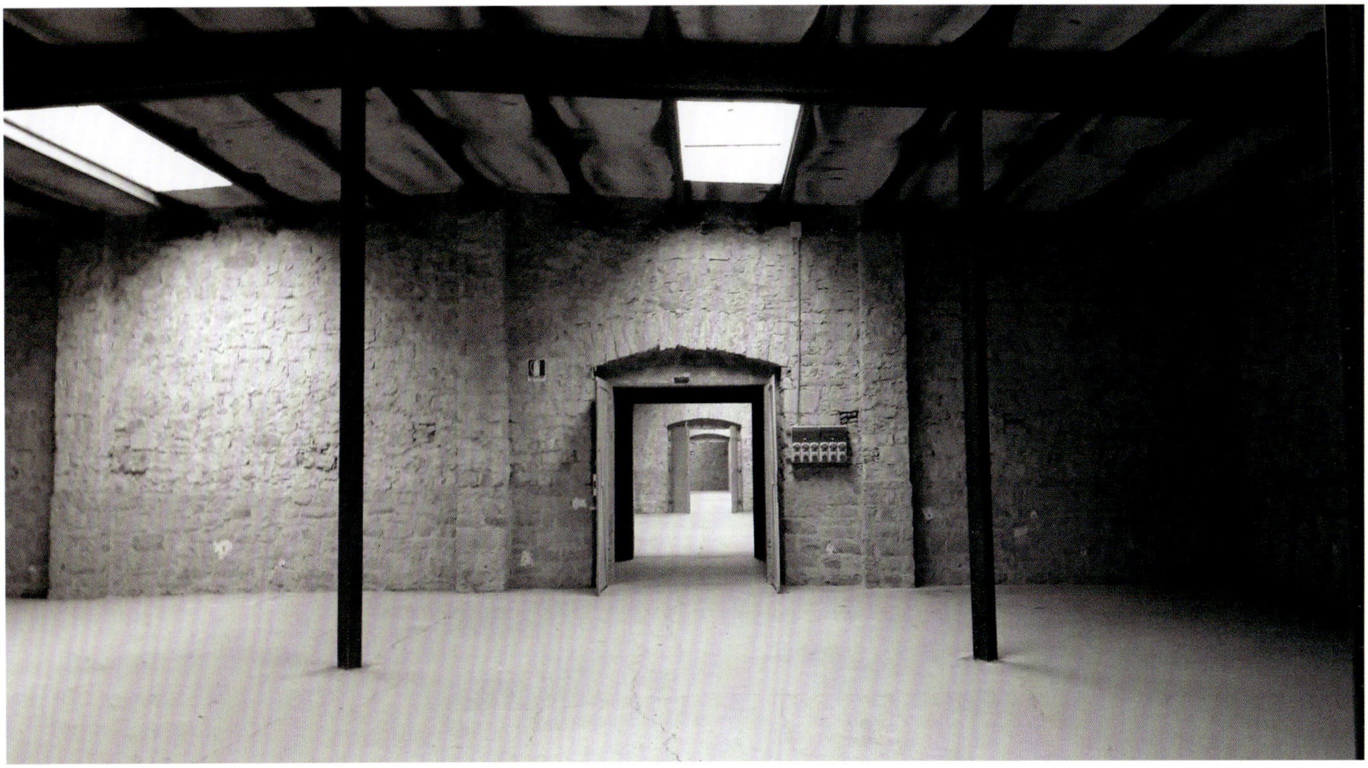

Pavilion 26 - old harbour - to host a new museum, Trieste

3.2. From a functional plan to an architectural plan

The list of functions and thus functional spaces is just the beginning. It leads to defining the relations between exhibition galleries and other facilities. Of course this does not mean that all the functions listed above are vital for the museum or that all museums can afford to have such an articulated architectural plan, but certainly it means that you must have clearly in mind what is essential and what not, and what is the minimum space necessary to offer your public a good service.

In most cases we know this exercise of what is really needed leads to a functional plan, which is the basis for the necessary briefing to the architect(s). It then turns into an architectural plan. An architectural plan will have an estimate of the costs, whether it is in the to be renovated museum building or in a completely new one. It will not come as a surprise that the final result often leaves the permanent exhibition less space than wished and originally aimed for. The costs are almost always higher than calculated, and this often diminishes the possibilities for the exhibit spaces and for some special functions.

The architectural plan might lead to proposed changes in the relationship between the exhibition galleries and the other functions. Be aware and have your arguments ready for those defining moments.

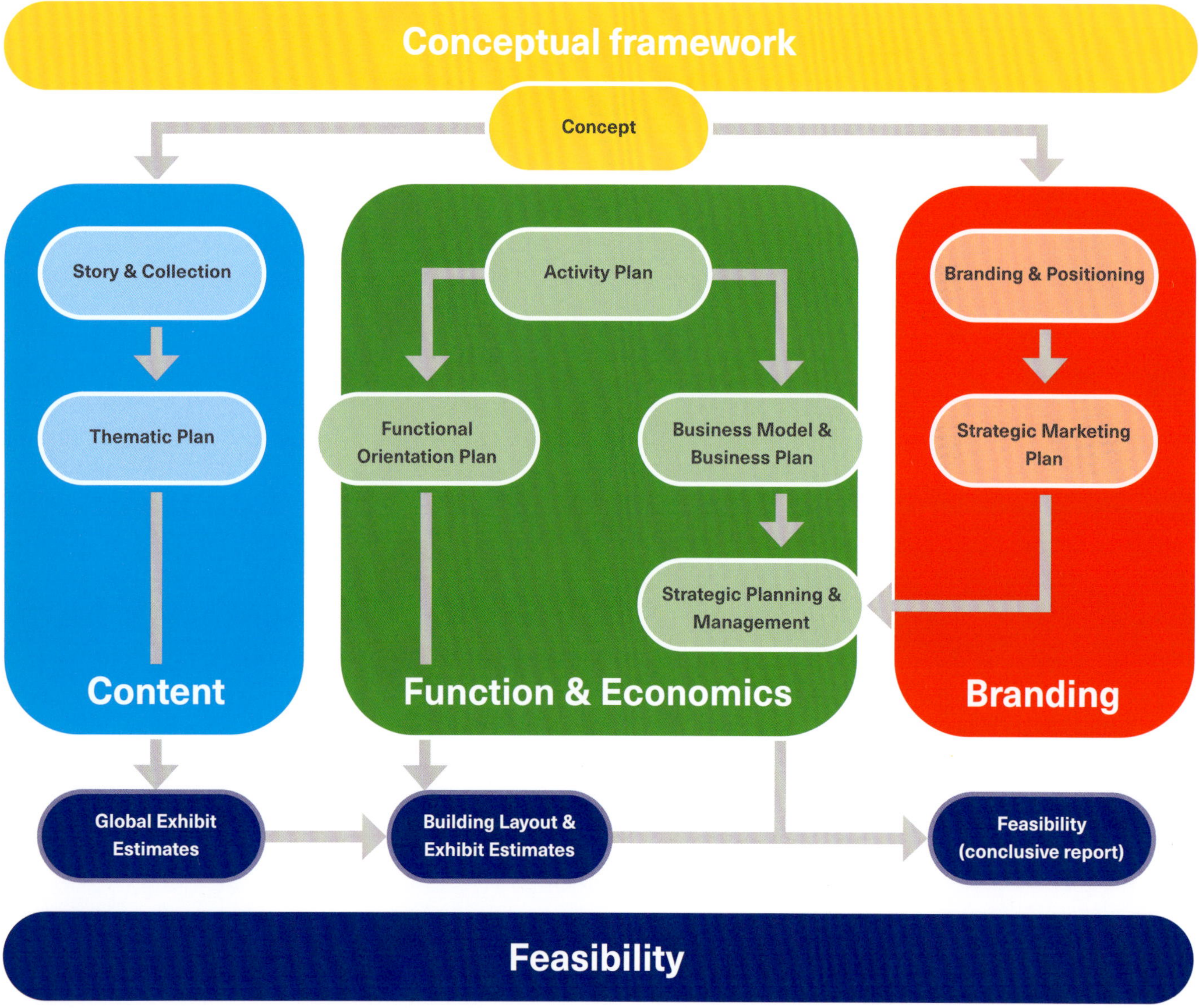

3.3. Feasibility study

If you are at the beginning of it all, there is another structural approach needed. You have to come up with a feasibility study, which consists of several components and steps. Not least there is a concept needed and a thematic plan. It also describes “the reason why” and an estimate of the costs.

How to get those content elements will be part of *this* manual.

3.4. The request of an estimate for the exhibition costs right at the start

It always happens that one or the major stakeholders (typically: the municipality) wants to know the approximate costs of a museum or a temporary exhibition. If not an exact figure, at least a range. And their consent is crucial. Without it, there will be no exhibition.

However, we do believe it wise to work through all five ingredients as named in the previous paragraph, before handing over some calculations. Though calculations must be made.

When a new building is involved, the building costs are often not a problem as the architect and the technical services of a municipality can come to a figure even if the so-called executive project is not yet formulated. There are standards that can be adopted and brought to a reasonable conclusion.

However, we do not yet have yet uniform standards for an exhibition infrastructure. You can find, though, average square metre costs for recent projects – whether or not your own - and so have a kind of guideline. When it is not within your own institution, it often is too rough a calculation. It is rather difficult to come to plausible conclusions if you have not yet defined a certain level of detail in the storyline, have not put it into the context of the architectural space, or have yet to decide the interpretation philosophy and consequently the exhibition equipment. Of course, this is different in the case of a very traditional gallery, as it is based on basic elements (lighting, security, graphic layout, display cases, furniture) but these traditional galleries are on the brink of extinction.

How then to get there? You need reference data. Before that, however, get an approximate idea of the square metres, the type and quantity of objects and an idea on a storyline and a scenography. Rework the spaces into blocks of different levels of 'intensity' of the exhibition equipment, such as (a) low intensity level, (b) a standard level and (c) one or two high intensity levels (scenography, complex multimedia installations, air-conditioned showcases, interactive devices, replicas and models, etc.). For each of these levels you can decide a range of estimate costs per square metre on the basis of reference data collected. All added up you get a rough figure. Then add a plus of 20 or 25% and you might have a first idea of an appropriate range.

Intensity	Area	Description	Estimate € / m2	Total
Corridors	.... m2		€	€ .....
Low level	.... m2		€	€ .....
Medium level	.... m2		€	€ .....
High level 1 (scenography)	.... m2		€	€ .....
High level 2 (ICT)	.... m2		€	€ .....
Other	.... m2		€	€ .....
			Total	€ .....
			added 20% / 25%	€ .....
			Range (grand total)	€ .....

Mind you, this approach is only for this first phase when there are no straightforward reference data available. In a (much) later chapter we come back with a much more refined system.

By courtesy of the Vintage Calculator Web Museum, a virtual museum. www.vintagecalculators.com >

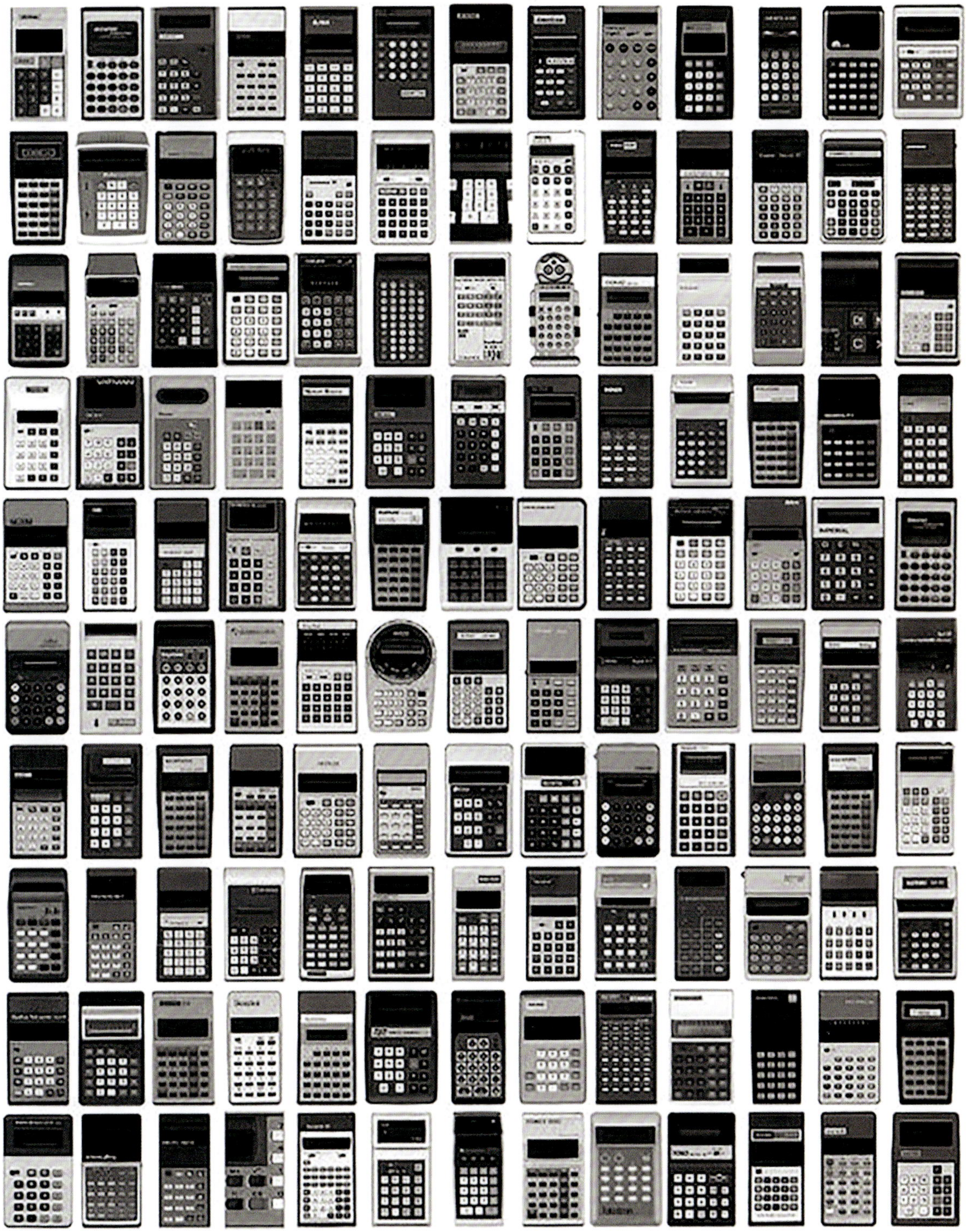

3. In the context of a functional plan

4. Some thoughts on networking the museum: the museum as a 'hub'

4.1. So what?

Museums historically started as places of reflection on our world and our heritage. Museums do 'map the world'.

What does it mean that museums do have a history of 'mapping the world'? Well, it means that their origin is one of documenting, understanding, showing and telling. Although museums do use the scientific methodology, they are not scientific institutes at heart. That role was historically taken by universities in the 19th century. Museums however have a historically based role in organizing the ideas of the organization of culture and of its outcomes.

Where they developed later on in collecting institutes and again later on into knowledge institutes within their domain, the new role of museums – we would argue – is to put technical, cultural and natural developments into a sociocultural context. So, knowing, organizing the patterns and, from that base, storytelling is at the heart of a museum.

Does that have any substance to the average museum worker whether an educational officer, a curator or an attendant? No, we would say. It does not change their role in the museum of today, as this basis is ingrained in the daily routine of most museum workers.

It does however have its importance for the strategic course of any museum. It helps to rethink its positioning in relation to its competitors (in its broadest sense) and the societal role it has to move to.

4.2. From 'a museum with a network' to 'a network with a museum'

Nowadays there is a substantial layman base of workers on almost every topic, often interested civilians with an extensive knowledge. They are not always organized in formal organizations, though they do find each other on the internet. It is the internet also who made this knowledge base explode.

In addition the growth of the science industry has also led to many new insights, experts and connecting fields of knowledge.

So more (lay)scientists and a explosion of exchanging information. Where does this lead the museum? We think it leads to a new role for the museum, different from what it has been, but based on the historical groundwork.

Becoming a hub in a (heritage) network

A museum can and should take up a role as a hub, as a node in a network with a specific role view. In a well organized network, there is no such thing as a 'spider in web'. It is all about 'connecting, connecting, connecting...' where a museum will be just 'one of the boys'. The museum might not be the core of this network, but it does have a major role to play within it and thus has the possibility to position itself clearly.
What stays: a museum still takes the role of an aggregational organizer, a gathering point for knowledge and for the telling objects. It still is where experts exchange and find a home base. It still is one of the few places where knowledge and objects can be shown in a contextual story. So the museum still is a gathering point, where knowledge and objects will 'condensate'. It is the role of a generalist and the keeper of a systematic collection.

Where the change will come in, is the way the museum organizes itself in relation to society and the knowledge base. There will be no specialist curator anymore, to act as 'a master in the universe on a topic'. The curator will be the generalist, who *organizes* its group of experts and interested layman. The museum will help to organize and support many, many people, organizations and ideas - but none of the people are to be employed by the museum. The museum of the future is a very active organizer of people and exchanges. A broker.
So, a museum will get out of its corner, shake off the shackles of a privileged collection-based institute, and reorganize itself into a very active broker in its domain. It invests substantial in relations, in building a (internet-based) knowledge base, in platforms – and thus expands its original core business into new areas.

Exhibitions

This said, it does affect the organization of museum exhibitions. An exhibition becomes a way of connecting interested experts and layman. It will be their way of reaching out too. The exhibition thus will become part of the network activities – in which the museum (can) remain in charge, but where the 'outsiders' (have to) have impact on the subject matter, on its content, and with whom to develop it (together). An exhibition is going to be a network 'thing'.

The organization of an exhibition then will be even a more daring job than it is today. The good part however is, there is a real need for this role switch – for a museum to become an organizer and a (physical) platform - and there is no one yet to fulfil this need. Yet. We think this could lead our museums and exhibitions to a bright future. And do not forget, the exhibition language has gone beyond the museums' walls, being adopted in a variety of venues.
Having said all this, there definitely is a need for a shared exhibition language or methodology. It will make cooperation and co-creating way easier.

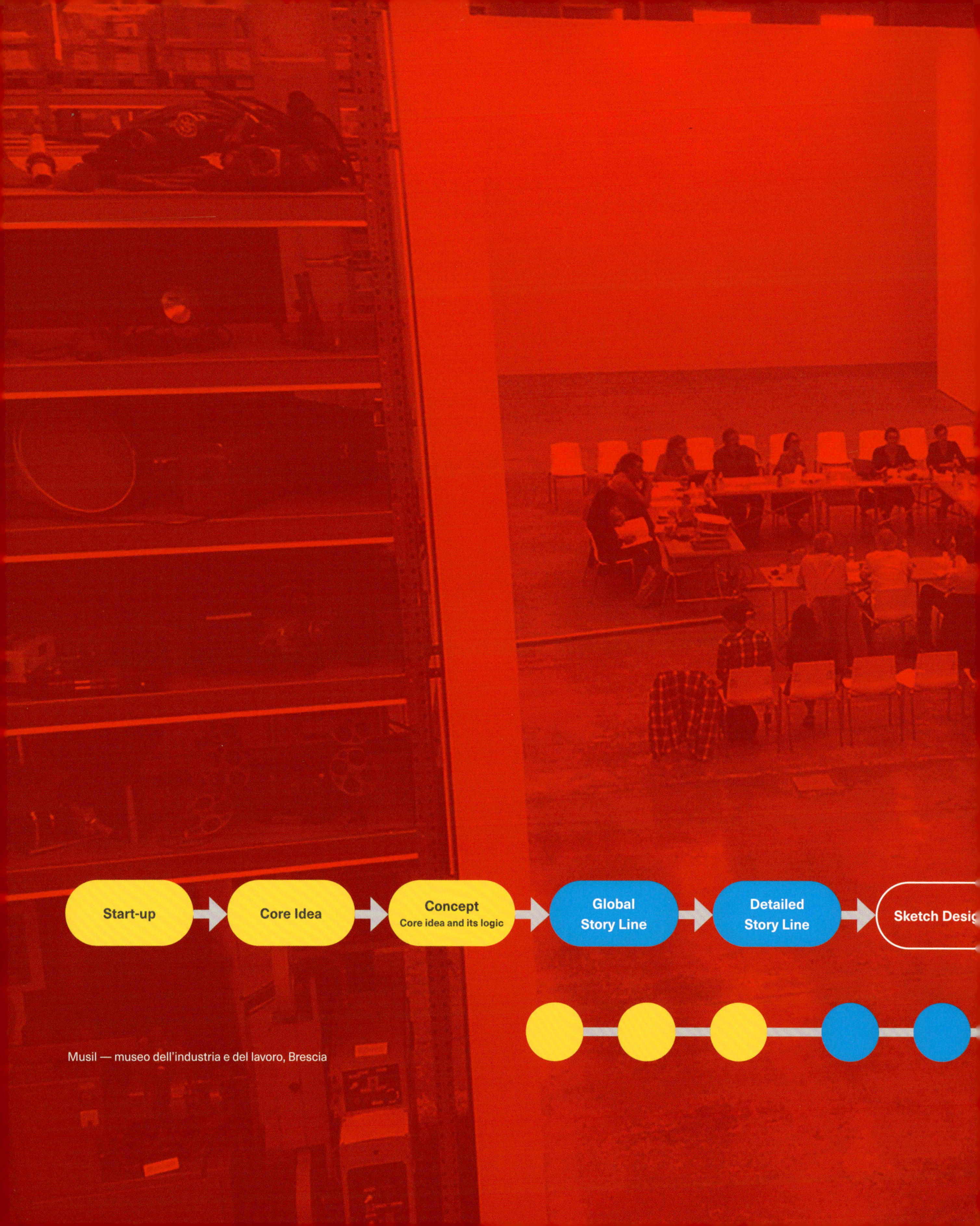

Musil — museo dell'industria e del lavoro, Brescia

Section 1

The overall workflow & start-up

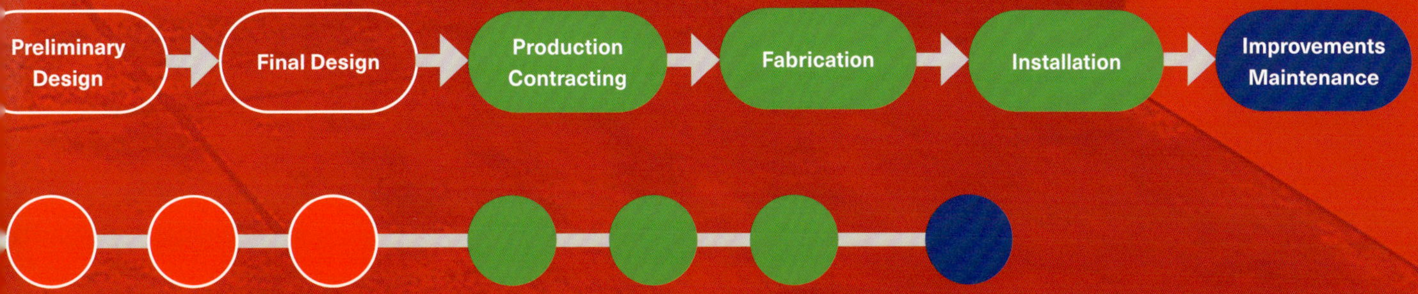

5. Stages and ingredients

For a museum to proceed from a general idea to a fully realized installation involves a process with four stages, and a fifth afterwards, along with key ingredients that are part of those stages. These aspects of planning for a museum installation will be reviewed as a whole in this section. A more detailed analysis of the five ingredients of the process will then be presented in the subsections that follow.

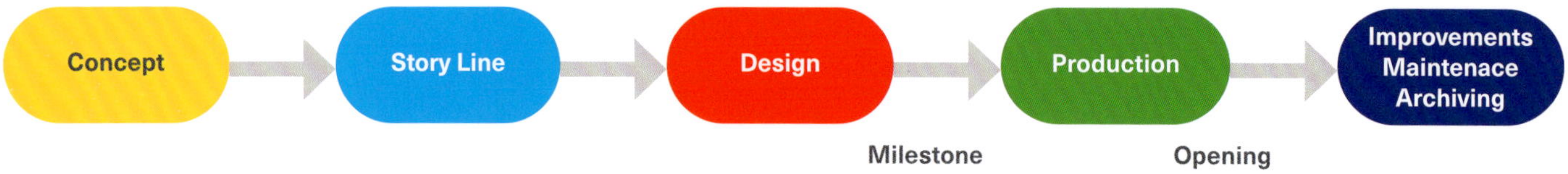

5.1. Five stages

The overall process that moves an exhibition from a core idea for a single display or an entire museum gallery plan, through its design, fabrication, and installation, usually involves five stages. It typically includes the:

1. establishment of the concept;
2. creation of the storyline;
3. development of the design; and
4. realization or production of the exhibition.

It results in the opening. And then it comes to
5. maintenance and improvements. Archiving.

As well, each of the phases of the overall development process does have its own underlying sub-phases and parallel processes, which can be advanced in tandem before eventually leading to the production of all the components of an installation. Each (sub)phase has a deliverable, a timeslot and an 'owner' who is responsible. A milestone is a decision moment and defines, for one, what is needed to end a phase.

In the next chapters each phase will be explained in some detail, including the various deliverables outlined in the appendix.

5.2. Tooling: ten additional ingredients

This book focuses in more detail on specific ingredients or components that it considers to be the methodological backbone of exhibition development as well as the master-planning process. They do have their own emphasis in each phase but will be dealt with separately in the forthcoming chapters.

The ingredients we emphasize are:

1. the knowledge and information that the museum wishes to transmit, referred to as the **content**; and the translation of the content into two- and three-dimensional **designs** (starting from the DNA of the museum and its vision / mission)
2. the **educational model** used, and the importance of **educational tools**
3. authenticity and objects versus **storytelling**
4. the composition of the exhibition development **team**
5. the **stakeholders** organized
6. **visitor and visitor research** in the concept, storyline and design phases
7. the **timeline** organized, i.e. the dependency of (sub)phases and staged decision moments
8. the **budget** needed and organized to accomplish the project
9. the **digital toolset** adding exhibition options, and as an extended world in itself
10. **text writing**

There is more. Exhibition planning will most likely also include components, such as security, retail, the development of marketing and PR-plans, fund-raising plans and such. The opening and maintenance of an exhibition will require additional considerations too. While important, the items listed we consider essential to the installation development process itself and therefore are examined in greater detail.

More on content development

We make an extra effort to introduce our tools for the establishment of the exhibition concept and then its spatial storyline, leading to the development of the design and text components. There is a reason for this. We do consider the content of an exhibition, in its broadest sense, as an essential power we museums have. It is at the same time one of the 'thorny' issues in the development phases. A clear work process really can relieve the inherent tensions here.

5.3. Anything new?

As said before, the whole process as such is established museum practice, though with significant variations. This practice is hardly ever written down however, and many of us have to learn it by doing. So, a written manual can be of great help. And we do come up with some new elements on content development. Though still not rocket science, these tools could be really helpful. Anyway, there is no absolute truth and more ways are leading to Rome. The methodology is a frame. Feel free to adapt it to your culture, institution, organization or personal experiences and beliefs. The only warning here: if you have your own elements, do it beforehand, do write them down, and communicate the adapted methodology. In any other case: just hand over this book to everyone involved.

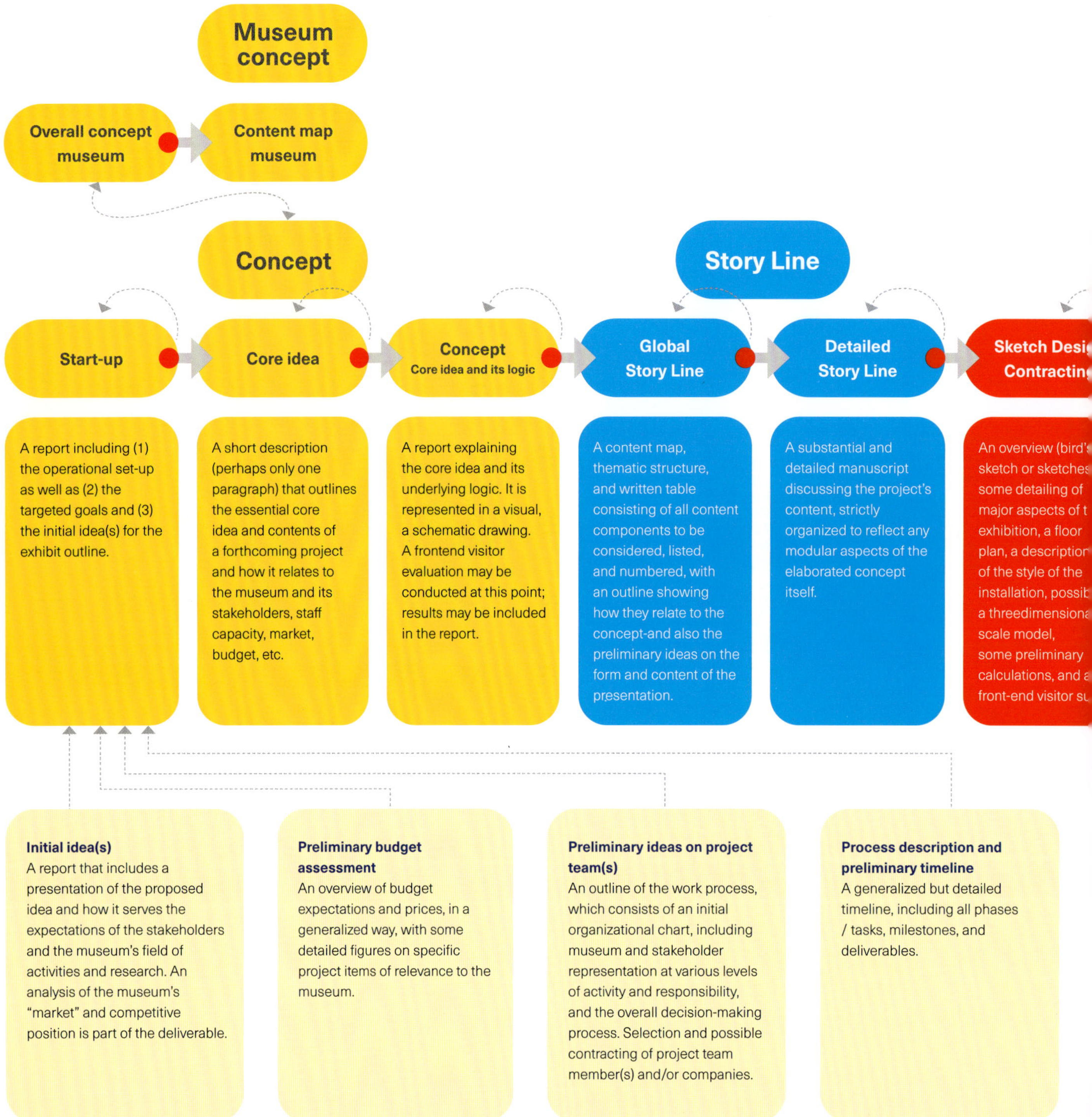

Museum concept
Overall concept museum
Content map museum
Concept
Story Line
Start-up
Core idea
Concept
Core idea and its logic
Global Story Line
Detailed Story Line
Sketch Desi
Contractin
A report including (1) the operational set-up as well as (2) the targeted goals and (3) the initial idea(s) for the exhibit outline.
A short description (perhaps only one paragraph) that outlines the essential core idea and contents of a forthcoming project and how it relates to the museum and its stakeholders, staff capacity, market, budget, etc.
A report explaining the core idea and its underlying logic. It is represented in a visual, a schematic drawing. A frontend visitor evaluation may be conducted at this point; results may be included in the report.
A content map, thematic structure, and written table consisting of all content components to be considered, listed, and numbered, with an outline showing how they relate to the concept-and also the preliminary ideas on the form and content of the presentation.
A substantial and detailed manuscript discussing the project's content, strictly organized to reflect any modular aspects of the elaborated concept itself.
An overview (bird's
sketch or sketches
some detailing of
major aspects of t
exhibition, a floor
plan, a description
of the style of the
installation, possib
a threedimensiona
scale model,
some preliminary
calculations, and a
front-end visitor su
Initial idea(s)
A report that includes a presentation of the proposed idea and how it serves the expectations of the stakeholders and the museum's field of activities and research. An analysis of the museum's "market" and competitive position is part of the deliverable.
Preliminary budget assessment
An overview of budget expectations and prices, in a generalized way, with some detailed figures on specific project items of relevance to the museum.
Preliminary ideas on project team(s)
An outline of the work process, which consists of an initial organizational chart, including museum and stakeholder representation at various levels of activity and responsibility, and the overall decision-making process. Selection and possible contracting of project team member(s) and/or companies.
Process description and preliminary timeline
A generalized but detailed timeline, including all phases / tasks, milestones, and deliverables.

6. An overview

6.1. The baseline

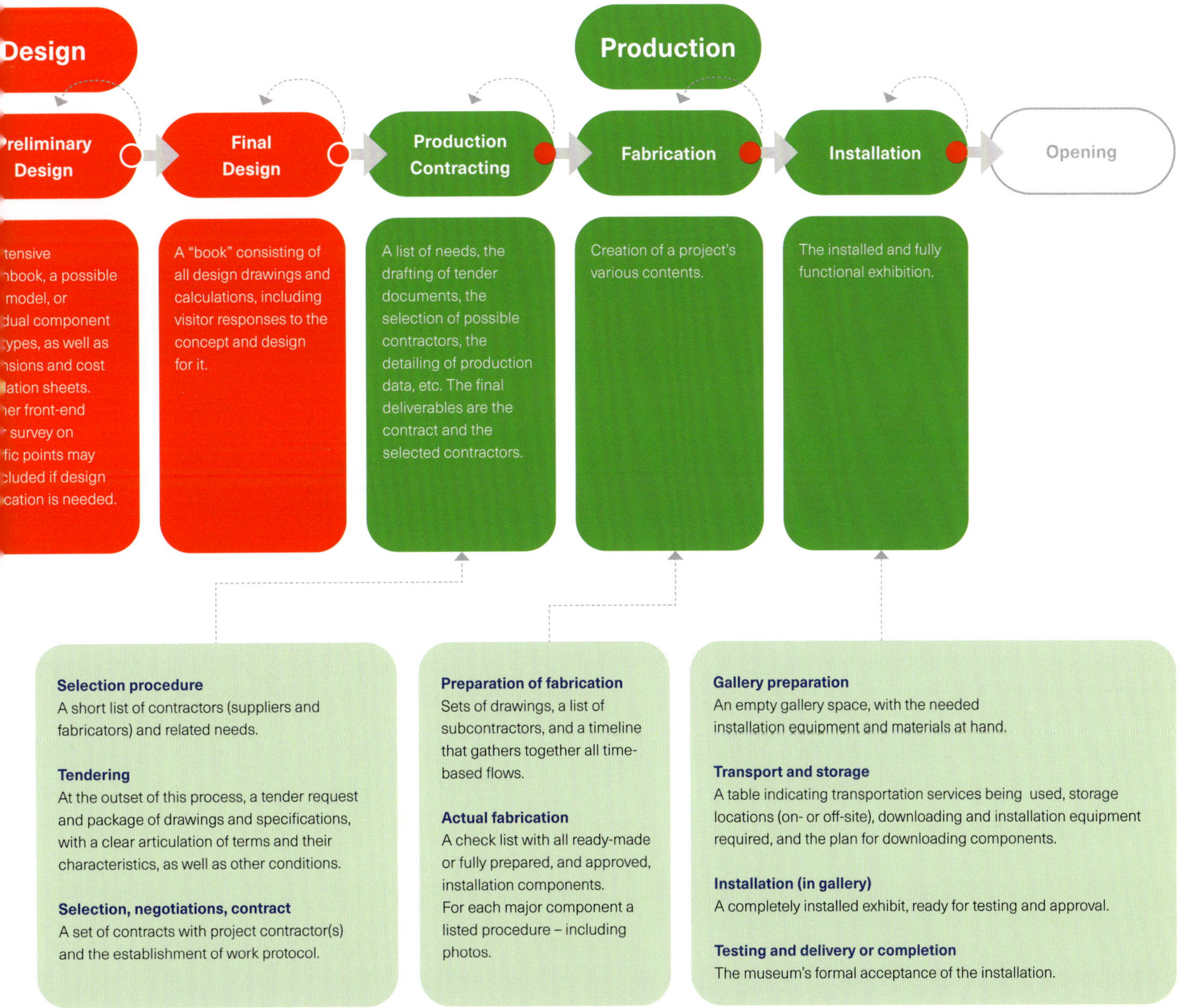

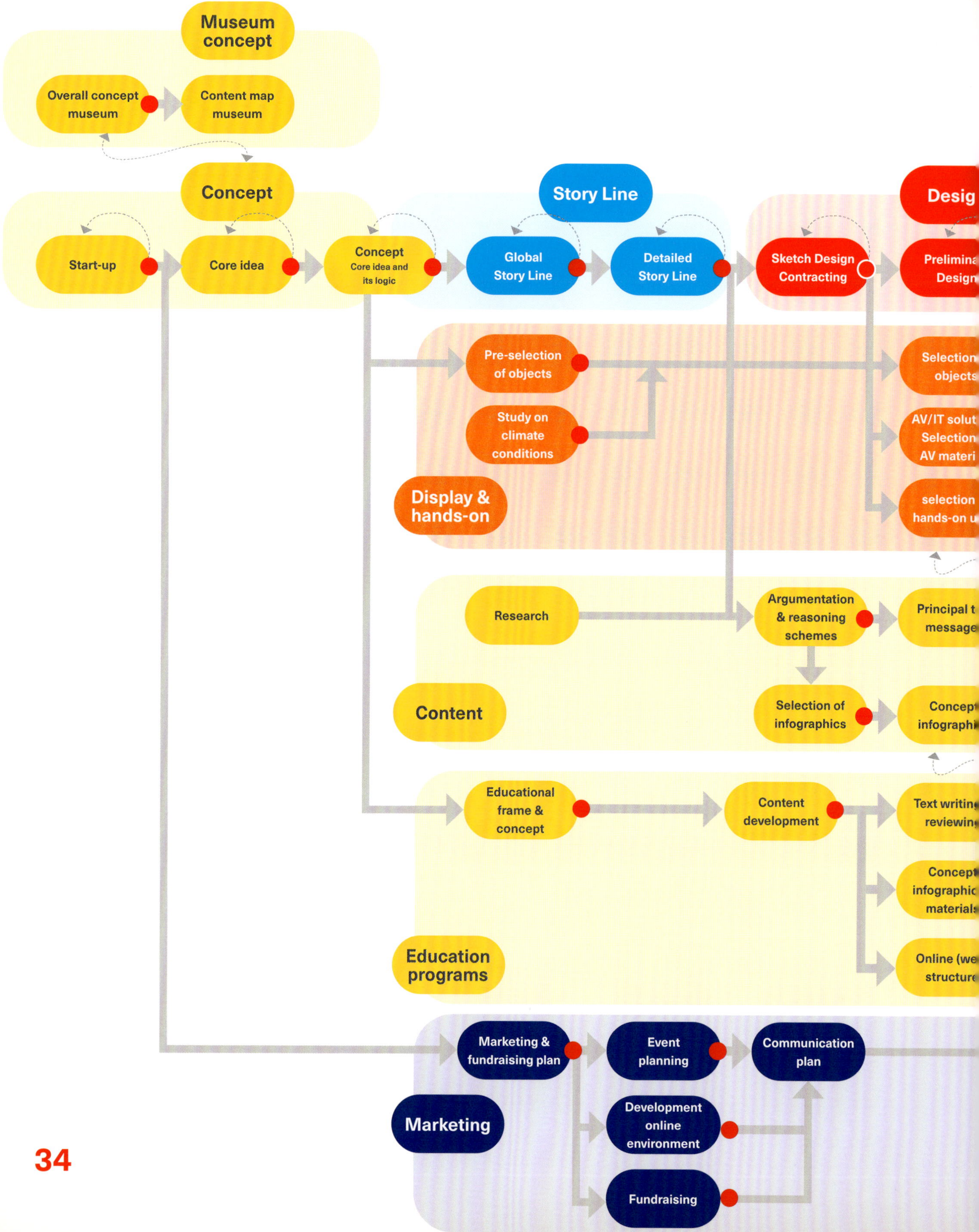

Museum concept
Overall concept museum
Content map museum
Concept
Start-up
Core idea
Concept Core idea and its logic
Story Line
Global Story Line
Detailed Story Line
Desig
Sketch Design Contracting
Prelimina Design
Pre-selection of objects
Study on climate conditions
Display & hands-on
Selection objects
AV/IT solut Selection AV materi
selection hands-on u
Research
Argumentation & reasoning schemes
Principal t message
Content
Selection of infographics
Concep infographi
Educational frame & concept
Content development
Text writin reviewin
Concept infographic materials
Online (we structure
Education programs
Marketing & fundraising plan
Event planning
Communication plan
Marketing
Development online environment
Fundraising

6.2. ... and some additional (sub)processes

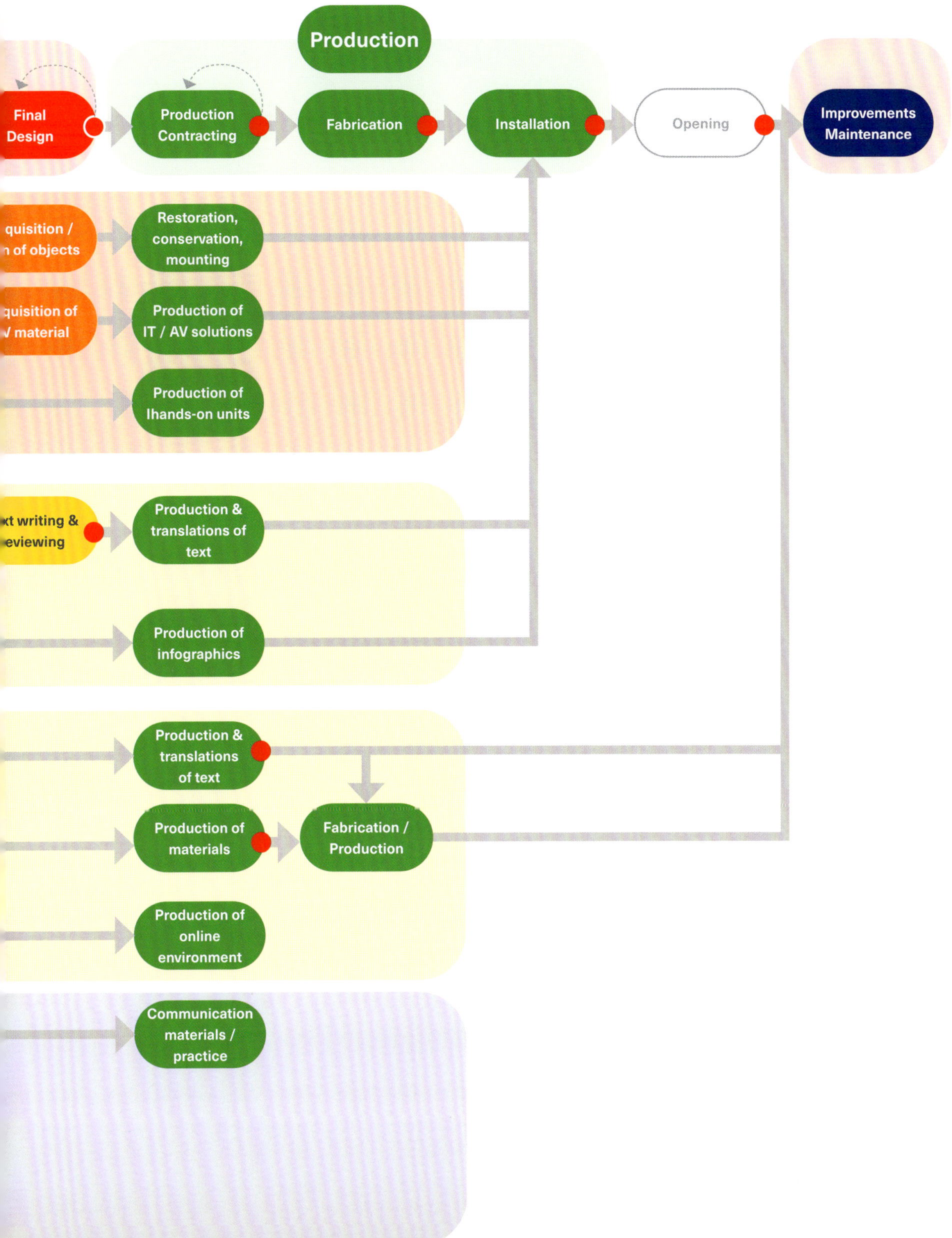

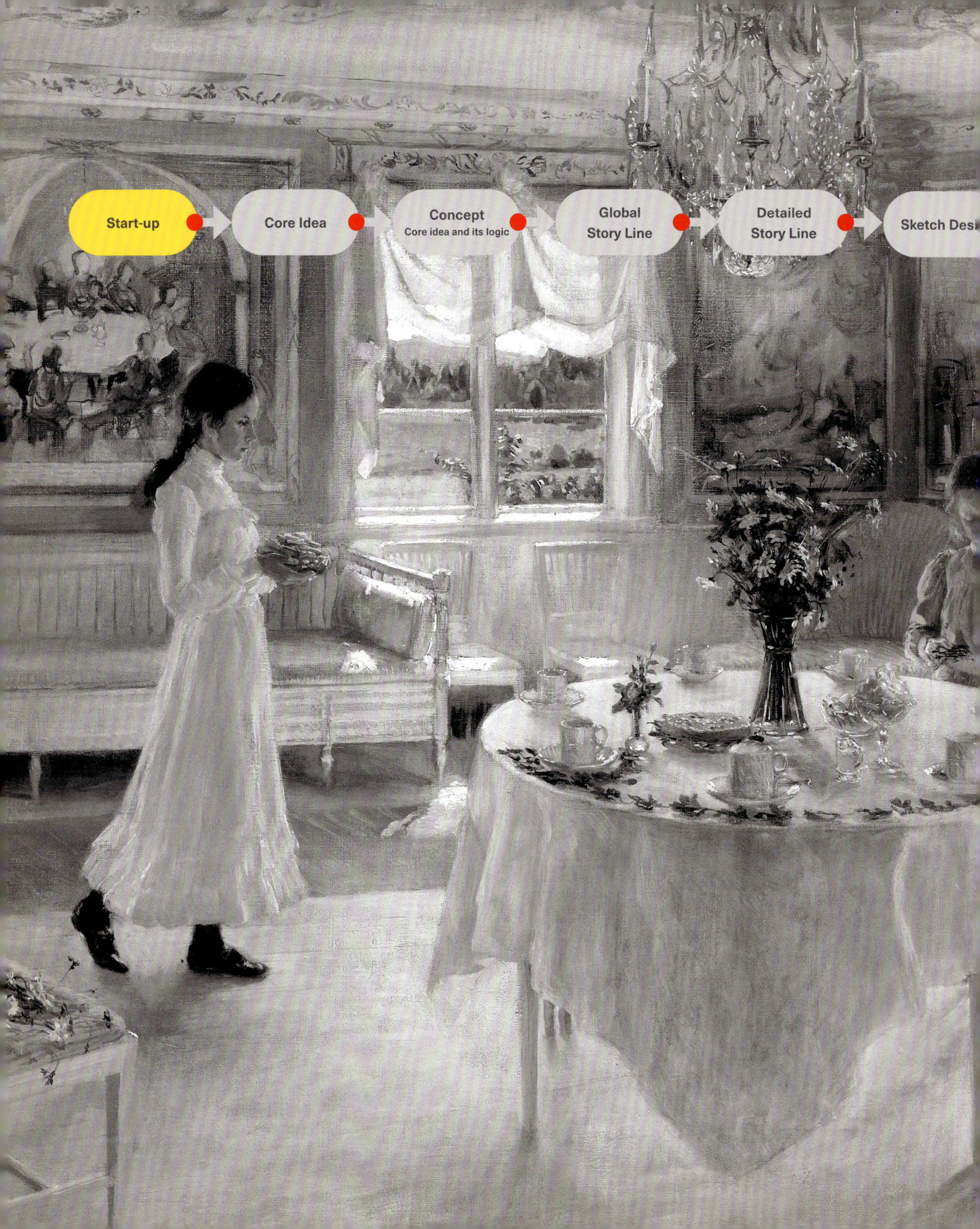
Start-up
Core Idea
Concept
Core idea and its logic
Global
Story Line
Detailed
Story Line
Sketch Desi

7. Key to success: setting the table

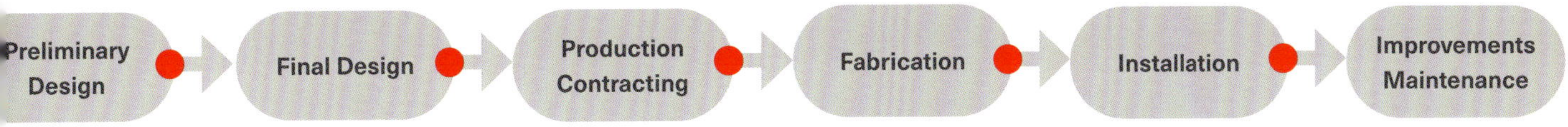

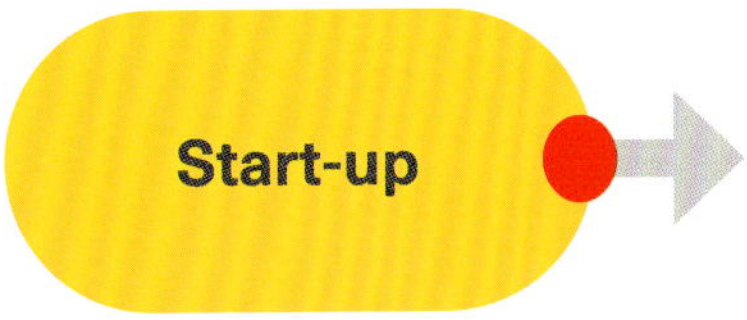

Before entering the development of a temporary exhibition – or any new permanent exhibition – there are some choices to be made and announced to everyone involved. It is to be seen as 'setting the table'. It establishes the way you are going to work.

Have it clear how the process is organized

It has to be clear to everyone how the process will be organized. Which steps are to be taken, in which order, with whom and how organized? There is an order of things to be done, which we will describe. It has to be clear who is doing what kind of job, how responsibilities are divided, and decisions taken. And to keep the flow going, who needs what kind of information and decisions for his job? And who need to be informed, for whatever reasons, if only for support and acceptance by the stakeholders.

Is there a project management methodology adopted? Some museums might have done so. As this book has a fully worked-out system, we will assume this as the outline taken. But as said before, you are free to adjust as you please. Just make it clear on the outset, to everyone involved, what it is and/or how you have adapted the process described here.

The reason we emphasize this start-up so much is the experience that often the rules of the game are developed, and worse, changed during the game. That is bad enough – and should be discouraged – but if you have not set your way of working clear right-on, this lack of clarity will lead to uncertainty, ambiguity and often downright confusion. It will definitely hamper the flow.

The resulting Initiative report

The startup phase will be concluded with a detailed report – we call it an initiative or start-up report - on the how, the whom, the timeline and the money involved. This report has to be agreed on by all decision-makers. This is the way you are going to do it. The result might be a 'no-go' too. Or some redoing might be needed. Be sure however, that you won't start until the setting is clear, and you know how the 'table' will be organized.

Detail from A Day of Celebration, 1902, Fanny Brate, National Museum of Fine Arts, Stockholm

7.1. Operational set-up

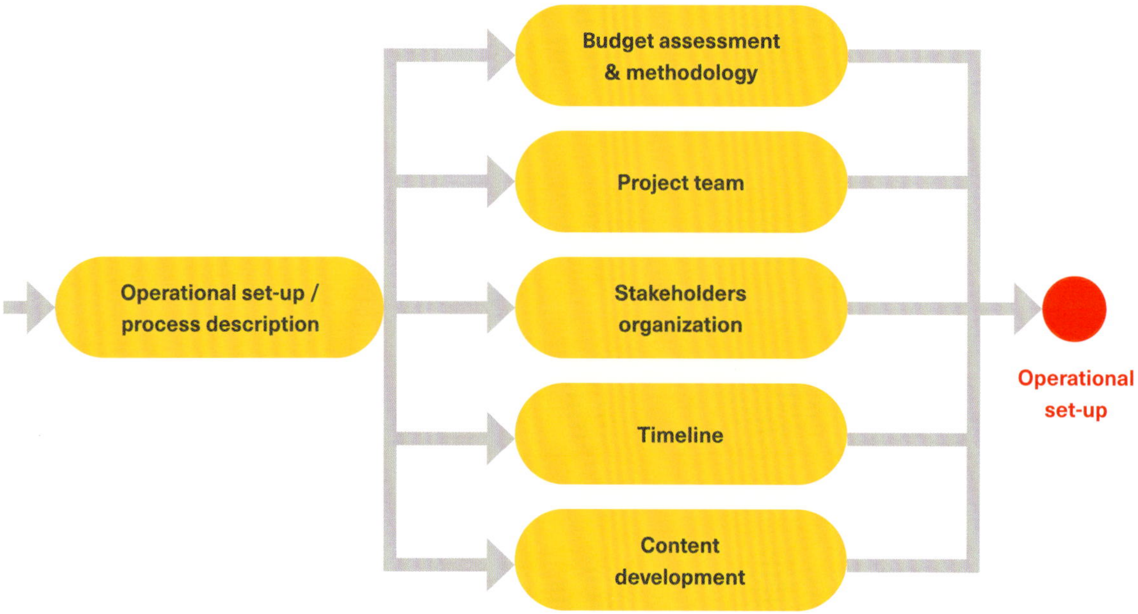

The operational set-up describes what we have written earlier in the introduction, and to be shortly repeated here. There are different types of components to consider.

- The process scheme itself and its (sub)division in sub- and parallel phases – which describes the process flow in detail, including decision moments. This results in a global timeline.
- Additional structuring tools – ways of doing things within certain (sub)phases of the process
- Structures for organizing people and teams
- Structures for controlling the budget

Many of the additional and organizing tools described here are connected with the five ingredients. So, before you enter the process, have it clear which process and tools you are going to use.

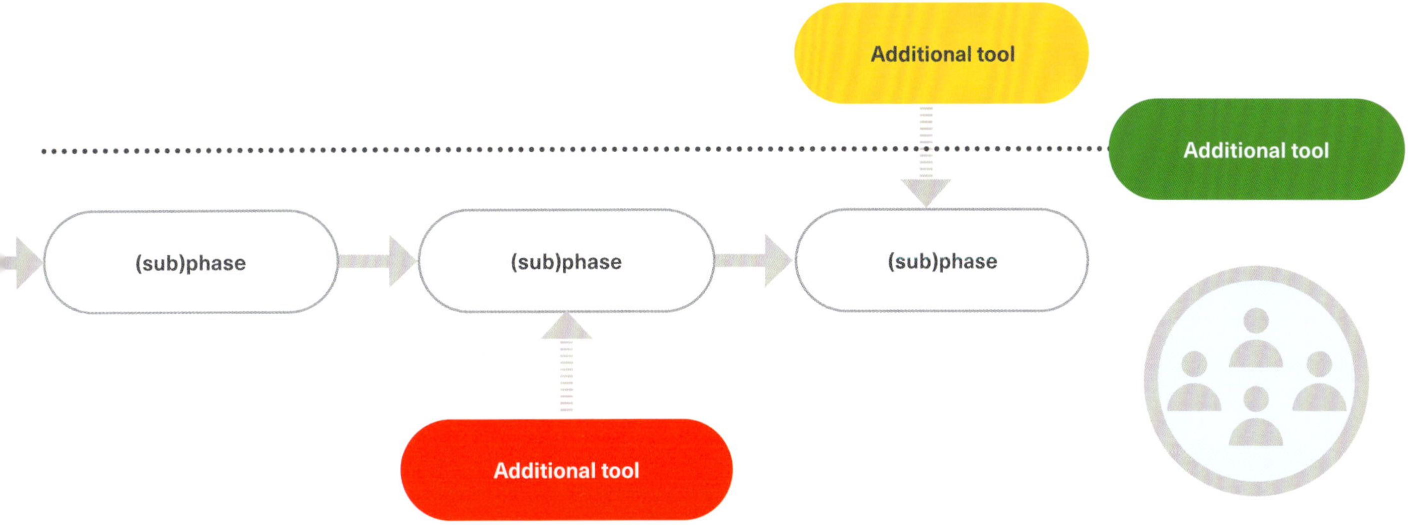

The five ingredients in the operational setup

We consider different aspects, which have to be described as pretty conclusive. This includes the results – the filled-in outcome - of the five ingredients below. Each topic has its descriptions in later paragraphs and chapters.

1. What is the budget set? How does it compare to the standards in our business / your country, your close peers? Note: the comparison might be handy to play down (or up) expectations. This part also includes the way the budgeting and control is organized. It too encompasses the expected income generated by visitors.
2. How is the project team organized? Who is going to do the job, in which roles, in which different phases?
3. How are the stakeholders included, in which phases? What is their mandate and how is dealt with corrective feedback?
4. The timeline includes the proposed process as well as the crucial real-life dates. If you keep this methodology, you hand over the book. Otherwise, you have to point at where you will do things (a little) differently. This description also involves the actual dates of crucial importance as the process should be fitted into a concrete timeline. Though we will have a template ready online, you have to adapt it to the proposed opening time, and adapt different phases according to the experience in your museum and the type of exhibition requirements (AV to be expected? Objects needing restoration? And so on.)
5. How is the development of content organized, in which steps, by whom, in which roles? Though many museums do have a fixed way of who is in charge – curators, interpretative planners, content developers – it can be a source of serious disputes or internal dissatisfaction. Therefore, we propose to discuss the methodology as well as the tools beforehand.

7.2. The DNA of the museum

What we would call the DNA of the museum is more than what is described in mission statements. It describes the current identity in all aspects. Who are you, and what is your role in society? What is your tone-of-voice, your reason-to-be? How much of this is shared within your staff? Is it congruent with your stakeholders' and visitors' expectations?

The reason to have the expectations – stated or underlying – clear, written and known beforehand actually is quite simple. The exhibitions will be judged on them. The more concrete you know what these parameters are, the easier it is to set meaningful goals to accomplish.

7.3. Goals set

Expectations are to be considered beforehand as they influence the development process and the choices made. It is to be set in parameters in your dashboard. What is it you want to measure and what are acceptable and good scores?

Parameters	Minimum	Satisfied	Great
Amount of visitors			
Score given	7.4	7.8	8.1
....			
Cost-benefit (financial)		Break-even	
.... etc.			

Table 1: an indicative table. As every museum and exhibition asks for a dedicated 'personal' version, do give ample considerations to what you are going to be put into it.

The second part of the initiative report (or starting note) thus describes what it is all about in the exhibit, who you are aiming at, with what kind of results should be there. Have them in a table and make sure they will be measured.

We have a 'wishful thinking' warning too. As we all know, lists could easily turn into a less realistic summary of wishes and hopes, not least by the museum management. It is not uncommon too, that unrealistic figures are communicated to potential funders. Therefore include a range whenever possible, be sure to put it into an historic perspective, and stick to the important matters.

There might be some obvious important parameters, such as is the visitor review, the average or media time spent, the attracting power i.e. the amount of visitors attending and in congruence the public relations attractiveness. And it is often felt important how competitor / collegues and experts judge, so take them into account too.

More business-based parameters would be the budget use (did it stay within budget, is 5 to 10 % saved for alterations and repairs), the time pressure (easily done or fairly stressed), or the cost-benefit ratio. What is the ratio of sponsoring involved.

Try to quantify some of the strategic perspectives, however hard. You can always measure the reputation of the museum with visitor evaluation and stakeholder discussions afterwards for example.

Groups of parameters

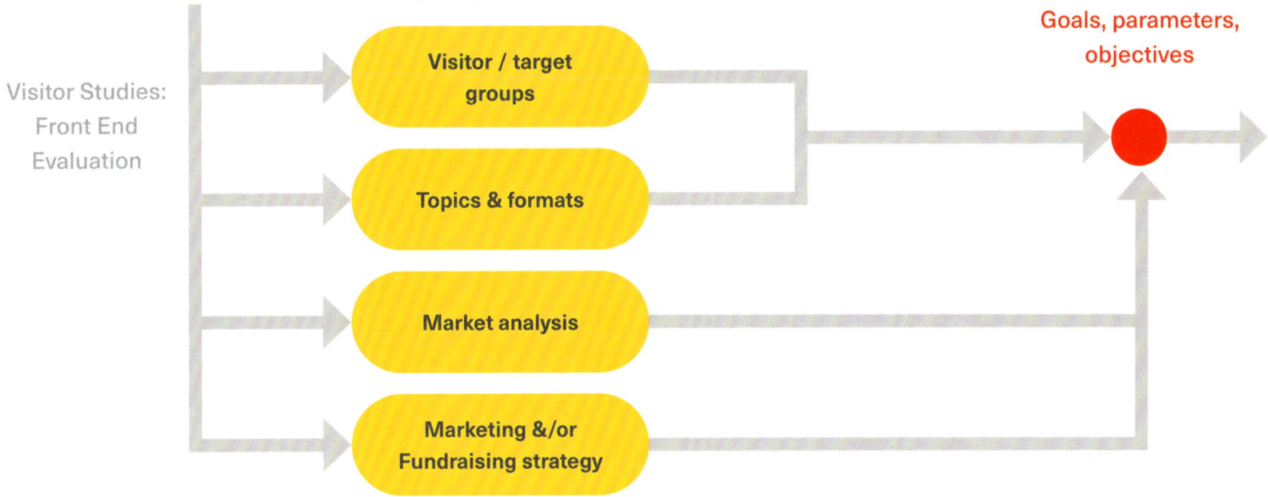

Audiences

Regarding the audience you want to reach, describe your target groups as clearly as possible, as well as the key messages and 'feelings' you want to get across. To get there, you do need some knowledge on what is there already with your audience(s). Which experiences do they want, what basic knowledge is there, and so on.
As we said before, when determining target groups, be sure you can 'measure' them. They have to be addressed, quantified and counted within your audience. It is of no use to speak of 'the general audience'. In principle, each specific group can be described, though sometimes roughly, and quantified. It is better to have an incomplete and partly inaccurate picture at the start than none at all.

See later for a more extended discussion regarding audiences and some basic visitor research to be done beforehand by yourself.

Topics and content matter

The same applies to which exhibition themes (topics) you address, balancing the intellectual and collection capital to the needs and interests of your audiences. See later for a description of a methodology for a deliberately choosing process.

Market analysis

A market analysis combines the above with an overview of your competitive environment and business considerations. It also positions the attractiveness of your museum in the context of alternatives visitors can make, how the proposed exhibition theme may stand out.

Marketing and funding

There often is an implicit or explicit strategy too for external funding and positioning / marketing the exhibitions. It is best to dedicate some strategic lines in the setup – and what happens if the expected or hoped for external funding does or does not work out.

It also includes some serious considerations on marketing perspectives to be included in the exhibition development, from the perspective of external funders as well as what is known from your audiences and front-end visitor research.

The more strategic perspectives and considerations are harder to put into concrete numbers. Does it strenghten the strategic positioning and reputation of the museum? Does it 'fit' with what the museum stands for? Is its current positioning – its reputation and position with civil groups, funding agencies and so on – as it should be? Should there be a repositioned mission and strategic perspective?

Internal marketing

Internal marketing indicates the package of public relations actions which are addressed to the staff of the company itself, and normally at all levels. All workers and decision makers involved must have knowledge of the motivations of a specific project or rule and ideally to underwrite them.

First and foremost, this means it is directed to the major decision makers and/or funders, like a director, a mayor or the foundation which is close to the museum. The so-called "selling propositions" of the project vary according to the interlocutor and the first aim is to make of him/her a solid partner. There might be quite a lot of politics involved, not only in the metaphorical sense, but also in the practical sense. Due to the variety of possible interlocutors, it makes no sense to enter here into the details of the possible formats to be adopted, but a few things are common to all possible approaches and strategies: to know well the governance of the body to which your 'client' belongs, to be aware of his / her perception of the project as far as you can envisage and have a clear idea what the consequences are for him/her when supporting you openly in the public arena.

However, do not forget the powers within a museum. So, do make time to think of a strategy for ''targeting' the museum staff too.

7.4. The conclusive initiative report

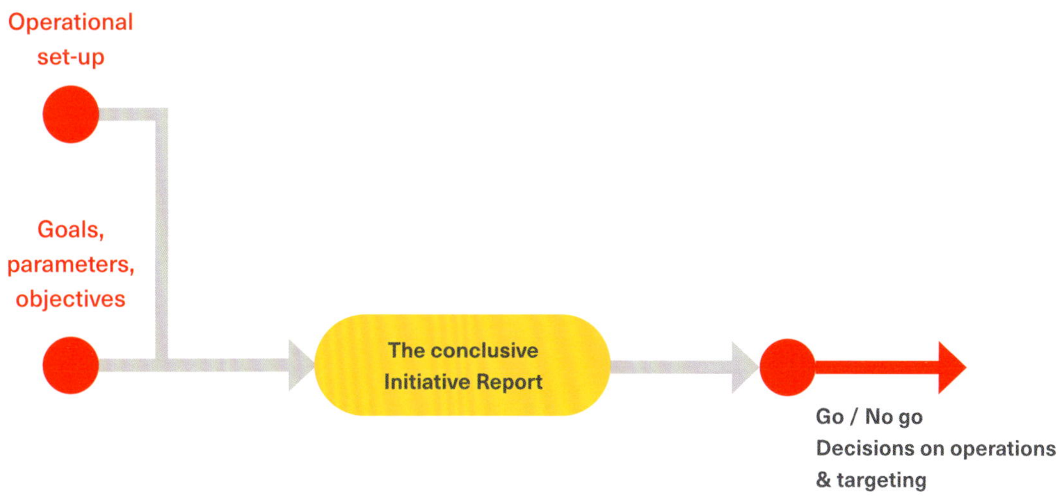

The resulting report gives a pretty clear picture of the expectations set – and the way you are going to get the work done. It is the starting point, to be set before actually starting the project. It is preemptive too for false or unspoken expectations.

This report is to be decided on by management or a (to be set) steering committee. A steering committee might be a temporary one of decision makers, but most probably will be the steering committee all along the process – to decide on other milestones too.

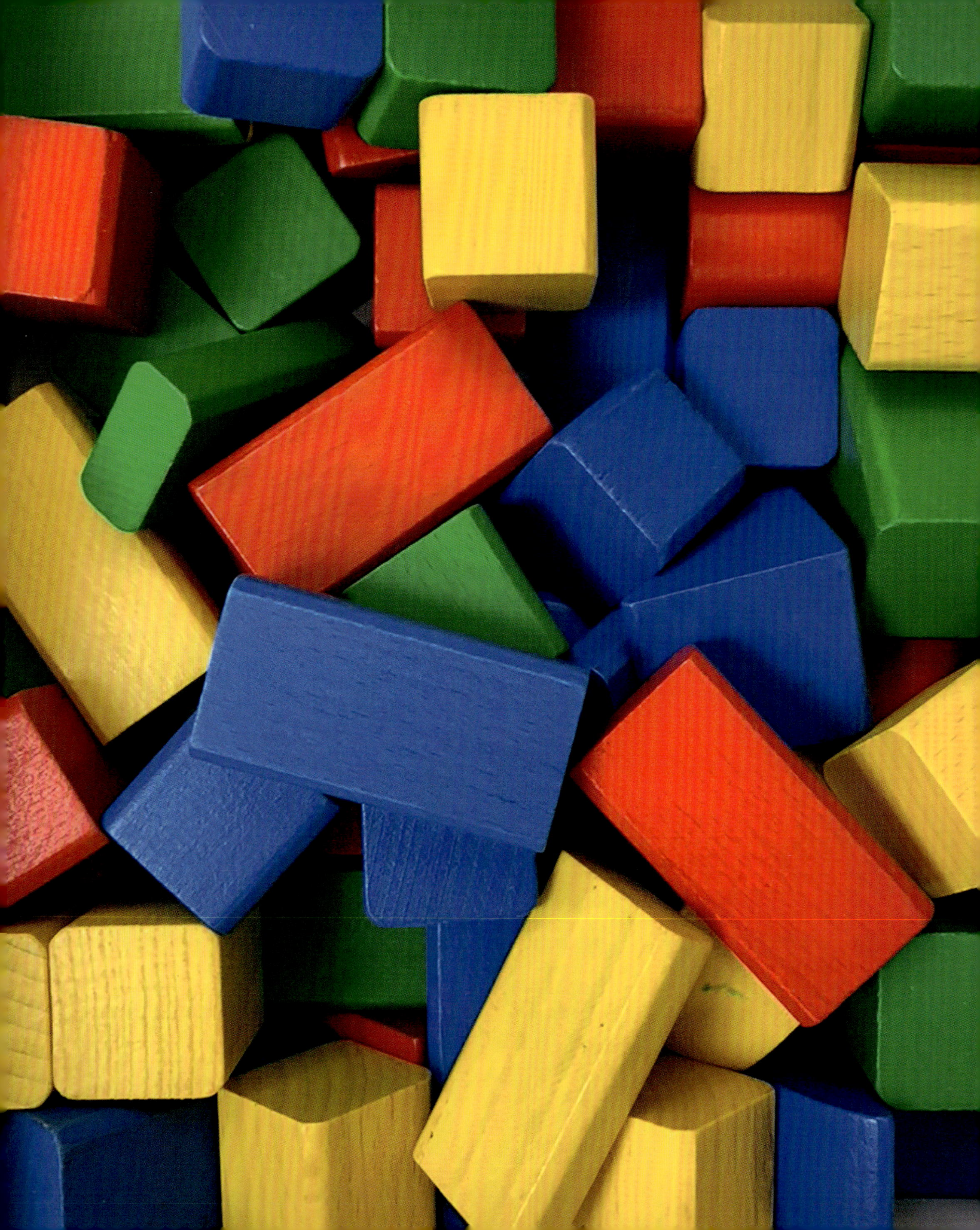

8. Building the network of tasks and timeline

8.1. The principles

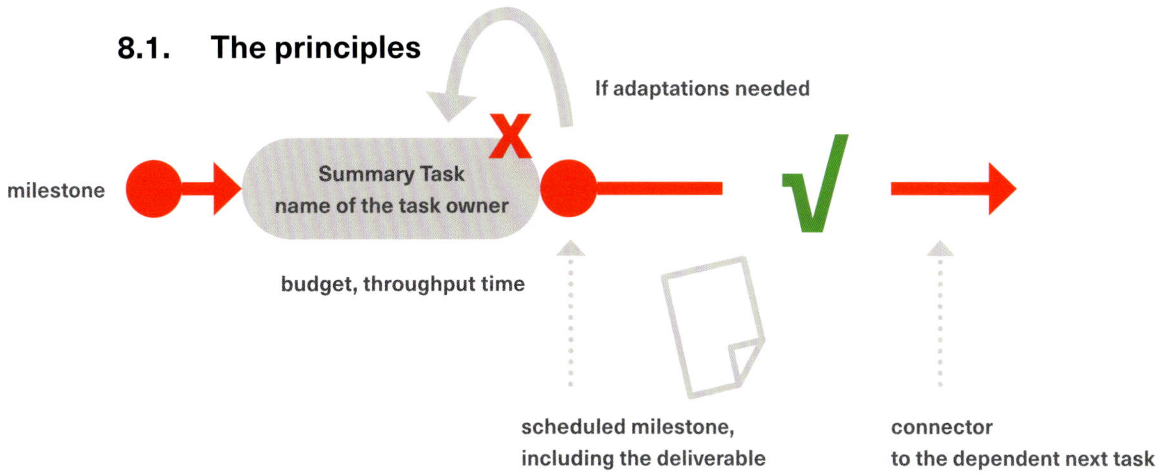

The overall scheme, the global outline of the major (summary) tasks in their sequential order, will be more or less the same to all of us. On a more detailed level however, there will be differences, aligned to your own situation and way of doing things.

There are the following building blocks:

- Tasks, i.e. something to be done, with a clear-cut finish
  - name of the task
  - description of the task
  - who is to do it and/or responsible (task-owner)
  - the given amount of throughput time
  - the budget available (max)
- Deliverable, i.e. a description on what the result should be, and eventually to be judged
- Milestone, i.e. a position in the process, after the accompanying deliverable is accepted
  - eventually how a decision by the stakeholders is to be organized
- Connectors, i.e. the connecting arrow implying which task is the next in line (and dependent on the previous finished one).

Who is to develop and draw this overall scheme, geared to your own institution? As it will be too much of a luxury to have your own planner in the team, the task will be shared between the project manager and the production manager. It takes some to learn the appropriate software, but it is worth the effort. More than we would say.

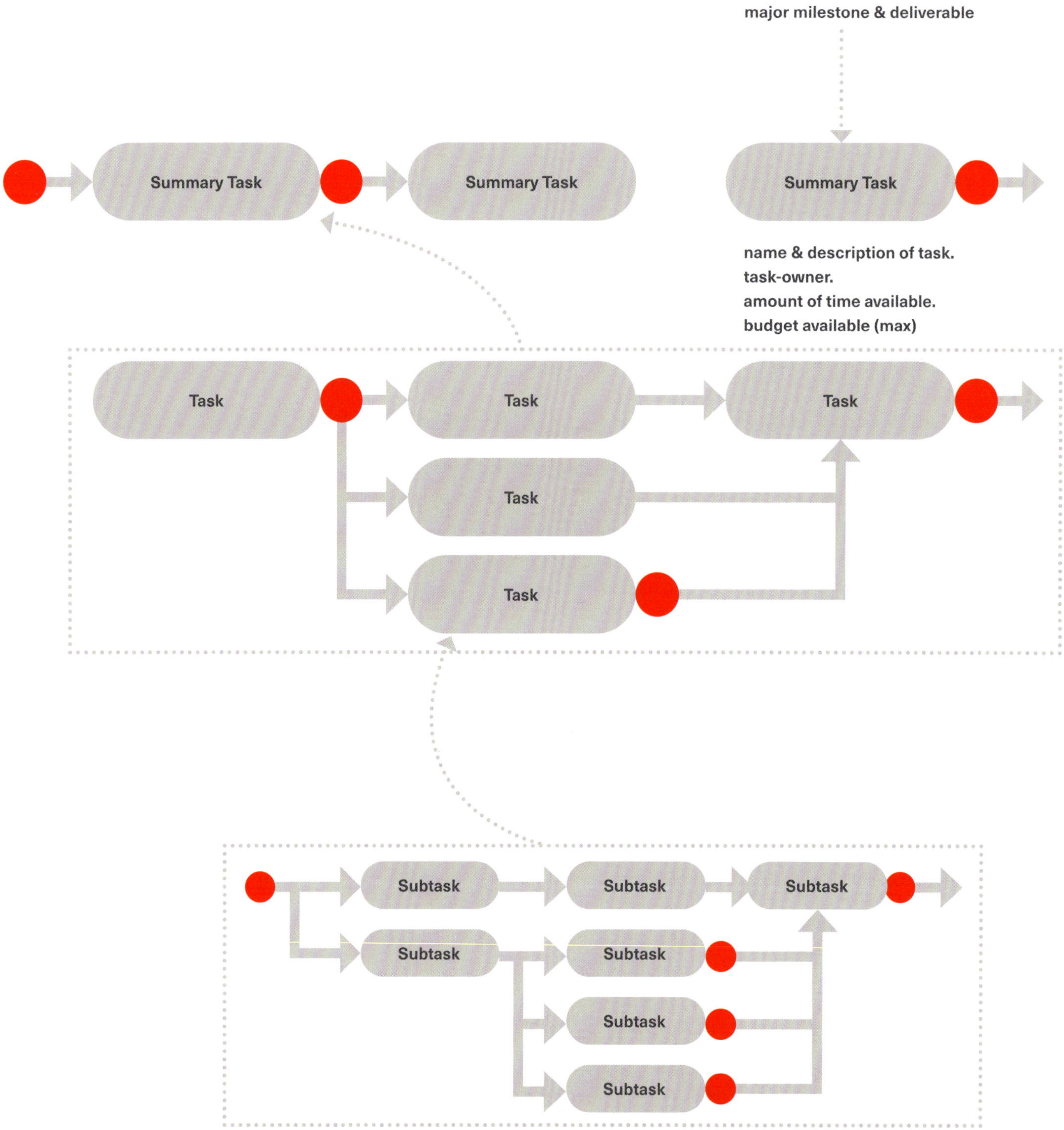
major milestone & deliverable
Summary Task
Summary Task
Summary Task
name & description of task.
task-owner.
amount of time available.
budget available (max)
Task
Task
Task
Task
Task
Subtask
Subtask
Subtask
Subtask
Subtask
Subtask
Subtask

Build a networked cascade of tasks

Each task can in itself consist of a group of (sub)tasks. It is a nested structure and can be detailed as much as you like. And it should be. We certainly recommend doing so. A detailed structure in general means a well-considered structure. Building a cascade of tasks is most easily done starting from the summary task. It is therefore often called a work-breakdown structure / way of building the network.

What are the reasons not to do it? For one, it is tempting to build a timeline on summary tasks only because it is quicker, easier. Because you think it is obvious what should be done and in which order. Because it saves you from nagging doubts that you do not know yet how much time things will take, and you will, to be on the safe side, come up with unrealistically long timeline. And not least, it saves you the discussions within the team.

Wrong. You are wrong. It really is better to start upfront with a timeline which includes as many small steps as you can think of. They might not all be included in your visualized timeline, but you had better have them noted down. It will help speeding up the process, as we will see when we arrive in the paragraph on slack time.
And you can always adapt when you, once in a while, come up with a new and updated version.

It turns out the planning practice more often than not is based on experience and organizational practice. There often is a timeline, albeit a simplistic 'spreadsheet' version. There hardly ever is a meaningful detailed manual. **There should be**. An instruction and operational manual, including a detailed timeline, will save you money, time and a lot of frustrations. Use this book and schemes – if only as a starter.

An example

Take for example the phase of the sketch design. You enter the phase after the selection of a design company. This will be different when it is all done in-house. But assume you do as we say. A possible roadmap could be as follows. There is (a) a first phase of selecting several companies, (b) write out a tender or call for a proposal or pitch- including the contract draft, (c) have the choosing process, (d) select one, (e) finish the contract, (f) and start the actual sketch design phase with the chosen design company.

In the sketch design you start with (1) a complete descriptive start document (deliverables from the previous phase(s), (2) some days of study by the company, (3) followed by several start-up meetings, (4) and a period of sketching and thinking by the company, including (5) requests for additional information to you and to companies, (6) accompanied by several meetings for discussing and testing ideas, (7) leading to a preliminary document, (8) including a preliminary cost calculation, (9) to be decided on and (10) reworked into a decision document for (11) meetings with the steering committee and advisory groups, eventually (12) leading to some adjustments and (13) a final 'go' to move on.

8.2. Each (sub)task is defined by a result and thus a deliverable

A task – most tasks - thus has a predefined result to be delivered by the task-owner, which can be 'ticked off' when it is 'done'. This predefined result – a 'deliverable' - most often is input for the next phase. In the first phases of the exhibition process, a deliverable takes most often the form of documents, mock-ups, drawings or calculations.

So, have a clear outline what this deliverable, this 'result to be approved' should be. What form, what quality, what level of detail? What kind of decision is needed before going on? And by whom? It will definitely be very useful if the asked-for-result is clearly circumscribed in the operation manual.

When there is no definite 'tick off' possible with a predefined result, as for example for 'time for study', then still have a procedure ready in which you can mark it as 'done'.

Finish before moving on

As we said before, but state again, in our experience it is much better to have a process or task fully finished before moving on to the next phase or task. Everybody will agree. In theory. In practice, for reasons of time and thus money, there will be pressure to 'go on' and adjust in the next phase. This will be especially the case when outsiders, for example a design company, are part of the process. Try to withstand the pressure. The process will be much clearer, controlled and contained when you stick to the baseline set.

Decision-making on milestones is serious business

A milestone is a marked point in time, and often a decisive moment based on a result (deliverable). The result, the outcome, thus has to be approved before moving over to the next phase. This moment of deciding on a deliverable before moving on, a milestone, a decisive moment in time, has to be planned ahead so agendas of decision makers can be organized accordingly.

And as with any decision, there can be a negative outcome, and/or some work needs to be redone. This will take some time, especially when the re-done work has to pass the decision-makers again. Plan for it.

A steering committee will be needed when major decisions are required, as for example a storyline or sketch design has to be approved. These meetings thus are important and should be well prepared for and thoroughly organized. Decisions made during these meetings need to be clearly articulated. What is decided? If adaptations are needed, which ones? Is then a

new meeting to be organized (serious comments) or can it be handled by the project manager (serious too, but not fundamental).
All these decision moments, major and minor ones, in our view are to be taken seriously. You cannot go on with the next step if there is no agreement on the previous phase. On what is the basis to build on. So, a decision has to be taken if what is there, is good. Or good enough. This might include some adaptations which need to be asked for. So, for example, when there are some adjustments necessary on the sketch design, finish those before moving on. And decide too if the adjustments require a new meeting of the steering committee, or a meeting with an appointed member of the steering committee or can be handled by the project manager.

Plan milestones way ahead

As timeline components, at least their most significant items, are usually set at the beginning of a project's development, the milestones can be dated at least a year or half a year ahead, together with their deliverables. Thus, it is clear and planned to everybody when is to be decided on what.
One pitfall is being too optimistic. Take enough slack time and be sure there is some correction or 'repair' time planned after any milestone. The time is needed to accommodate inputs, corrections, and possible changes, particularly additions to the process that may result from consultations with the steering committee and/or advisory groups, etc.
To keep scheduling realistic means a precious balance between speed, pressure and slack time.

8.3. Throughput time and slack

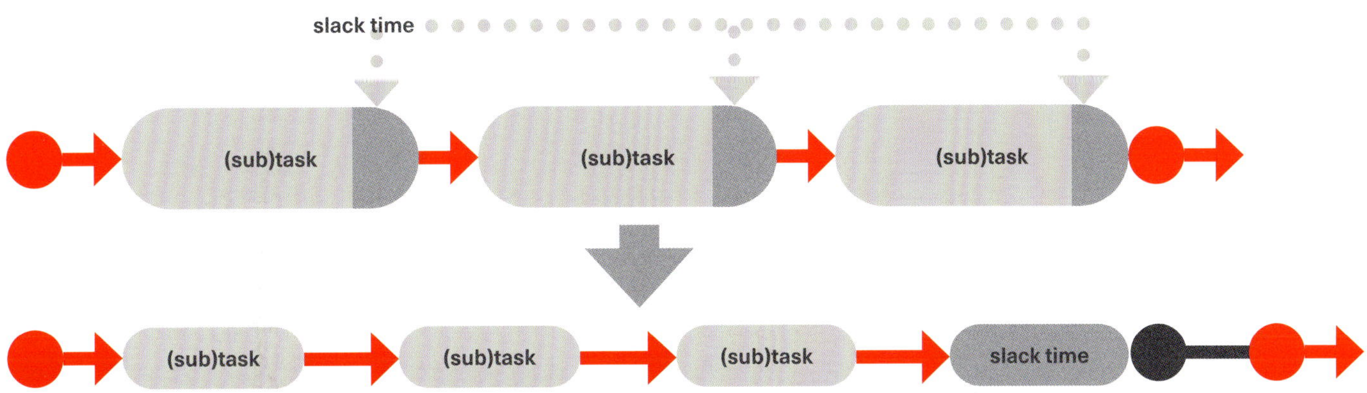

Most project planning software has too many features, like automatic scheduling based on the amount of work in hours needed and such. You will be tempted to use these. Don't. Too much detail requires constant adjustments and one of the main advantages of using only throughput time is that it keeps the schedule constant. You can concentrate on the overview.

As everyone knows (and does), we calculate a built-in reservoir of spare time 'in case of'. You know you need 1 day, with some dependencies it might be 2 days, but you tell others you need 5 days. So, you build in some reserve., i.e. slack time. Don't. Take the more transparent approach. Do ask for 2 days and hand the 3 days for an accumulated slack period at the end of a series of subtasks.

So, do not use the 'real' worktime. Use the 'throughput time' in which you think the work ought to be done. It is contrary to what people are used to do. Nevertheless, it is by far more convenient and transparent what the 'real' schedule is[2].

8.4. Stick to the decision

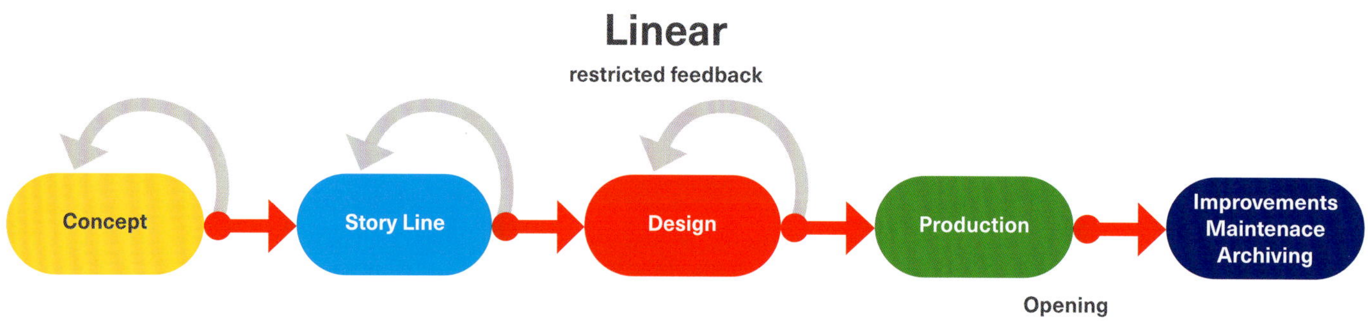

There are different ways how to move on after a decision is taken. When for example a storyline is agreed on, you will see that later some – experts – will ask for adaptations. Something of real importance is to be added. A decision is to be reconsidered.

This reconsideration of decisions is not what we would advise. When a decision is made, stick to it.

However, in museums there often is a more continuous feedback loop, the so-called 'spiral' way, in which adjustments on previous decisions are made along the way. It is more open to change and might even result in a return to or reinvestigation of an earlier part or aspect of the process.

As you can imagine, having read the previous paragraphs, we strongly advise not to walk that way. We think it a strict linear reasoning is by far the best, the most efficient and clear. Upon

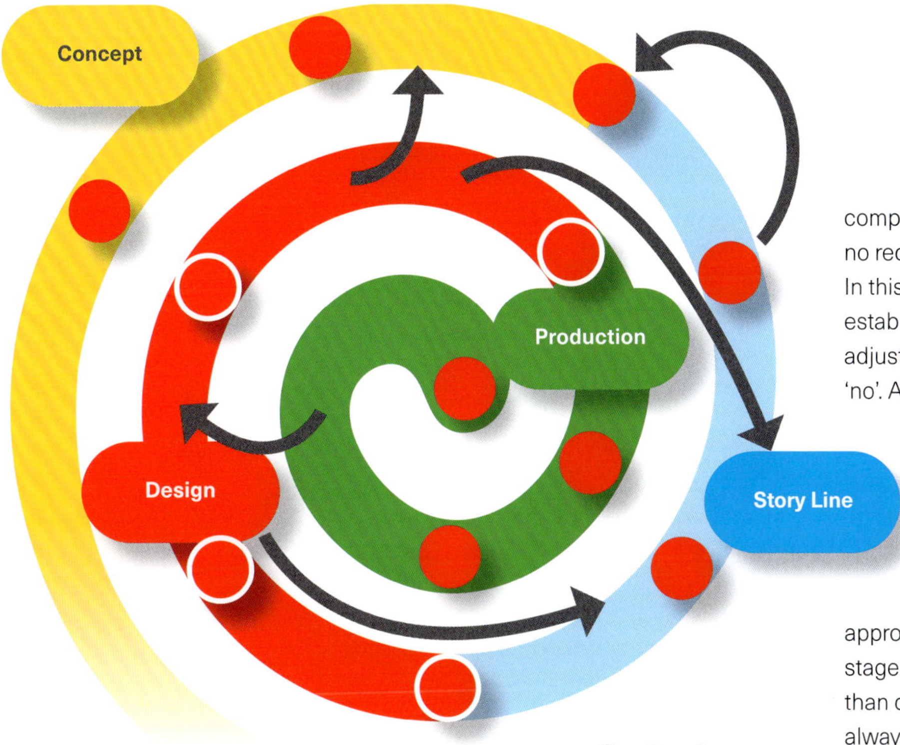

Spiral
continuous feedback

completion and approval of one phase, there is no reconsideration of decisions already taken. In this process, each phase has its deliverables established, and when agreed, set. If later on adjustments are asked for, the first response is 'no'. And the second response is to see if they can be resolved within the current phase, without much trouble. If not, it cannot be done. Sorry.

This process results in a very focused, efficient, and clearly defined approach, with outcomes determined for each stage. However, we know this is easier said than done, especially when the local culture always has been different and/or when is a more hierarchical one. Who dares to say no to the director? Do try, however.

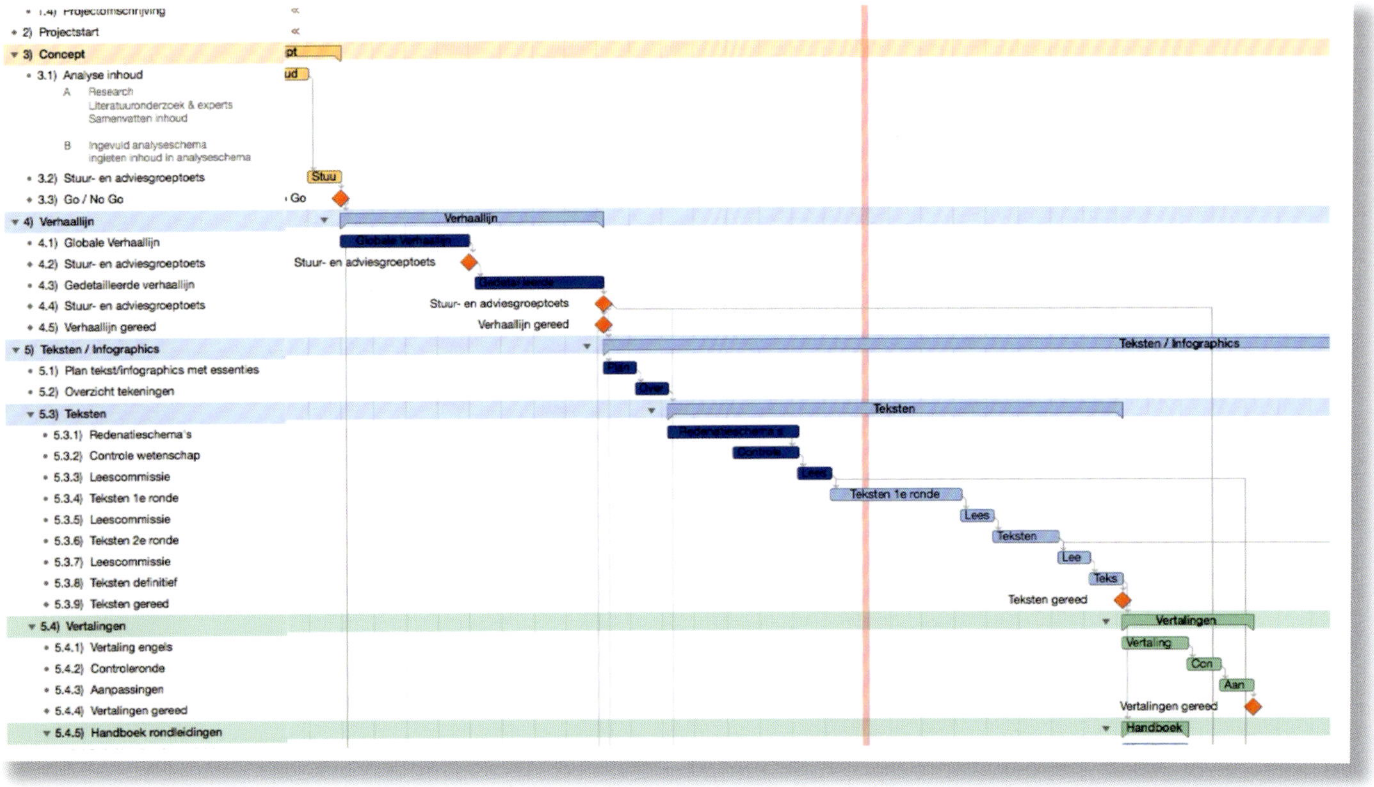

8.5. Come together: the project planning

A network diagram converted into a Gantt chart

The way to start is building a network diagram – the networked cascade of tasks - is a graphical way to view tasks (boxes) and dependencies (connecting lines, i.e. connectors). It is the way we show our drawings in this book.

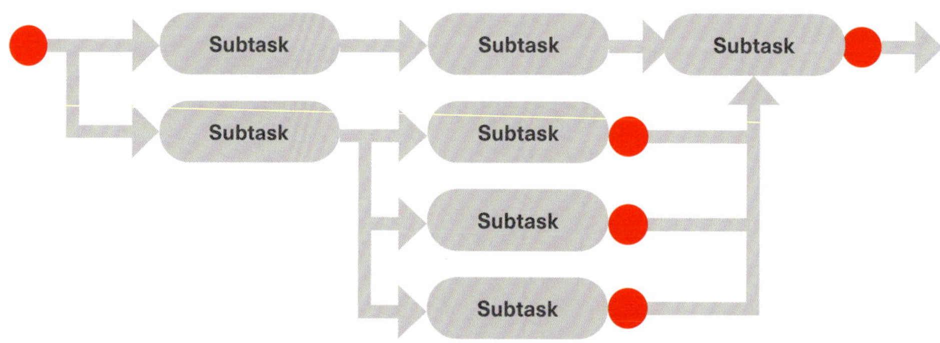

When done, set time with each task, you transform the network into a Gantt chart. A Gantt chart is just another representation of the network diagram, but better equipped for tracking progress in time. Both charts can be easily transposed into each other's format. However, when you are on your way, having built the logic and depth with a network diagram, after the transposition, you usually stick to a Gantt chart.

For building such a project planning timeline the way it should, you have to include:
- all tasks and the further breakdown in (sub)(sub)tasks, in the proper phases
- in their sequential and interdependent relationships
- including all milestones
- including blocked periods for slack, for holidays, etc.
- The estimated throughput time, leading (automatically) to the dates, timetable

8.6. The importance of a detailed Gantt chart

A detailed timeline for a project – a Gantt chart - including any connections to related activities, is an indispensable tool for mastering a museum plan. Its importance cannot be overestimated. By and via the timeline, each of the exhibition development phases and their elements are 'connected' through time. It shows to all involved: this is how we are going to do it.

If done correctly, a well-constructed timeline-in-the-form-of-a-Gantt-chart acts as a communication tool for the exhibition team and for the stakeholders. It shows the goals and expectations for any given period of time and for all players. It is transparent to everyone.

Standup meetings in front of a large print

The truth is, not many people find a project planning (Gantt chart) an easy read. So, do not expect individuals to study it carefully or actually use it as a guidance. The reason to have it, first of all, is to have all dates and milestones ready and communicable. By building the Gantt chart, you have an in- and oversight which you then have to share, preferably in standup meetings in front of the planning, with all co-workers together. It is then easier to show the consequences of certain (inevitable) delays on the planning. Is it on a critical path? How serious is a delay to be seen? It is thus really very helpful for the project manager to gather the team around periodically and walk through the weeks to come.

Thus, make sure your scheme is available to everyone, best positioned at a place where you gather and a place for small talk. Besides a large print where all the meetings are – the 'war room' – a copy may be placed at the coffee machine, for example.
Any exhibition process, small or large, scheme is too large for a series of A3 papers, to be glued to one large sheet. Try to get hold of a plotter – and use paper with a minimum size

of at least A0. The paper maybe cheap, the colours weak, but the size should be good. It is worthwhile investing in a plotter for very big paper sizes in order to produce these detailed, clearly readable, large-scale timelines. And if that fails, do glue the different A3-prints on one large lower plate of carton or multiplex.

As time goes by, the scheme needs to be redone once in a while, so there is no need for a careful treatment. Actually, it is the opposite. Feel free to make notes on it, directly or by using post-its.

Software and the sparse use of features

There are several dedicated software applications available, such as Microsoft Project, OmniPlan and such. The investment is worth it – money- and timewise. Regarding the time-investment: there is quite a learning curve involved. For this reason, most of the museums have their planning in a rather simplistic spreadsheet. The main advantage of project planning software however is the way it works with dependencies and the easy to map in full detail. As long as you keep the outline simple, KISS, the use of project planning software is a vital help.

Some words on KISS - 'keep it simple'. Most project planning software has far too many features, like automatic scheduling based on the amount of work in hours needed. You will be tempted to use these. Don't. Too much detail requires constantly adjustments and one of the main advantages of using only (1) throughput time, (2) interdependencies, and (3) task owners is that it keeps the schedule fairly constant. You can concentrate on the overview and there is no constant adjusting.

New versions of your timeline: only once in a while

Changes to timelines should be avoided (or made rarely and for exceptional reasons only). Consistency pays. Adjustments do confuse and make people tend to take the planning less seriously. And as said earlier: the major milestones with the meeting dates of the stakeholders are not to be changed at all. Sticking to the ones you've said early on signals you are in control. It is important though to have frequently new prints of the current timeline – adapted for results achieved or delays of significance. When a task is finished, or nearly finished for example, you put it onto 75% or 100% 'done'. The colours will directly change according to your pre-set definition. And if you have a serious delay, put in an extra module 'delay' in fire-engine red.

So, they should be updates, no new versions where adjustments do influence the whole timeline.

On the positive side, milestones are worth celebrating, not only with the team involved but with as broad a group as possible. They not only are dots on the horizon to look forward to, they function as moments of 'internal communication' too.

9. A detailed description of each phase

As said, each task is 'done' after a certain time. A task – most tasks - has a predefined result to be delivered by the task-owner. If this result is a building block to be used, we call it a 'deliverable'. In the first phases of the exhibition process, a deliverable takes most often the form of documents, and/or mock-ups, drawings and calculations.

In the tables on the forthcoming pages the different tasks, its subtasks and its deliverables are set in some detail. This is still not as extensive as your elaborated schedule could and should be, but if it gives you a pretty good baseline.

Notes: There some subphases added which are not visualized in the general framework. The validation of the deliverables is described in the decision-making process later on.

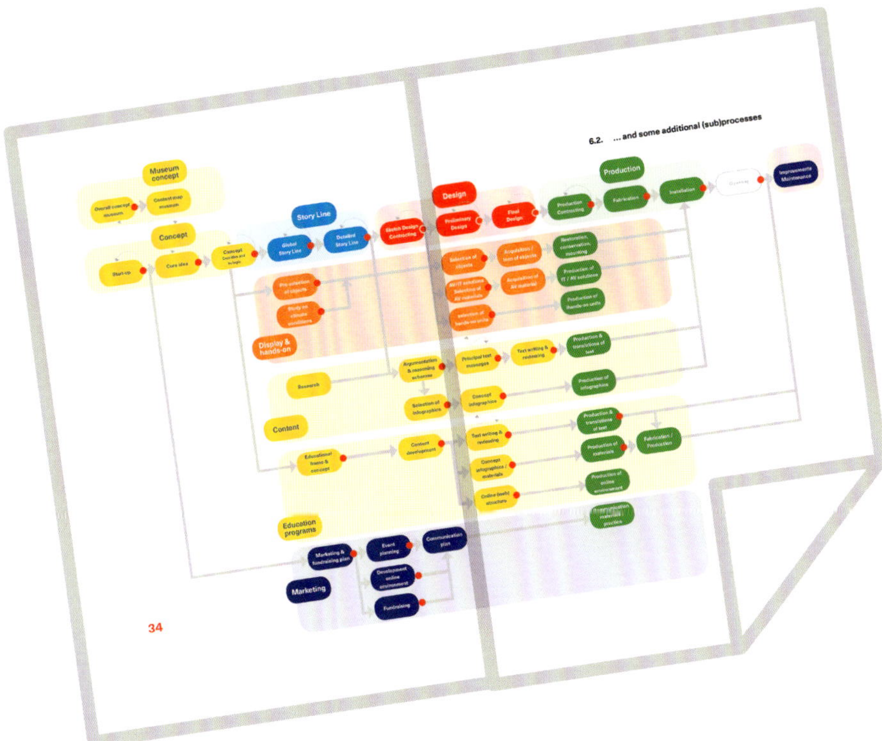

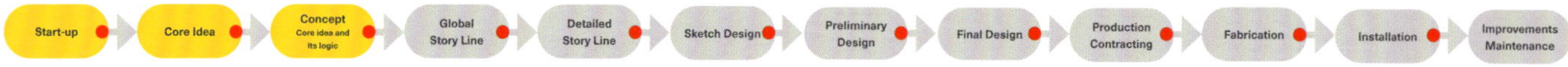

9.1. Concept phase

Phase	Description	Lead	Deliverable
Concept Phase	The concept phase takes the museum through the process of considering and fully defining a central or core idea for an exhibition – and of the way it is going to organize its development.		There are two deliverables: A concept that defines the core idea and its logic in detail, as well as a description of the process and its organization. You might call this report a ***Preliminary museological study*** as is the custom in some countries.
Start-up	The start-up phase sets out the basic terms of the proposed project and its objectives. It includes the operational setup and its boundaries, as well as the targets (goals made testable) and preliminary ideas on positioning and content		A (initiative or start-up) report including • the operational set-up, including a project description, a preliminary timeline, an initial organizational chart, and a budget estimate • as well as the targeted goals • and the initial idea(s) for the exhibition outline.
Initial idea(s)	What is the initial idea (or ideas) for a projected exhibit, and how well does it meet the expectations of the museum and its main stakeholders (including the museum's audiences)? How does it fit within the museum's philosophy and activities? How does it relate to the competitive environment?	Content director	A report that includes a presentation of the proposed idea and how it serves the expectations of the stakeholders and the museum's field of activities and research. An analysis of the museum's "market" and competitive position is part of the deliverable.
Preliminary budget assessment	What is the range of prices pro square foot/metre for a project of this size and substance? What is the estimated or potential overall budget for the project? What are some key budget figures on items such as the acquisition of specific objects, building renovations, technologies, travel expenses, etc.?	Project manager	An overview of budget expectations and prices, in a generalized way, with some detailed figures on specific project items of relevance to the museum.

Phase	Description	Lead	Deliverable
Preliminary ideas on the project team(s) and steering committee and advisory groups	What team(s) should be in place to run a project and to oversee it? Does the existing museum staff have the capacity to undertake the entire project or just specific parts of it? Who are the most significant stakeholders and how should they be represented on the teams established in conjunction with a project? Who needs to be on an overall exhibition steering committee (whether one already exists or not)?	Project manager	An outline of the work process, which consists of an initial organizational chart, including museum and stakeholder representation at various levels of activity and responsibility, and the overall decision-making process. Selection and possible contracting of project team member(s) and/or companies.
Process description and preliminary timeline	A description of the work process (for example, as outlined in this appendix), adjusted to institutional conditions and translated into a preliminary timeline with milestones.	Project manager	A generalized but detailed timeline, including all phases / tasks, milestones, and deliverables.
Core idea	The core idea reflects the essence of the new exhibition. What is the working title, the tagline? The idea must be consistent with the museum vision, mission, values, intellectual activities, audience, etc.	Content director	A short description that outlines the essential core idea and contents of a forthcoming project and how it relates to the museum and its stakeholders, staff capacity, market, budget, etc.
Concept	The concept is an elaboration of the core idea, now including the logic of its underlying structure. Often this involves broad research into the literature on the topic and discussion with experts. Stakeholders and visitors can be surveyed for their reactions to the proposed concept. The concept becomes the basis for the project's future development.	Content director	A report explaining the core idea and its underlying logic. It is represented in a visual, a schematic drawing. A front-end visitor evaluation may be conducted at this point; results may be included in the report.

9.2. Storyline phase

Phase	Description	Lead	Deliverable
Storyline Phase	This phase describes, in depth, the narrative or storyline of the chosen concept. In addition to detailing the storyline itself, this phase gathers examples, ideas, and options for transmitting the story. This phase is of crucial importance as the story is structured for the exhibition, the educational programming and the events as well.	**Content director**	A detailed storyline or storylines. In a separate addendum there could be stories and links outlined for educational, event and marketing purposes. The name of this deliverable should be in line with the accepted customs, as it is called a Museological study in some places.
Global storyline	The function of the global storyline is to outline the content of the project and to serve as a communication piece to inform all project teams, the designer, other stakeholders, future evaluation activities, etc. Therefore, it restricts itself to the major components, up to the second or third level of detailing. It consists of schemes, text, and drawings, and is the starting point for the sketch design (see Design phase, below)	**Content director**	A content map, thematic structure, and written table consisting of all content components to be considered, listed, and numbered, with an outline showing how they relate to the concept-and also the preliminary ideas on the form and content of the presentation.
Detailed storyline	The detailed storyline describes, in depth, all facts and figures related or relevant to the components concerned, up to the most detailed level. The project contents are strictly organized in a grid-like format that expresses the logical structure of the concept and serves as the reference for all involved in the development or approval of the project. As this is a major undertaking, it may end up as a book on the subject.	**Content director**	A substantial and detailed manuscript discussing the project's content, strictly organized to reflect any modular aspects of the elaborated concept itself. Visualizations – sketches, schemes – are an indispensable part.

9.3. Design phase

Phase	Description	Lead	Deliverable
Design phase	It is in this phase that project content meets design, and these essential aspects of a project must connect logically and visually. This very critical phase is divided into three distinct steps to guarantee an outcome that meets stated expectations.		The design phase, in the end, delivers a final, overall design for the production of the project. It includes (anticipates) elements for tendering purposes.
Sketch design	In the sketch design stage, the major concern is to connect content and space and deliver 'the big idea' of the design approach, as well as the voice and tone of the installation. Sketches developed during this stage are used in further visitor surveys and become part of the decision-making process.	Design director	An overview (bird's-eye) sketch or sketches, some detailing of major aspects of the exhibit, a floor plan, a description of the style of the installation, possibly a three-dimensional scale model, some preliminary calculations, and a front-end visitor survey.
Preliminary design	The chosen sketch design is now detailed to include all design elements, including objects, audiovisual presentations, interpretive components, etc. In addition to description for all content components determined to date, there is an outline of all necessary technical feasibility, prototyping studies and budget calculations.	Design director	An extensive sketchbook, a possible scale model, or individual component prototypes, as well as dimensions and cost calculation sheets. Another front-end visitor survey on specific points may be included if design clarification is needed.
Final design	The aim is to detail all design elements for production drawings. Corrections to costs, technical features, objects selected, etc., are indicated, but within the boundaries of the earlier proposals. The final design represents a clear understanding of all aspects of the design.	Production managerr	A 'book' consisting of all design drawings and calculations, including visitor responses to the concept and design for it. This deliverable recognizes and anticipates which elements are going to be used for public tendering purposes.

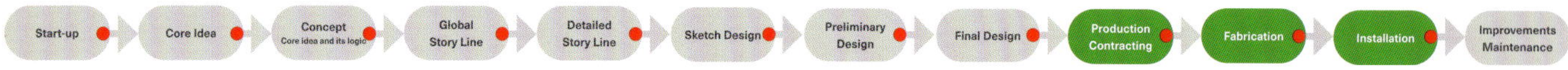

9.4. Production phase (and contracting)

Phase	Description	Lead	Deliverable
Production Phase	The production phase involves fabrication and installation of the exhibitions.	**Production manager**	Fabricated and installed exhibition.
Production contracting	This subphase describes various aspects of the production process, when developing an installation, including the outsourcing of fabrication. This is a phase, with several subphases, in which contractors are determined possibly by tenders, prices are set, and timelines and calculations are, if necessary, adapted. This part of the process might also be an integral part of the work of the design company if design and fabrication are combined in a 'turnkey' installation.	**Production manager**	A list of needs, the drafting of tender documents, the selection of possible contractors, the detailing of production data, etc. The final deliverables are the contract and the selected contractors.
Selection procedure	The search for suitable production companies as well as acceptable pricing (including specific costing for items such as showcases) requires considerable time. Reputable and experienced contractors represent a huge advantage.	**Production manager**	A short list of contractors (suppliers and fabricators) and related needs
Tendering	The tendering process will follow European as well as local and/or museum procedures, which might vary. The importance for a detailed tender-request package, including the procedures for decision making, cannot be overstated.	**Production manager**	At the outset of this process, a tender request and package of drawings and specifications, with a clear articulation of terms and their characteristics, as well as other conditions.

Phase	Description	Lead	Deliverable
Selection, additional negotiations, contract	Once the bids are received, clarification may be needed on prices, areas where the responsibilities of two or more contractors meet or overlap, technical descriptions, guarantees and support, etc. The selection of contractor(s) should not be rushed, so additional time may be needed for recalculating and/or amending the actual contracts.	**Production manager**	A set of contracts with project contractor(s) and the establishment of work protocol.
Fabrication	Fabrication leads to the creation of various components ready for the installation of a project's contents. This phase, in particular, may have interwoven parts from different contractors, which sometimes continues during the actual installation.	**Production manager**	Creation of a project's various contents.
Preparation of fabrication	The initial preparation results in (a) working drawings, (b) a detailed production plan, (c) orders for materials (considering also delivery times/delays), and (d, optional) contracts with small or specialized subcontract parties.	**Production manager**	Sets of drawings, a list of subcontractors, and a timeline that gathers together all time-based flows.
Actual fabrication	A considerable amount of time will be spent by fabricators, suppliers, internal suppliers, third parties, etc., to create the project contents, which include the components of an overall gallery setting, object display components, audiovisual settings, graphic displays, printed materials, etc. →	**Production manager**	A check list with all ready-made or fully prepared, and approved, installation components. For each major component a listed procedure – including photos – might be handy.

Phase	Description	Lead	Deliverable
Actual fabrication	This phase also include time for the conservation, preparation, and mounting of objects. As this is often a very time-consuming phase – it is best to have it started early in the time schedule with all presumed objects.	**Production manager**	
Installation	This stage involves the installation of all project contents.	**Production manager**	The installed and fully functional exhibition.
Gallery preparation	The preparation of the gallery (galleries) for installation consists of cleaning, refurbishment, and adding or improving lighting, electrical and information technology installations, etc.	**Production manager**	An empty gallery space, with the needed installation equipment and materials at hand.
Transport and storage	In a parallel process, the transportation and storage of all installation content materials and equipment need to be considered as well as the possible move of objects from a preparation facility to the galleries. This phase may be outsourced or included in the fabricators' responsibilities.	**Production manager**	A table indicating transportation services being used, storage locations (on- or off-site), downloading and installation equipment required, and the plan for downloading components.
Installation (in gallery)	In a parallel process, the transportation and storage of all installation content materials and equipment need to be considered as well as the possible move of objects from a preparation facility to the galleries. This phase may be outsourced or included in the fabricators' responsibilities.	**Production manager**	A completely installed exhibit, ready for testing and approval.

Phase	Description	Lead	Deliverable
Testing and delivery or completion	Testing, remedial evaluation, and fine-tuning of the installation are the focus of this phase. It is not unusual to have this phase extended until after the official opening, as often some problems become apparent only after initial use of the exhibition.	**Production manager**	The museum's formal acceptance of the installation.
Opening	The opening marks the formal end of the exhibition development process and the starting point for the presentation and maintenance of the installation. In practice, however, there is often an overlap, when the formal delivery has not yet been accepted by the museum and/or its maintenance has not been transferred from exhibition fabricators to the maintenance staff.	**Production manager**	There often is a set of instructions for the opening itself. Besides there is a need for a set of 'acceptance statements' to transfer the responsibilities to, for example, the maintenance staff.

9.5. Maintenance

Phase	Description	Lead	Deliverable
Maintenance	The maintenance of an installation is also part of the production planning procedure, although often not incorporated. There must be a consideration of, and budget for, the actual "wear and tear "on a new installation, and how to deal with its maintenance in financial terms as well as staffing, training, documentation, and responsibility. A visitor evaluation might be a very helpful tool for deciding on adaptations.		There are three deliverables: A maintenance guide, including the 'technical sets' (drawings, guidelines, and such), as well as a description of the responsibilities, the budget allocated, and procedures for reparations, including guarantees / responsibilities of the manufacturer (even after 'acceptance'). Then there is a visitor evaluation.
Maintenance, adjustments, and adaptations	A set of maintenance instructions and documentation is needed for maintenance staff and other internal services. The technical documentation is part of the contract(s) with the fabricator(s). Of equal importance is a procedure for handling or dealing with adjustments and adaptations that may be required as a result of technical, design, or other malfunctions.	**Production manager**	The documentation for maintenance staff and instructions for other technical staff, including budget and procedures for dealing with modifications (needed or desired).
Summative surveys and adaptations	Summative visitor evaluations, peer evaluation, and exhibition development staff evaluation are carried out during this phase along with, if needed, the installation adjustments that come out of the surveys or that are otherwise identified.	**Project manager**	
Deinstallation and reuse	The actual dismantling of an exhibit, including the possible reuse of infrastructure materials and/or the renovation of display items, if necessary.	**Production manager**	A preliminary list of components of the exhibit, their 'owners' (including the museum itself) and how/where to return items, as necessary, after closing of the exhibition.

Phase	Description	Lead	Deliverable
Archiving	Who is going to store what? Selected deliverables (display objects, infrastructure material, etc.) and installation documentation (e.g., video or photographic records), as well as all adjustments and maintenance experiences during the installation, need to be catalogued and stored in such a way that retrieving a record of the installation, or the physical components of it, is fast and easy. For example, the need for retrieving images and texts years after an opening is often underestimated. As archiving is necessary and important throughout the process, it is best to prepare for it at the start of the project.	**Production manager**	A plan as well as the end result, i.e. the archive of the exhibition development, production, and installation.

9.6. Concept development for an entire museum

Phase	Description	Lead	Deliverable
Concept development for an extended or entire museum	This subprocess considers how an idea for an overall group of exhibitions of a renovated or new museum must be developed so as to connect the individual parts of an idea logically and deliver a structured content that can also be connected to the floor plan of the museum's galleries.	**Content director**	
Concept	The phase is an elaboration of the single exhibition concept phase, but it includes the concept for the entire museum (the core idea in its major components), structured in a logical and visually consistent proposal. In this subphase, the proposal is restricted to the major components as it needs to correspond to the architectural spaces of the overall building facility.	**Content director**	The concept tor the entire space/museum (core idea and its logical structure), represented in a schematic drawing with sketches that capture the style of each part of the installation. A front-end visitor evaluation can be part of this report.
Content map	As most museums have an existing building, the content map for a new or renovated collection presentation would need to be 'laid over' the existing museum floor plan. It is important to maintain the logic/consistency of the core idea in the content map. The exhibitions should stay on the same level of abstraction and connect logically to support the overarching core idea, as the museum should strive for a logical structure of its entire installation.	**Content director**	A content map that lays out the exhibition floor plan of the museum, showing the designated themed galleries and, eventually, a suggested visitors' path.

9.7. Selection of the display materials

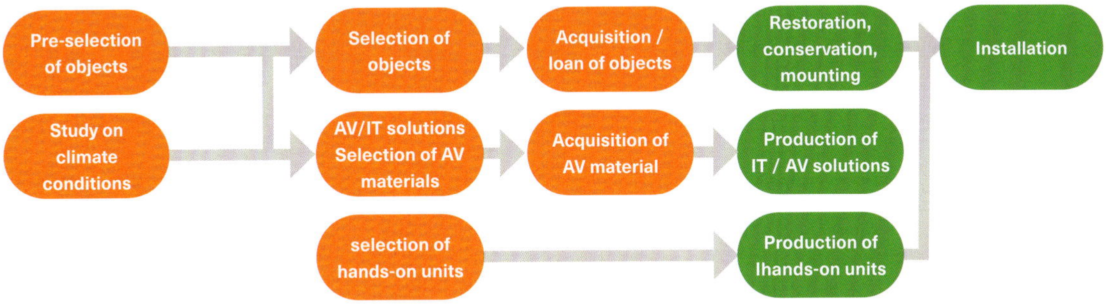

Phase	Description	Lead	Deliverable
Selection of the display and hands-on materials	The visual carriers of the storyline can be the objects themselves, audio-visual materials, infographics, texts, etc. The selection of objects, as well as the development of audio-visuals (including interactive software) for installation, is a task not to be underestimated. Often it requires more time than originally allotted to it and is a challenging logistical procedure. These tasks therefore require separate phases and planning.		
Study on climate conditions	There often are restrictions to the range of climatic conditions – temperature, light, humidity – allowed. Though often interpreted to strict, they are essential to know for the designer and for the ones choosing the objects.	Production manager	A (yearly updated) report on the climatic conditions in the exhibition galleries during the day and the seasons. Part 2 consists of specific conditions on vulnerable objects known. The report will be essential to the designer and should therefore be accompanied with conclusions and directives.

Phase	Description	Lead	Deliverable
Selection of objects	Before the exhibition development process starts, there is likely to be an understanding on the part of the museum as to its key collection objects for display (the 'masterpieces' of the museum). However, many objects have to be chosen or confirmed while work proceeds on the storyline and the design. The desired objects, as well as the display characteristics they should have, are set out in 'wish lists' indicating their relative importance and possible alternatives.	**Content director**	An extensive database consisting of a list of objects (including alternatives), their material and display characteristics, their need for conservation and preparation and mounting, the cost of these procedures, and their need for conservation and preparation and mounting, the cost of these procedures, and the exhibition module to which they belong.
Acquisition or loan of additional objects	If necessary or desirable, objects need to be acquired or borrowed. Locating these objects and negotiating the terms of their use requires considerable time. Keeping track of the preparation status (conservation, mounting, etc.) necessary for such objects, as well as the budget required, is also essential.	**Project manager**	An updated database of all objects (including status, etc.) anticipated for installation.
Restoration, conservation, mounting of objects	As most objects need additional treatment, their conservation, preparation, and mounting need to be done by staff or outsourced. For an installation of an entire museum, thousands of objects need to be prepared. This may take years of work.	**Production manager**	A database that includes the tracking information on the location and treatment (including the duration and status of the treatment) for all objects. This also needs to include the 'production' flow chart for the objects and the protocols for their move, storage, and security.
Selection of AV	Choosing the kind of audio-visual presentations, photographs, film sequences, etc. to be used should be undertaken in relation to the stories and the choice of objects as they have to complement one another in their capacity to transmit the storyline.	**Content director**	As with the objects, the deliverable is a database listing all wanted images (moving or still) and their contents, including alternatives, and an indication of the display module to which they belong.

Phase	Description	Lead	Deliverable
Acquisition of audio-visuals	As is the case with the objects, the process of acquiring audio-visuals, or finding suitable alternatives, is costly and time-consuming and needs considerable attention.	**AV director**	A timeline, including the steps to be taken to acquire desired materials, as well as a detailed database tracking system.
Production of AV material	Photographs, film/video footage(s), and/or audio recordings may have to be made specifically for the installation in order to illustrate or present a certain component of a storyline. The process of producing such material is costly and time-consuming and has to be done in parallel with fabrication of sets.	**AV director**	Stills, video, or sound material ready for installation.
Selection of hands-on units	Some insights are much more effectively explained by infographics, AV and/or hands-on objects or units. They have to be balanced to each other. There might also be a use for hands-on experiences with real objects or added artefacts. Besides the explanatory power, there is an advantage in having a variety of means – not least for children.	**Content director & technical director**	A list of all (possible) hands-on installations wanted, preferably scored within a matrix of types of interactives.
Production of hands-on units	The actual production of hands-on units often is costly and time-consuming. It is therefore preferable to be part of the tendering procedure – except when you have your own technical staff.	**Production manager**	Hands-on units ready for installation.

9.8. Continuation of exhibition content development

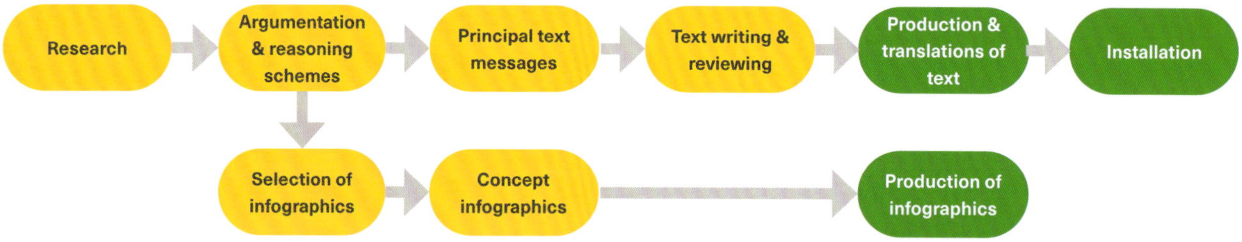

Phase	Description	Lead	Deliverable
Continuation of exhibition content development	Content development will be reflected in the overall design of an installation, including the organization of collection objects and interpretive support material such as text panels, audiovisual presentations, labels, etc. Texts and infographics are added to explain a display using either a narrative or visuals.	**Content director**	Texts and infographics to augment a display.
Research	A period of information gathering, transforming the content into a logic deconstruction of essential insights, cause-effect argumentations etc. The amount of time needed varies significantly.	**Content director**	A report describing the content of the exhibit, preferably structurally organized in building blocks / interconnected modules.
Argumentation (reasoning schemes) Analysis grid	The analysis grid and reasoning schemes are created to check the validity of the scientific construct, and its logic. They are a drawn up as a set of arguments, constructed in a logical, structured schema. The reason for undertaking this argumentation is to facilitate subsequent text writing and to check the content of the texts and their logic with experts.	**Content director**	An analysis grid and subsequent reasoning schemes for each and every module in the storyline. If correct and approved, they serve as input for the next phase in this subprocess (text messages, below).

Phase	Description	Lead	Deliverable
Principal text messages	In each and every module of the storyline, the text components are presented so as to distinguish their importance and, as well, to anticipate different levels of 'learning' interest that a visitor may have. These text messages (or 'content parts') serve as building blocks for text writing. The clusters of text components are also developed with the school curriculum and other target groups in mind.	**Content director**	An extended document consisting of all text messages
Text writing and reviewing	The draft texts are read and reread by a review group. Different members may be assigned different aspects of the text (logic, readability, attractiveness, number of words, comprehensibility, terminology, appropriate word use, etc.). Some visitor testing should also be included.	**Content director**	A collection of finished texts neatly organized in large batches by modules.
Translation and production	When necessary, the translation (and checking) of texts flows into the actual production of the graphic panels. All texts should undergo copyediting before they go into print. This phase is notorious for mistakes, misunderstandings, last-minute adaptations, etc. A well-organized flow of full-scale mock-ups will help reduce the level of stress and error.	**Content director**	A complete set of copy proofs (to be checked) and a finished set of panels for production.

Phase	Description	Lead	Deliverable
Selection of infographics	An infographic is a visual presentation that is closely connected to, or even substitutes for, text. They sometimes explain certain processes better than words. One challenge, however, lies in the time-consuming and relatively expensive production of infographics. Animations are considered 'moving infographics' and are part of this phase. Some preliminary cost calculations are also included in this phase.	**Content director**	A list or database of infographics, including some preliminary cost calculations.
Concept infographics	Each infographic is defined in terms of its location in the exhibition as well as its own intrinsic structure and principal message. This information is accompanied by rudimentary illustrations showing the process and perhaps highlighting certain components. The infographics are to be checked with experts. A style sheet is made under the direction of the design director to define the graphic style, use of colours, etc.	**Production of infographics**	A more detailed overview of all infographics to be produced, as well as their principal messages and, separately, a generalized example/style sheet for all infographics.
	The actual production of infographics by illustrators takes time and needs to be monitored carefully. The process will include reviewing the graphics and their texts, as well as any other texts in the same display. When outsourcing this task, the choice of illustrators or designers who can work quickly, easily incorporate changes, and deliver illustrations built up in digital layers (which allows components to be used individually) is an important concern, as is the cost per illustration.	**Production manager**	At the beginning of this subprocess, the deliverable is a detailed timeline, including ample time for corrections. The end result consists of the actual drawings, which will flow into the overall production of the various exhibition modules.

9.9. Education programmes

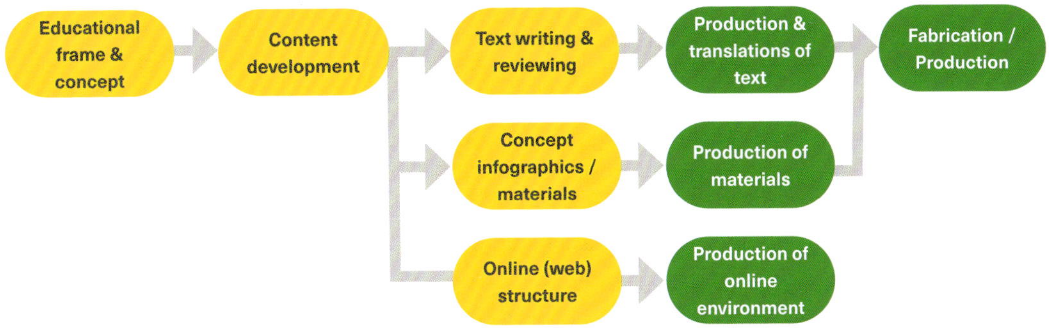

Phase	Description	Lead	Deliverable
Education Programmes	The production of accompanying educational programmes requires its own development process and production system. There is a mutual influence, as the exhibition includes input in the form of team representation, information, needs, etc., from education staff.		Educational programmes that resonate with the concept and execution of the exhibition.
Educational model (frame), concept and strategy	It is helpful to have an explicit educational frame or model, preferably as an extension of the frame used in the exhibitions. It describes the connections between examples and the underlying structure or system you want to get across. The educational concept might be described as the core insights you want to get across, as well as it could be used to express the strategy how the programmes are structured, and the insights are to be transferred and shared. There is in most cases a division to be made for the different school and/or age levels.	**Education manager**	A descriptive manual in three parts. One is the educational concept used. The second part is the educational model, describing the approach of how examples and underlying insights and structures are connected. This part extends to a third part explicitly describing your strategy or approach. Make it clear where there is a differentiation regarding the age groups and possible school types.

Phase	Description	Lead	Deliverable
Content development	Based on the educational concept and model, as well as the exhibition content concept (the analysis grid), the different modules are to be structured. This is to be differentiated for the different age and school levels. The division of what should become textual and infographical elements	**Education manager**	A modular grid – preferably (loosely) based on the analysis grid – with the different content parts and relevant context. Take into account where infographics should be added. For each educational programme this has to be differentiated. A different approach (strategy) for each class of age / school type might be added.
Text writing and reviewing	The actual writing of the texts. The system of decomposing text messages before the actual writing might be used. See the explanation in this book.	**Education manager**	A structured textbook.
Production and translations of text	The resulting appointments and work when additional work is to be done – like translations, contracts, or the development of booklets.	**Production manager**	The resulting contracts, forms, translations.
Concept infographics and illustrative materials	The different infographics needed are to be developed and detailed. Be aware you focus on the essentials needed for the transfer of insights. For production purposes it is needed to have an outline of what type of infographics you want. So, include examples and style descriptions.	**Production manager**	A list of all needed infographics, in descriptions and sketches, as well as a manual on the preferred style.
Production of materials	The actual phase in which the result is to be produced.	**Production manager**	The resulting products.
Online web structure and content	Alongside each exhibit, an online educational structure can draw upon the information and graphics developed for an installation project. In effect, it can reuse or adapt the exhibition content, storyline, texts, infographics, and audiovisuals, as well as the entire design style of the installation.	**Education manager**	A framework (interaction design) for web (mobile) purposes.

Phase	Description	Lead	Deliverable
	It might be an additional mobile tool for use in the exhibitions too. Especially for school groups, adaptation of /to the educational framework will be necessary.		
Production of online environment	There are two components to it: (1) building the environment and (2) the production of (filling in with) the actual content.	**Production manager**	A ready-to-use online environment.

9.10. Marketing, Communication and Fundraising

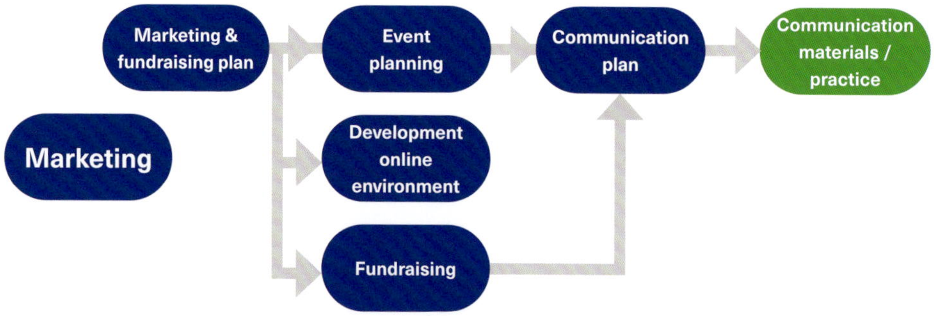

Phase	Description	Lead	Deliverable
Marketing, communication and fundraising	The strategic positioning of the museum within its knowledge domain, and within the realm of related or comparable institutions, is important. It is essential, therefore, from the beginning of the development process that the marketing group is represented on the project team and on the steering committee and is always present to understand and influence decisions being made. The same can also be said for the department responsible for fundraising.	Marketing manager	Ongoing fundraising and marketing activities set to realistic goals and a 'plan B' option when the results are not as they were supposed to be. A set of communication materials and practices, again set in relation to the objectives aimed for.
Marketing and fundraising plan	The marketing and fund-raising expectations or objectives are to clearly be articulated in written form. This includes a 'Plan B' when (financial) objectives are not met, as It can be very disruptive if plans or goals change during the development process because of changes in the possible funding sources after a project is under way.	Marketing manager	A marketing and a fund-raising plan, including outlined expectations, criteria, as well as strategic considerations and realistic objectives.

Phase	Description	Lead	Deliverable
Online environment	It is supposed an online environment will be part of the marketing, communication and fundraising efforts. Therefore, a dedicated web application should be available, whether as part of the current museums website(s) or as a separate domain.	**Marketing manager**	A ready-to-use online environment, filled with the content developed.
Event planning	To keep public and media attention going, additional public and educational activities (events, happenings) are required for different public groups. The planning - in synchronicity with holidays - requires systematic scheduling. Be sure to 'colour in' too all remembrance days, holidays, weekends, religious and other national days, and all types of special moments connected to the museum-topics. Not all subjects are there yet, but a baseline can be set. What (kind of) activity is required when? Think in series. There is a need for a plan in this stage, as it often is a tool in the marketing and fundraising perspectives.	**Marketing manager**	An event calendar, preferably a graphic, including all holidays, special moments and such, and all specific (series of) activities are to be planned for different audience groups. The plan will be used too in the communication story of the exhibition.
Communication plan	Communication of the museum's new exhibition is of crucial importance. It directly follows the museum's branding, strategic positioning and objectives, which will be outlined in the marketing plan.	**Marketing manager**	A communication plan, including all aspects of a marketing communication plan, such as target groups, objectives for each targeted group, means and such. The communication plan aims for all the different audience segments, as well as all other stakeholders of importance. It also takes into account the variety of activities.
Production & practice	The production of communication materials and their operational use.	**Marketing manager**	The ready-to-use materials as well as the campaigning itself, including the measurement of the results compared to the objectives.
Fundraising campaign	As external funds are quite often of crucial importance, a fundraising plan needs to be as clearly structured as possible, setting objectives in time. As fundraising is often not delivering, the need for a plan B is crucial for the development team. It is preferable to work as if there will be very limited success, so all new funds are an extra, allowing specific features.		The fundraising plan, as well as the actual results compared to the objectives set.

Panorama 1326 Bursa Fetih Müzesi

Section 2

Team, stakeholders and visitor studies

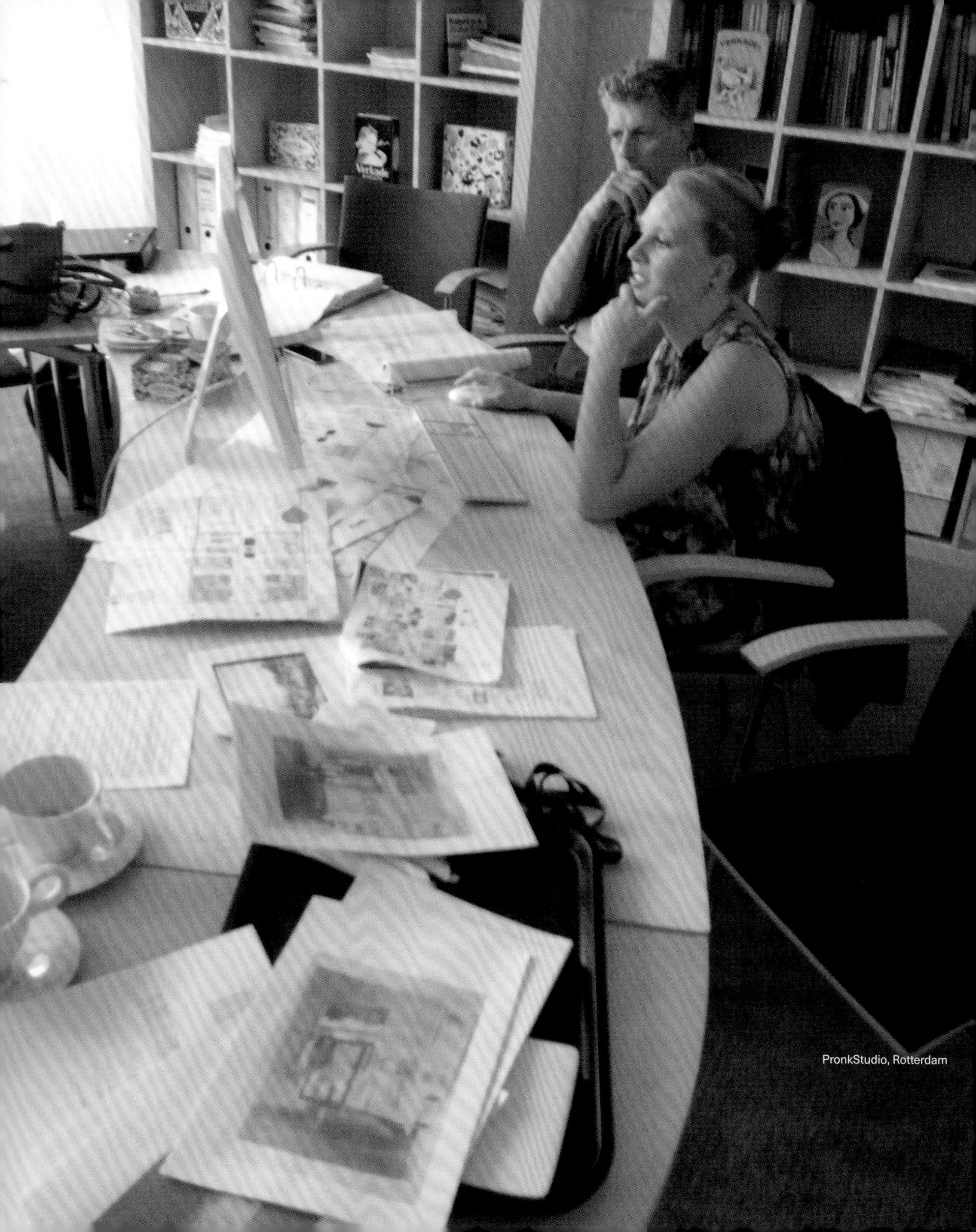

PronkStudio, Rotterdam

10. The exhibition development team

To build a good exhibition requires the engagement and management of different disciplines and people, often over a period of years. This is likely to be particularly so when renovating or building a new museum.

To have a team work together as a unit for many years might be one of the most neglected aspects of the exhibition development process, as well as one of the most important.
Like a sports team, an exhibition development team is more than the sum of its individual parts. Building such a team is not just about getting the best people, although the quality of individuals is very important. It is about the dynamics of the group, its joint vision and working style. It is also about finding the right people for the specific subject matter, with the presentation of the subject matter being influenced by the nature and quality or experience of the team members.

10.1. Exhibition team members and their roles

There might be an exhibition team on an ongoing basis at your museum, which develops, monitor and/or oversee exhibition development activities or needs. For large-scale exhibition development, however, it is most likely that a specific team (or teams) will be established when the project gets under way. We describe a team composition and a way of working in the chapter below. Where we do speak of *members*, that might as well be *roles*, as in smaller museums they sometimes have to be combined. And we do acknowledge there are different names attached to them too.

The key members of an exhibition development team are usually: (1) the project manager/ director, (2) the content director, (3) the art/design director, (4) the production manager, (5) a supporting technology director/designer (electrical, multimedia, new media, etc.), and (6) the administrative/ finance coordinator. They might come under different names, as a content director often is called an interpretive planner in the Anglo-Saxon world.
In addition to these members, a core exhibition team will have other regular players, including curators, interpretive planners (content developers), lighting designers, graphic designers, educators, marketing or fundraising experts, and administrative support staff.

There are different ways of dividing the roles and responsibilities among the players on an exhibition team, as well as ways of structuring the team. However, some general circumstances seem to prevail. The project manager, the content director, the art/design director, and the production manager tend to be the principal players in the process of developing exhibitions.
In our belief, the project manager should be a (supervising) content director (interpretive

planner) as well, for reasons we think that storytelling is most crucial, but other combinations might do as well.

Whatever the choice, the synergy and dynamics of such a group (personalities as well as roles and work structure) determine the working style of the entire team.

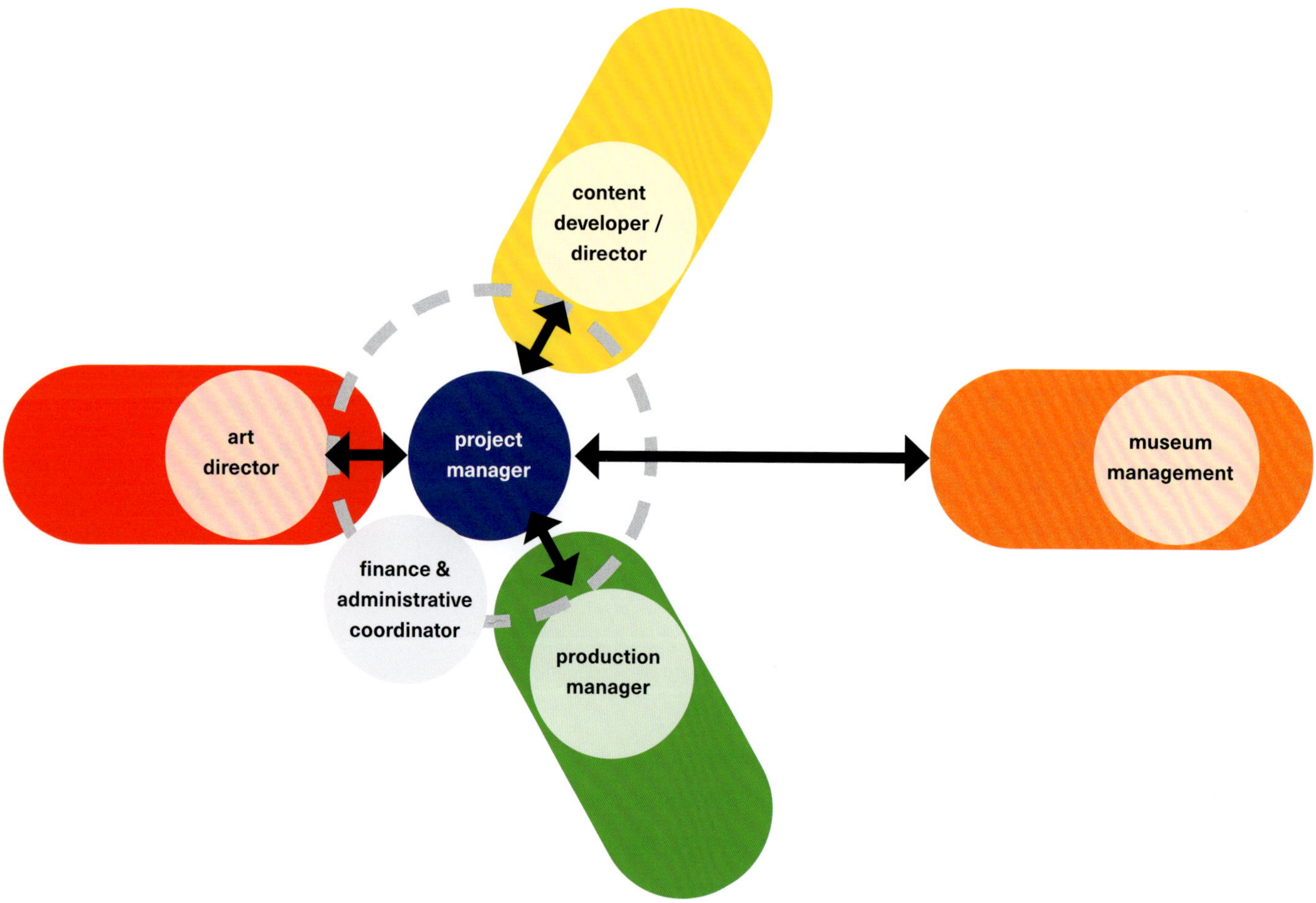

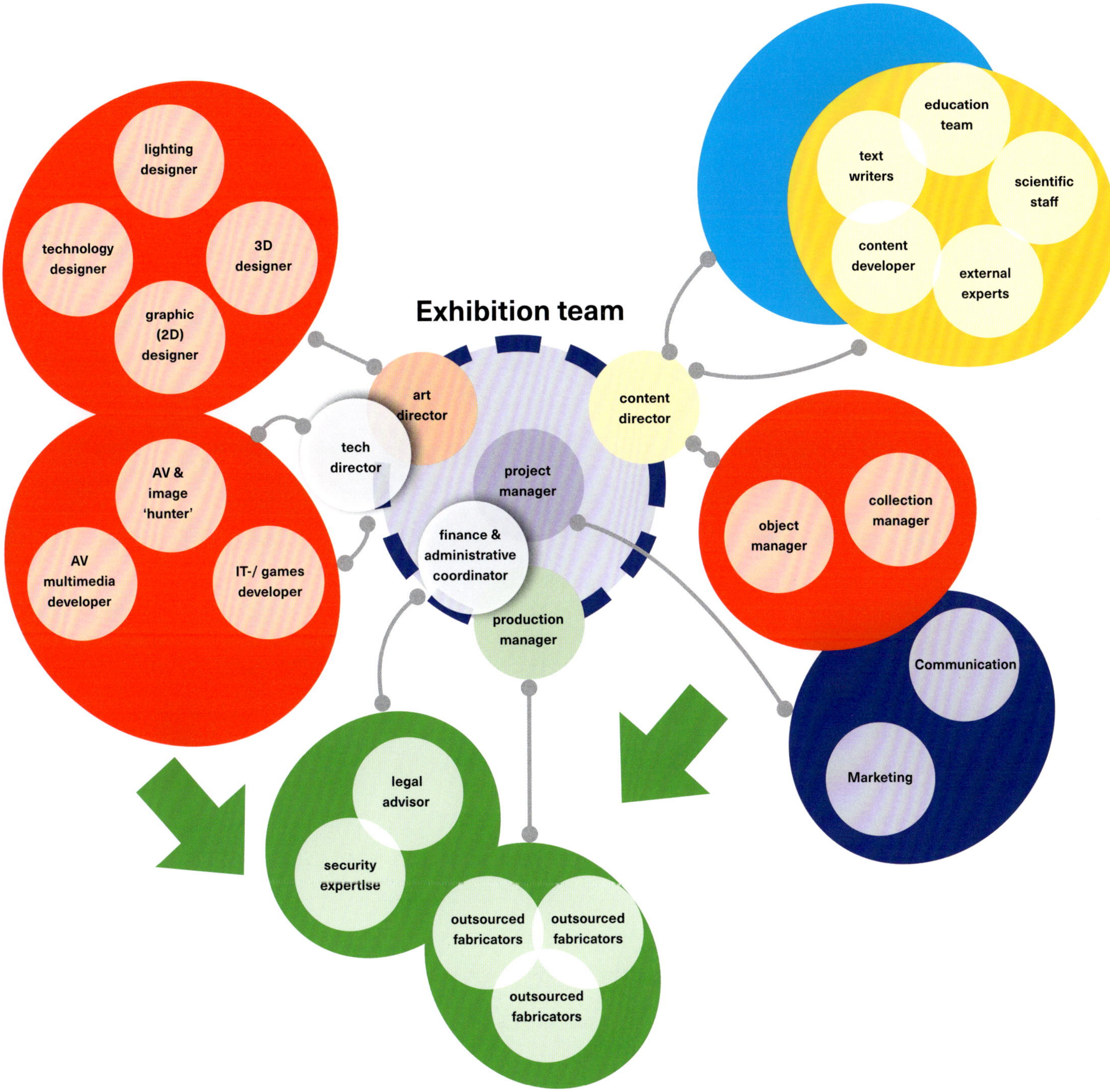

10. The exhibition development team

Project manager and content director

The project manager/director, who is usually the leader of the project, organizes its meetings and drives its processes while reviewing the overall progress of the timeline, and budget for the project. This position reports to the museum's director.

At first, the development of an installation must be driven by content, not by design or production. Thus, the project manager and the content director often share a background in the discipline to which the exhibition or the entire museum is devoted. In many cases these two roles are combined, and the project manager is also in the lead for the content development, though supported by a team, of course. We would recommend a science journalist type of thinking, as this discipline is focused on the story and the way it to be told. They might or might not be curators, although we regard being a curator requires different skills. The ability to communicate and popularize the subject, whatever it might be, is crucial. Either the project manager or the content director will also lead the evaluation and stakeholder input processes.

The content director may be supported by one or more content developers, who are in charge of the creation and management of the project content. Their responsibility is to be in contact with content sources (including those in the museum); to select, organize, and present the relevant research findings, collection material, and other information; and to distinguish primary from secondary information.

The role of content development is often combined with the duties of an interpretive planner (one or several, depending on the project), who will transform the content into written form. Curators, collection specialists, educators, and outside experts from different disciplines will provide essential information for the concept and overall content development, and its subsequent transformation into written texts. The graphic designer(s) should closely follow the work of the interpretive planner and, through collaboration, play a critical role in the visual presentation of the content, particularly when infographics are involved.

Art director and a design manual

With innovative exhibitions and displays, the role of the art design director becomes more prominent, although never to the point of overtaking the development of the content itself. The art/design director creates interpretive strategies and either serves as the principal designer or supervises the design work that leads to the two- and three-dimensional components that will deliver the developed concepts and content. This team member also provides an overall aesthetic for the museum's exhibitions.

Producer

In many ways there are similarities between the production of an exhibition and a movie or theatre production. This is true both from the management and from the methodological point of view.

From the management point of view: a movie *producer* (the project manager in our book on exhibitions) is the group leader and responsible for managing the production from start to finish. He or she also finds the money, selects the director, supervises the casting in the context of the financial resources available, negotiates the rights and the distribution, etc. It is the movie director who is to supervise all the phases of the productive process including the scenography, the costume design, the casting and selection of locations and the postproduction work, of course in a constant dialogue with the others involved.

From a methodological point of view: the concept of an exhibition is very similar to the subject of a movie, while the storyline is like the script, the stage director is the project leader, the designer is like the scenographer.

Why are we looking for these similarities? Because the idea of the museum space as a movie or theatre stage and the exhibition as a scenography, is becoming more and more accepted. This view might lead to rearranging some of the more traditional tasks and roles in an exhibition development process.

A design manual is of crucial importance here, consisting of guidelines and rules of thumb, regarding all aspects of design, 2D as well as 3D. This is especially the case when there are several outside designers involved. You could see it as a tool in directing and overseeing the design process, in the same way as a detailed timeline is for the project manager. There are two reasons this manual should be there. It does help to direct designers and correct where necessary, by in a sense 'objectifying' the choices and corrections. It will temper heated discussions.

A design manual unifies the design throughout the museum too. Beware, however. We do not plead for one design style throughout the museum. In the contrary. We do think that variety on a common fundament is key to combat museum fatigue. So the manual is to secure a common fundament, a common ground, as for example with families of colours and fonts, style of text, spatial arrangements, style of displaying objects and so on.

Production manager and technology director

The production manager oversees the production process. As this part of the exhibition consumes most of the budget and delays due to last-minute changes are not uncommon, it is essential that this key player is involved in the development of a project from the beginning. There is the importance too of value-engineering solutions to the design of the installation.

This role also includes supervising the production of technical drawings for fabrication purposes and overseeing production meetings during the fabrication and installation stages. The production manager, together with the art/design director, also harmonizes and supervises the designers if the exhibitions are being created by a number of independent design groups.

AV, multimedia, and lighting play a prominent role in the development of exhibitions. Interactive devices and immersive environments have also become increasingly important for effective visitor experiences. As a consequence, another member of the core team is the technology director/designer, who plays a key role in determining the appropriate technologies for use in a project. Working with a lighting designer, the technology director/designer and the art/design director collaborate to realize a project's visual communication. These three designers need to have a compatible outlook and style in their aesthetic language and approach.

The technology director, however, is in a way 'subordinate' to the art director, as the proposed components are to fit in the overall story and design, as well as to the production manager, for which he guides part of the production process.
It should be pointed out however that for smaller projects roles can be combined. Moreover, some individuals may possess more than one expertise, and this may influence the division of team tasks.

Financial coordinator and administrative assistance

Administrative and financial support varies depending on the size of the project. For extensive installations or large renovations, we think it helpful to have a designated project office under the overall direction of the project manager. This office has to include an administrative/finance coordinator, usually a must in any large exhibition development process, along with an administrative assistant. Their roles would include administrative tasks related to the management of contracts, budgets, and general administration.

As the financial system in most museums cannot react as quickly and in as much detail as needed in significant exhibition developments, there is a need for a separate accounting system. This system is not to replace the formal museums accounting system, but to function as a supplementary, additional system tailored to the needs of the exhibition budgeting needs. It is the financial coordinator who should lead this particular system. See the chapter on Budget for more details.

10.2. Shifting leads

Over the course of the exhibition development process, the lead role changes as the project progresses. For instance, the content director often takes the lead during the concept and storyline development phase and remains present and vigilant throughout the remaining stages. The art/design director takes up the lead role through the design stages, with the production manager playing an increasingly important role. In the production phase it is clearly the production manager who heads the process while keeping in close contact with both the art/design director and the content developer.
The project manager/director oversees the entire process.

During the development of a project, regular meetings will occur with the executive, marketing, and communications staffs, as well as the fund-raising department, in order to ensure that the essence of the project's intention, content, and progress is known and shared. Indeed, for large projects these departments may have regular members on the core development team.

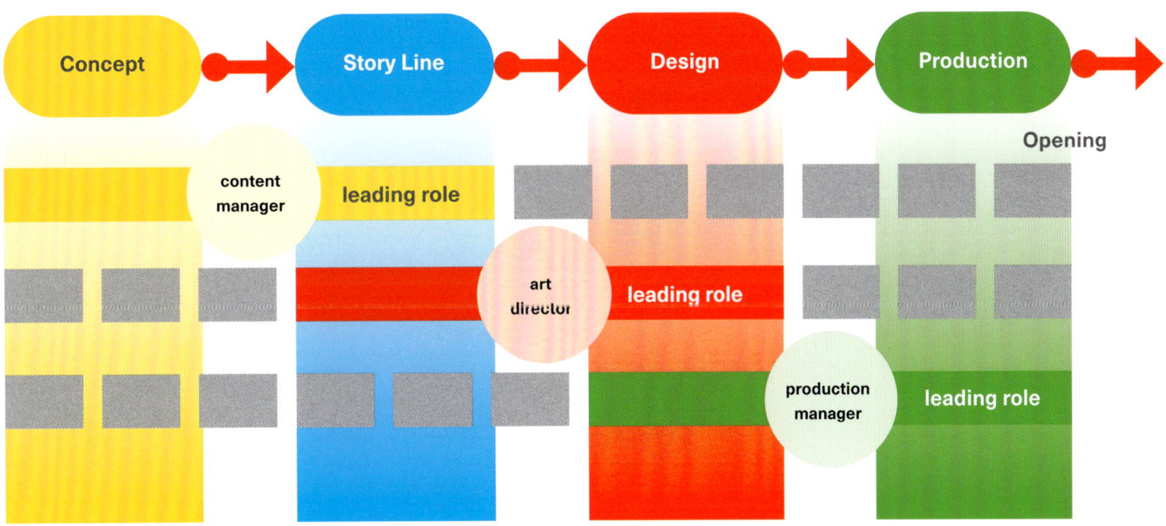

10.3. Small museums

Admittedly, the ideal constellation consists of more people than many museums can afford. Most museums are small. Therefore, the listed approach can serve them as a baseline of capacities and qualities you might consider, to be adjusted according to their possibilities.

We do recommend, however, a minimum of a two-person team - in our view the project manager with the assistance of a production manager. With this formula, the project manager steps in with a content responsibility, while the production manager also takes responsibility for the art director's role, whether by management of the design company or otherwise.

It would serve any team well if there could be an assistant for or assistance with financial management, as practice shows there is ample room for major savings if managed with focus and dedication.

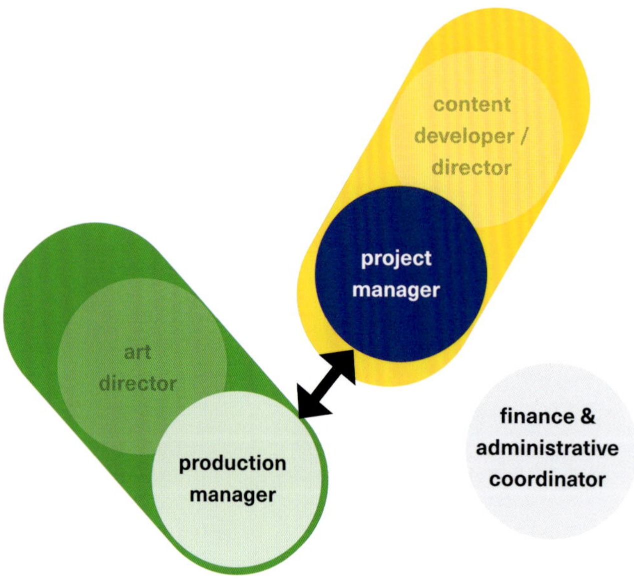

11. The stakeholders and decision makers

In addition to the exhibition team, there are many who need or wish to contribute to (have a voice in) the exhibition development process. And some are just plain interested. Think, for example, of community or special-interest groups, schoolteachers, scientists, artists, members of the board of directors, and so on. Keeping a project on track while managing or responding to these many stakeholders and opinions is not always easy. And then there are decision-makers who need to have a say in the major decisions, the major milestones.

The often quite large interest and sometimes emotional involvement is a beautiful thing to have. It is something to cherish. At the same time, it is not feasible and also undesirable to have too many of the not-directly-involved having a say, and even more so, having a decisive vote. We propose therefore a decision model to 'direct' all these voices, and which has been proven effective.

Besides this decision model, to sustain the process and maintain the enthusiasm of all participants or contributors, it is essential to have the process, including this decision-making process, well organized and transparent. Continuous communication on milestones and the resulting decisions are therefore essential. The themes described in this chapter are, in a way, part of the public relations of the project.

11.1. Milestones done formally, an often-neglected tool for stakeholders

Before entering the subject of organizing all these voices, we emphasize the value of having your milestones set in the phasing of exhibition development, as they are key to the decision-making process and guiding all those voices. We discussed it too in the chapter on the timeline, but we will repeat it here in the context of decision-making.

As said before, a milestone represents the decision-making moment after a certain phase has been completed. It is the moment to say 'yes' or no' or 'yes, with these amendments' to the results of the phase to close down. If 'agreed' the exhibition team can move on to the next phase. And if some major rework is to be done – we'll get back to this later – there will be a repeated milestone moment after the rework.

Milestone report

For each major milestone there is a report (and associated drawings, calculations and so on) on the table. This report is an essential key element in the decision process. The content of each report is the description of the phase closed, and it reflects too the core of the decisions to be taken. They may be even spelled out in 'decision points'. See the chapter on 'deliverables' in the earlier chapter for a more detailed description of each milestone report.

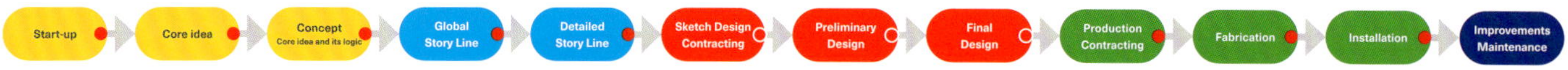

The major milestones (red circles) for which a meeting of the steering committee is necessary. For each meeting a detailed report with decision point will be on the table.

The steering committee decides on the key issues, so they will only meet on the major milestones after major phases. The many 'in-between' milestone moments are for decision-making in the exhibition team, though the results will be on the table in the major milestones.

The need for a break

The steering committee often will come up with some criticism and/or new ideas. It is essential to make a clear distinction between essential criticism and thus an obligatory task to change, and ideas who might be incorporated or discarded.

With essential changes asked, the process will halt. There has to be some significant redoing, and sometimes even a new meeting on the changed result, before the next phase can start. This break for rework is important. It might feel as a setback, but if not done properly the next phase will get 'cluttered', resulting in confusion and mixed decision-making.

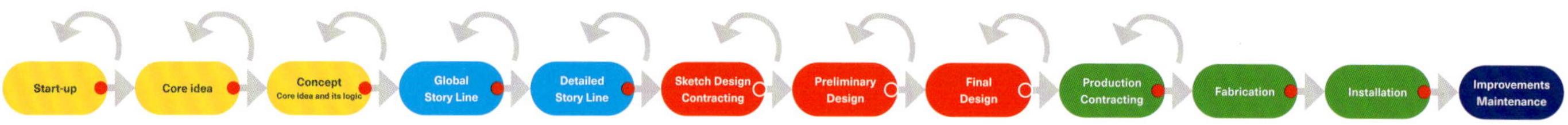

Each major phase – as in the graphic above – is 'closed' by a final agreement by the steering committee before it enters the next phase. If some major issues arise, the larger part of the work has to be redone, and the next phase cannot yet be entered.

Strict but not rigid

The idea behind this strict way of working is simple. If a decision is made, it is made, you cannot reconsider what has already been decided. This is a key rule: what has passed the steering committee cannot be undone, not even by the steering committee itself in the next phase. And though this type of 'rigidness' is difficult to accept in certain museum cultures we think it advisable to go that way. It will pacify the process as it is very clear and thus counters confusion when new ideas and opinions pop up. Everyone experienced in exhibition building knows the danger of decisionmakers or key 'influencers' reconsidering some crucial parts. There often is – not least when scientists are involved – a so-called progressive insight. New ideas 'we should really fit in too' or the like. In this proposed methodology this is not possible and even strictly forbidden. That might sound harsh, but it does work very well once stated clearly at the start.

The other side to it that you have to be very open, and 'asking' in a phase itself. If amendments cannot be made later on the process, it should happen where it ought to happen. And that means that all ideas should be received, researched and discussed in the proper phase. The experience is that if you are not receptive and listening when it matters, it will get back to you later on.

We know there is a cultural bias attached to it. In some of our national cultures there is a much greater 'power distance' than in others. And when this distance is rather large, it is very hard to impose this rule on the ones in power. Who dares to say 'no' to your general director or president? So, the clearer this rule is set, the more open and inquisitive you are at the right phase, the more it naturally works out.

Some might fear the development process will be too fixed this way. The fear of losing flexibility. This is, however, deceptive. When the content and process is organized well, all ideas count at the proper time slot, and important choices are clear and outlined. We would even argue a so-called 'flexible' decision process in the end is counterproductive, costly and hampers top quality as it brings a certain acceptance to have decisions postponed. "we will decide that later", which then often will be done in a rush. And as said, this continuous flexibility is fuelling unrest.

Another reason a decision or choice can be challenged in a later phase, is when the proposed solution turns out to be too expensive or budget cuts are needed. Though there is not always a solution to this, there are some precautions possible. One is to include alternatives in your design proposals when solutions might turn out to be too expensive. In other words, when you see the risk, propose an 'in case of' alternative in the decision-making process.

Then there often is the assumption that some money will be available, and it turns out it is not. The only solution to this is quite simple and in line with the above: do work with the budget which is there for sure. Eventual extra budget can be dedicated to specific and knowingly costly extras. So again, have scenarios ready, but with budgets it is wise to take the lowest amount as the baseline.

This all said, it is clear that the proposed milestone-decision-making structure does have consequences for the milestone reports. It does require scenario thinking to be inclusive in the proposed solutions.

11.2. Steering committee and advisory groups

In the case of development of a major exhibition or extensive gallery renovations, there is usually a formal decision-making group. We will name it the steering committee. The task of this committee is to evaluate, judge the incoming decision-report on a specific (major) milestone and decide if and eventually what adaptations should be made.

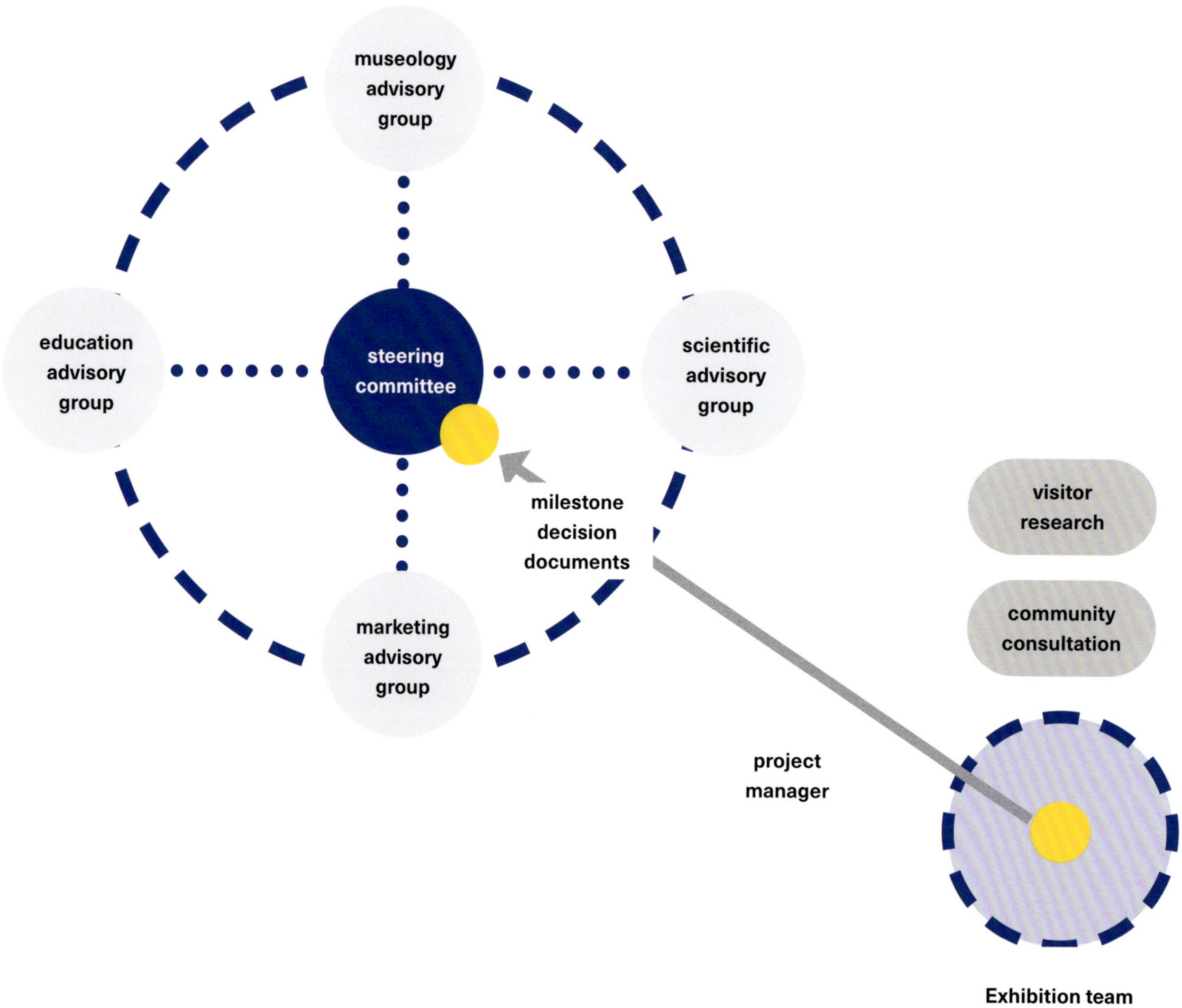

The composition of the steering committee

Depending on the size, the importance and the museum's culture, the steering committee may consist of the general director and/or the director responsible for the public services and one representative of each advisory committee (see below).

The project manager is, by definition, a member of the team. He also functions as a secretary, noting all decisions in bullet points with the reasoning added. It is wise to have him or her to be accompanied by relevant team members (art director, production manager, financial coordinator) for supporting explanations where needed. We advise however not to bring in the external suppliers, as for instance external designers, as we learned through experience it will become a pitch and members will not speak freely.

Two-stage decision process using advisory committees

Another way of dealing with a diligent decision-making process in steering committee is to bring in two stages in the decision making. First, the proposals will be discussed in the advisory committees. Each committee is qualified on a certain component – for example scientific content (scientific group) or visitor experience (museology peers and other outsiders). Each advisory group will discuss the results as presented in the milestone report and reflect with their specific expertise on the results.

So, the (dis)agreement of a specific advisory committee on their field of expertise is summarized in an additional report. This may be accompanied by strong opinions on other matters, but those will be set aside in an addendum.

The advisory group is chaired by a member of the steering committee, preferably a peer of course. It is his or her job to bring the comments, critiques, compliments and proposals to the steering committee. The project manager is also part of each advisory group, organizing it and noting all decisions and relevant argumentations too. The project manager/director thus has a liaison-role.

The meetings of the advisory groups follow the same pattern as the steering committee, but a little earlier in the process. In our experience it works satisfactorily to have them all in one or two days and a little less than a week ahead of the steering committee.

Planning

The process described here does take time. As it is a significant part of the process – in time and importance - and has to be planned accordingly.

The planning is to be done way ahead, already at the start of the process. A significant exhibition might easily take at least a year of preparations. So, the meetings of the steering committee and advisory groups can be planned right at the start and function as absolute deadlines. Everyone involved knows exactly on which dates the meetings will take place, and what there has to be on the table. This does mean something to the exhibition team as those dates are sacrosanct. Whatever happens – these major milestones and their reporting cannot be postponed.

We can imagine some of you are sighing. For many involved in the exhibition development, this might seem impossible as it almost never works this way. But it can be done, and it is far easier than you think when you have your process well organized head on. And of course, the project manager has to be a bit of a terrier.

And it might help to know that when it is done as described here, there is a significant reward. It gives peace of mind to many involved, and it most certainly makes the deliveries on time. The experience of one of the authors, a complete new permanent exhibition and over 150 temporary exhibitions, they were all on time, within budget and often with some 'repair money' saved.

Contracting, especially with external design and contracting companies

This way of working does require good contracting with outside companies, especially design companies. The rules should be stated in the contract. We mentioned it before.

Let us repeat one rule: if the steering committee decides changes must be made, they have to be made, whatever is decided during the work in progress by the exhibition team. This rule logically means that a design company has to take some time calculated for reworking their designs. And this is the opposite way they normally work. There is a tendency to have decisions made during the work-in-process and have the exhibition team complicit. This way of doing thus is not feasible.

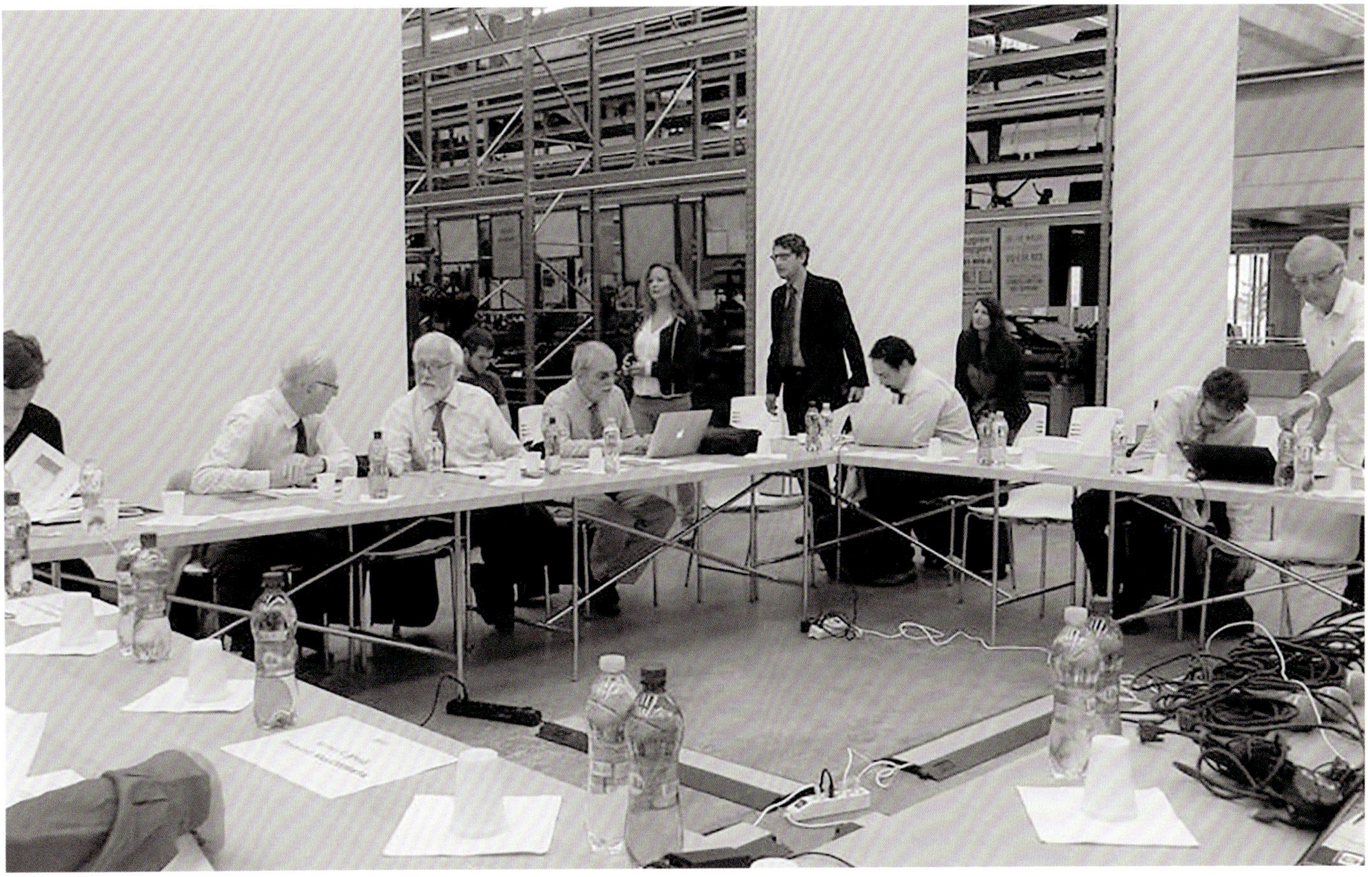

Musil — museo dell'industria e del lavoro, Brescia

11.3. Visitor advocacy

Some might argue visitors should be included in the group of stakeholders, as there should be a representative for those we are working for. There is some logic here, although for several reasons it is not a practical solution. Some museums therefore do have reference groups of visitors which they periodically consult. Some do use their volunteers for that purpose.

To keep life easy, we propose that the task of including visitor experience – the visitor advocacy - is dedicated to both the group of museology peers and the marketing (and communication) group. There is then the need to bring in objective information, so to stay away from strong opinions without figures upon which to be based. It means there should be visitor surveys and prototypes testing, having the results on the table.

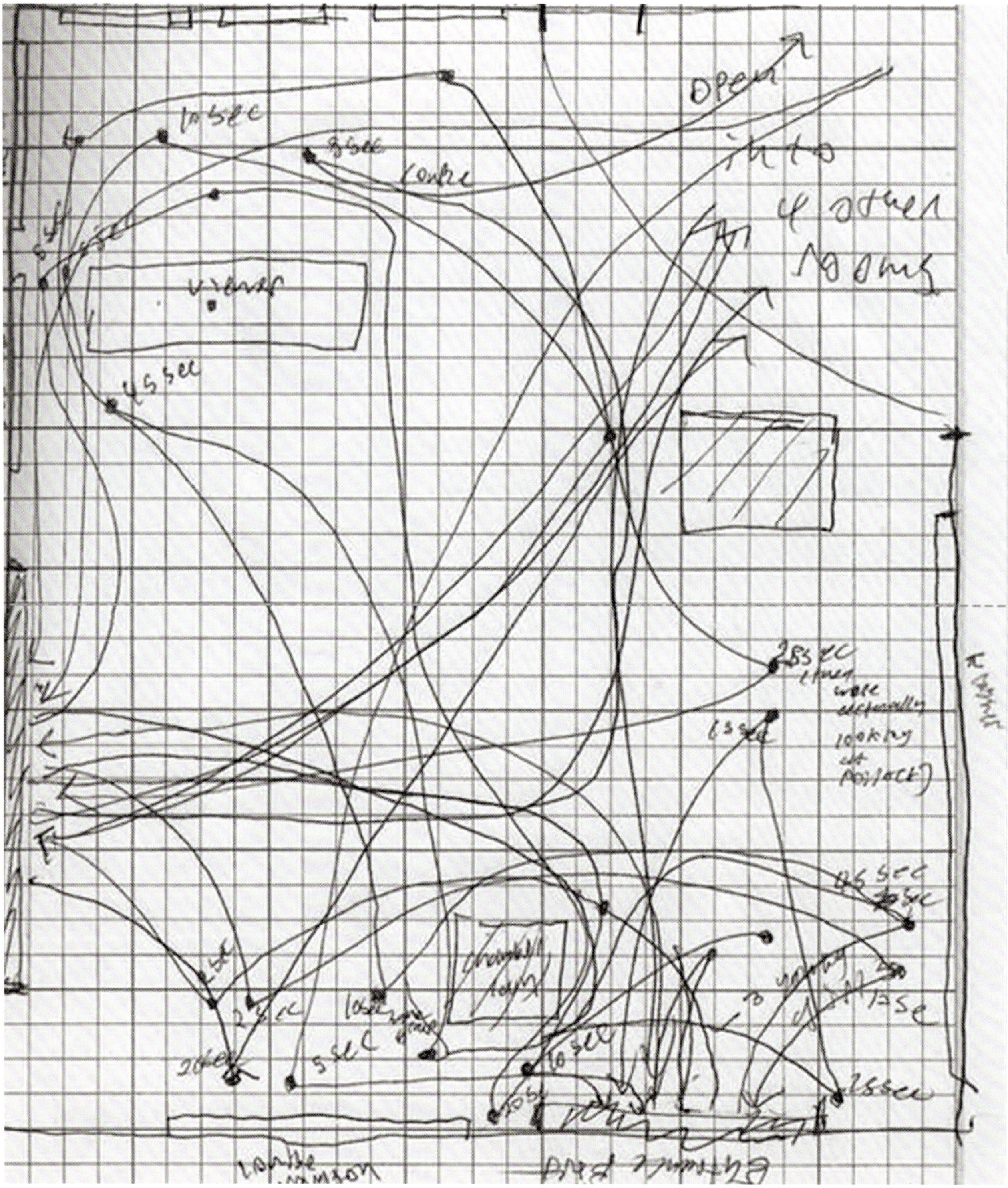

12. Visitor studies[3]

To invest some of your resources in visitor studies is not a waste. On the contrary, it does almost always save money and time. It helps to identify and prevent mistakes, prevents developing units which are not fulfilling expectations, improves your storyline and stimulates fresh thinking in design choices. We would advise setting aside something like 5% of your total budget to test whatever you have prepared upfront, before moving on to the next phase.

Having said this, for many purposes it can be done on a shoestring, by keeping it thoroughly simple and using your own staff. Let us be clear: visitor research is a profession, so get yourself coached by a professional. But stay in control, keep it simple and have the basic work done by your team. The big advantage of doing it by yourself is twofold. The experience of the direct exchange with (potential) visitors is priceless in itself and cannot be overrated. Secondly, it makes adapting and quick retesting much, much easier.

There is a third purpose for testing and that is to inform the discussions within the team or, in some cases, the opinions of the director. As is often the case on developing exhibitions, there are some quite strong opinions. Testing helps to counter them if needed. Politically it is wise to test many things, quick and dirty, just to make sure there is not too much effort spent on fruitless discussions.

12.1. Audience analysis

As described earlier on, you not only want to know who your (potential) audience is, but also their prior knowledge and their areas of interest regarding your exhibition themes. You need as well as to differentiate, i.e. describe your target groups as clearly as possible regarding the above, as well as what kind of publicity might work, and the key messages and 'feelings' you want to get across.

When determining target groups, be sure you can 'measure' them. They have to be addressed, quantified and counted within your audience. Each specific group can be described and quantified, though sometimes roughly.
If figures are available, you might come up with quantified statistics of the different groups within 'visiting distance' of your museum. This requires some desk research on available sources.

Movements in a gallery of Modern and Abstract art. Drawings by Andrew Oriani.
In: What a Physics Student Can Teach Us About How Visitors Walk Through a Museum, Henry Adams, smithsonianmag.com, May 16, 2012 www.smithsonianmag.com/arts-culture/what-a-physics-student-can-teach-us-about-how-visitors-walkthrough-a-museum-96782621/

The way you segment your current audience can and has to be easy. Keep it simple. Ask a sufficiently large group where they are from, the group composition (which is often easy to be seen too) and what made them come. And if needed you can ask the rating they will give your museum, noting if they are on their way in or on their way out. For this last group, you might ask what time they entered, so to calculate the time spent.

Keep it that simple, ask them yourself (no questionnaires) preferably in three to five questions and where possible with tick boxes.
If you do want to know more regarding their previous knowledge, then have for example some additional statements on facts and figures. Again, keep it short. You might differentiate for example if you have more than five questions into different questionnaires, taken separately.

12.2. Concept testing (front-end study)

When you have finished your analysis grid, or any other way you have organized your core messages and underlying themes and modules, it is time to relate this to the knowledge and insights of your audience.

As is described in the paragraph above, this can be done by asking some questions on statements and relations between subject matters. So as not to make your audience feel interrogated and stupid, please keep it simple and stay out of right and wrong answers. Keep it in the line of '*do you believe A or do you think it is more like B*?'. Or: '*what do you think happened in which order*?' '*what do you consider most interesting and important, module A or module B*? and suchlike.

You might ask them too, what would need to be added or outlined to make them come to visit you.

12.3. Testing potential titles

One of the most striking experiences we had was when testing exhibition titles. The titles we devised, often with quite some effort, were discarded or approved within asking 10 visitors. There is no need for any statically sound analysis at all. Just ask and you know within minutes.

There are two ways to go. The first is to have a very short description ready of your exhibition and two alternative titles. Read your punch lines on the topic and just ask the visitor which one (or none) of the titles they would be prefer. And ask if they like the title. Alternatively, you might just ask for the preference of one of the titles, without prior knowledge of the exhibition content.

The second option is to state one title to a visitor and ask what they think it is all about and if they think it interesting for them to come. It serves to see the potential of the title and the prior knowledge of the specific visitor.
This way you get an opportunity to ask them, after their answer, if they have some elements they think important to add (to the exhibition, to the title or to a short description).

12.4. Storyline testing

Testing your storyline should happen in the first phase, building the global storyline. This testing is of a more complex nature than the previous tests. It needs some visuals on how the story unfolds itself to a visitor. In the testing the potential visitor has to be guided, step by step, through the options and circuits. On many of those options and crossroads there can be questions asked.

The way to build up the storyline has to be done by presenting grouping of themes, by visualizations. On each crossroad one or two questions can be asked. They can be simple (*what direction would you choose if you have these options?*) or more complicated (*what do you expect when presented by this display or set of displays?* Or: *Can you tell me what you see and what it is supposed to tell you?*).

The main insights, however, you get by the discussions with the participants on what you present. Do they understand what you are presenting? Are they aware of your key messages in each module? What is most interesting and eye-catching?

For this reason, storyline testing can be done best by a qualitive research approach, and especially in focus groups led by experienced market researchers. It is only by the exchange and questions that the underlying ideas and choices can be understood.
As exhibition developers you normally will be able to watch the recorded interviews in separate rooms, which sometimes can become an enlightening, gratifying as well as frustrating experience.

This testing is more costly than you might expect. It requires visuals and a professional bureau. It is, however, crucial to build the argumentation underlying your choices and can help prevent some costly mistakes as well.

12.5. Design and text testing (formative evaluation)

In principle testing the proposed graphic and 3D-designs can be done again quite simply. How you do it depends on the questions you have. Regarding texts it can be straightforward on matters of understanding, readability and such. How it is judged and if visitors capture the essence quickly is to be asked directly. There is no rocket science involved.

With 3D-designs it is a matter of taste. If you are doubting you can easily put forward one or more alternatives – whether on specifics or on the exhibition as a whole - and ask which is preferred. Be aware though that if a sound image is to be presented, the real-life situation could be vastly different than what is presented on paper.

12.6. Summative evaluation

The resulting exhibition and its visitors can be evaluated on all aspects named above. The major point however is how the exhibition is judged in full and how it reflects the image of the museum. How satisfied are your visitors? Did they really enjoy and grant you a 'good' or higher? Keep in mind that a judgement like 'satisfactorily' normally does mean it was not good enough.
Please add some measurements to be taken by just looking around. Where do people stay longest? How long do they stay?

These kinds of judgements and figures become more valuable over time, when you can make comparisons between different exhibitions.

A second and often forgotten element is on the key messages your audience take home. What would they say if they have to summarize the key points in one or two essentials? Could they outline the important elements of the story?

Summative evaluations can be as short as above and as long as you want. Again, it could be done by professionals, but it is of greater value to your team if they do it themselves. They might need a hand in developing the methodology and questionnaire as this is a profession in itself, but the act of interaction with the audience does give extra insight for forthcoming exhibitions.

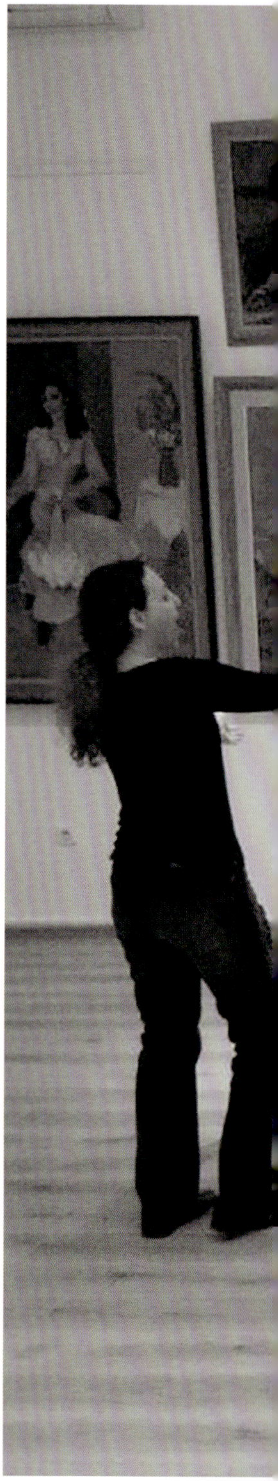

Gallery of Matica srpska, Novi Sad

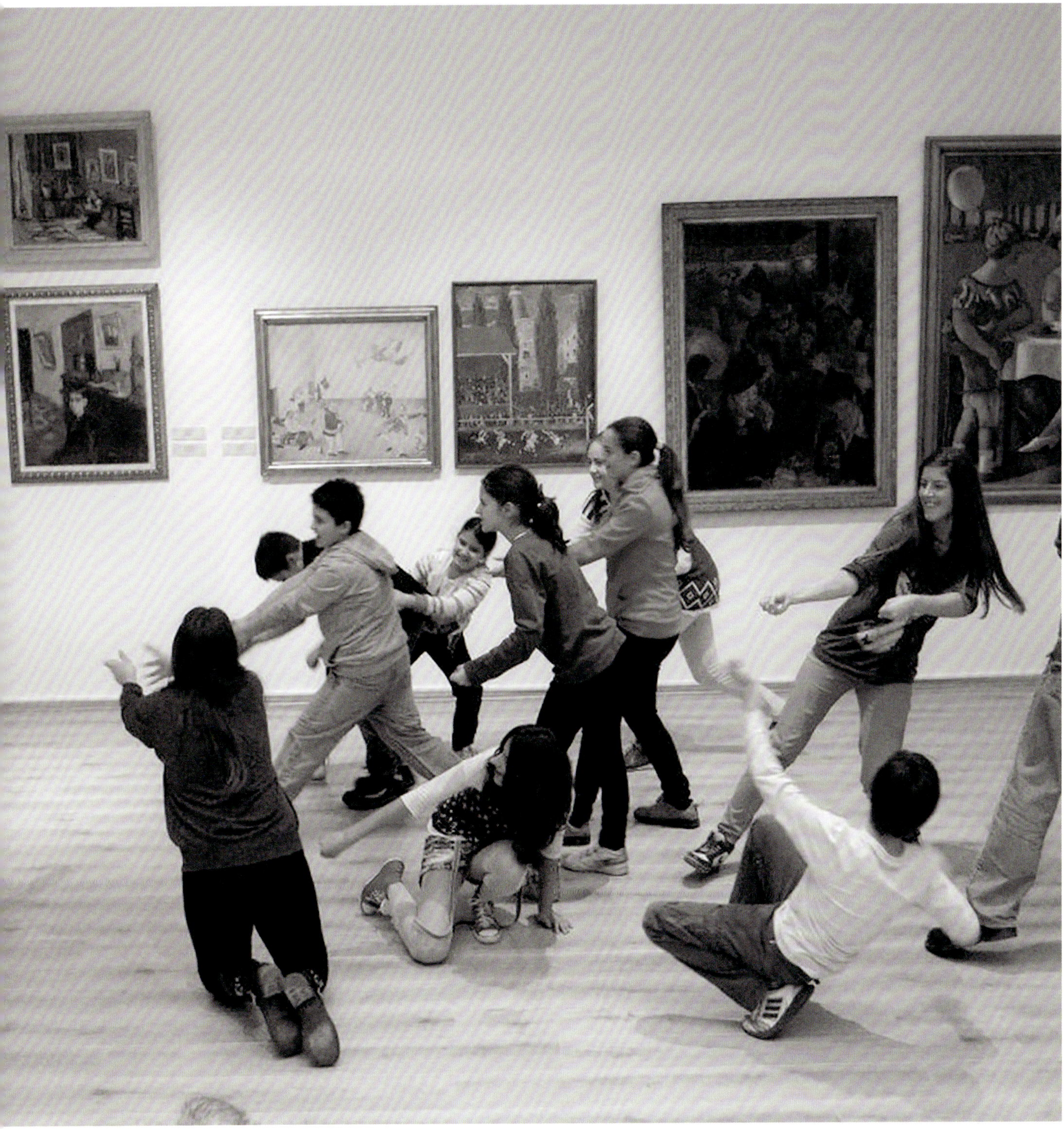

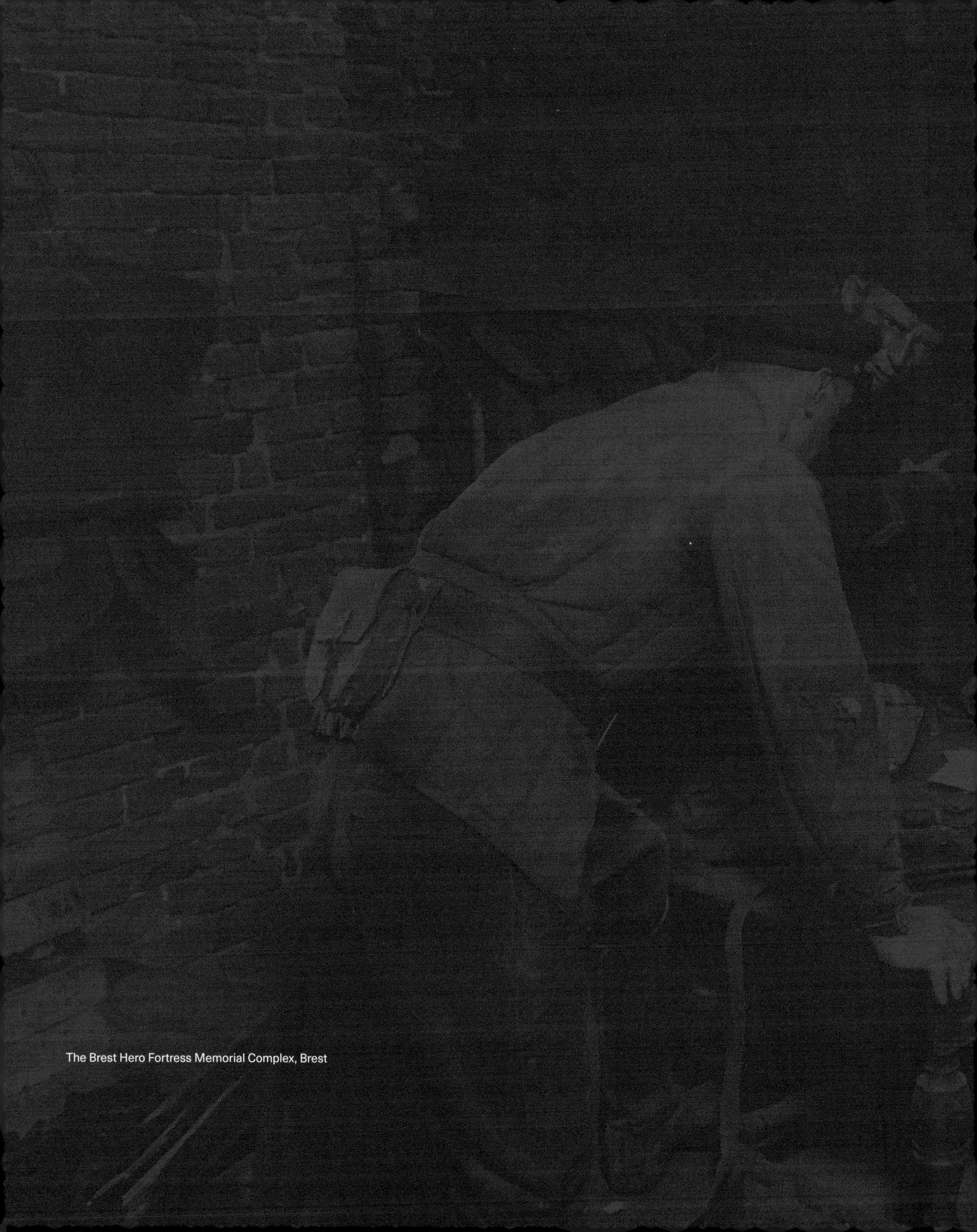

The Brest Hero Fortress Memorial Complex, Brest

Section 3

Some process elements in more detail

Start-up

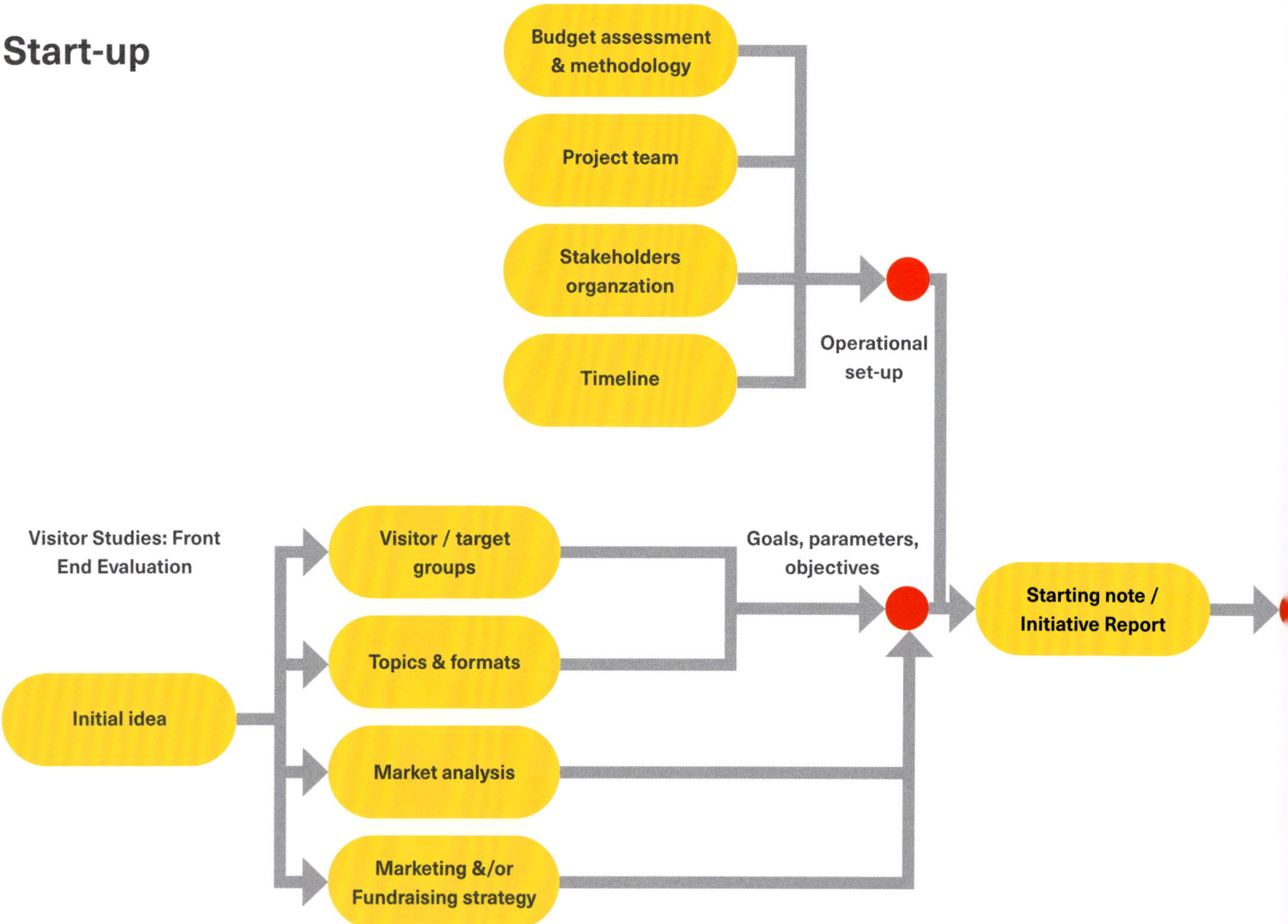
Budget assessment & methodology
Project team
Stakeholders organzation
Timeline
Operational set-up
Visitor Studies: Front End Evaluation
Initial idea
Visitor / target groups
Topics & formats
Market analysis
Marketing &/or Fundraising strategy
Goals, parameters, objectives
Starting note / Initiative Report

13. Content development: the use of an analysis grid

A museum is not 'a book on legs'. There often is no clear beginning and end as in books, and visitors definitely do not follow structured pathways. So, to get your stories and concepts understood, a smart and effective structuring of the intellectual and material content is essential. It has to be in such a way that no matter how visitors choose their way, the 'bigger picture' should be clear to everyone. And for each and every module it has to be clear how it fits within this 'bigger picture'.

This is a difficult requirement as we all know, as many museum exhibitions do not have as strong a content structure as they could have. This often is true of the individual displays as well as the overall installation of the institution's galleries. Most museums offer a patchwork of exhibition themes, which often function at several different conceptual levels. The reasons are frequently historical: most museum displays were developed over time and reflect different ideas, practices and points of view.

Go / No go
Decisions on operations
& targeting

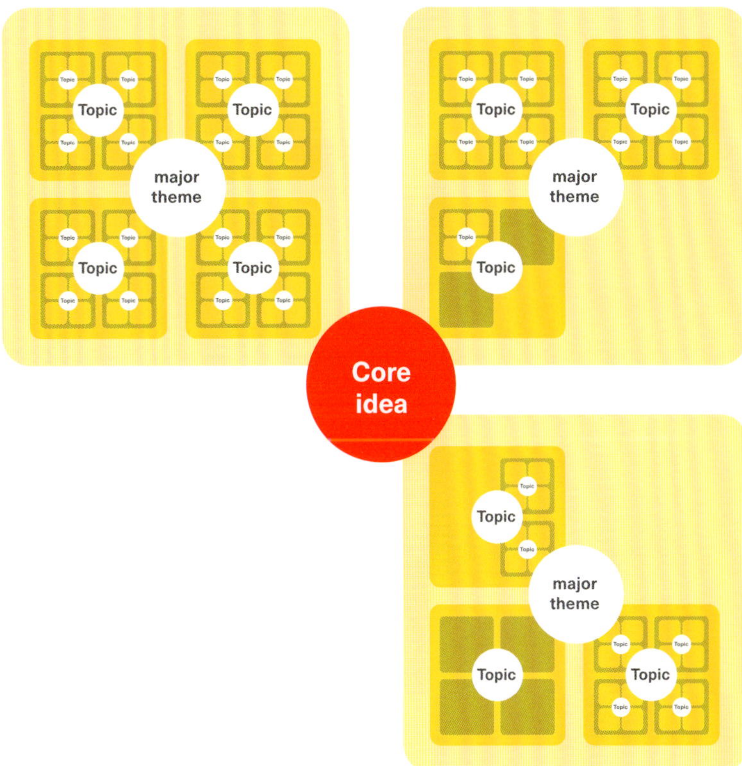

This section outlines the use of an analysis grid – a boxes-in-boxes structure - as an approach to construct a strong intellectual and narrative structure throughout a museum. In effect, it is the museum's essence translated into a core concept, which then resonates through thematically linked galleries and to individual thematic modules within a single space.

As it is all about a logical and coherent clustering of content (information units, stories, objects), it might seem a relatively easy and straightforward to do. Alas. We would like to say it is, but it is not. It takes 'blood, sweat and tears' so to say. And time. It needs to be done, however. If it is properly carried out and a strong schematic structure is developed, the rest of the process is set on solid ground. Once established, it saves time and discussions during the planning process, and visitor confusion later.

The following chapters describes the methodology stepwise.

13.1. From core idea to concept

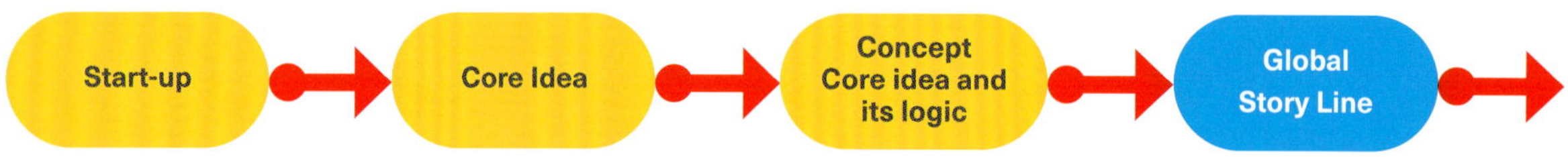

The development of the content for an exhibition or museum-wide installation will start with a core idea. The core idea represents what the exhibition is about. An exhibition's core idea may come from any number of sources and normally reflects the strengths of the museum's collection, its research activities, its interests and expected attractiveness to audiences, and its expectations. It should definitely fit the museum's DNA. Having a clearly articulated core idea gives a museum an intellectual context or framework, which then also serves as a guide to the content of individual exhibitions, galleries, and other programming activities.

Once the core idea is defined, a patchwork of underlying components in a hierarchical framework is to be established. Components need to be elaborated and the logic and their 'connectedness' determined and explained. This process of providing the core idea with an underlying logic produces the concept.
This applies for the museum plan as well as for a temporary exhibition.

13.2. The analysis grid: boxes in boxes

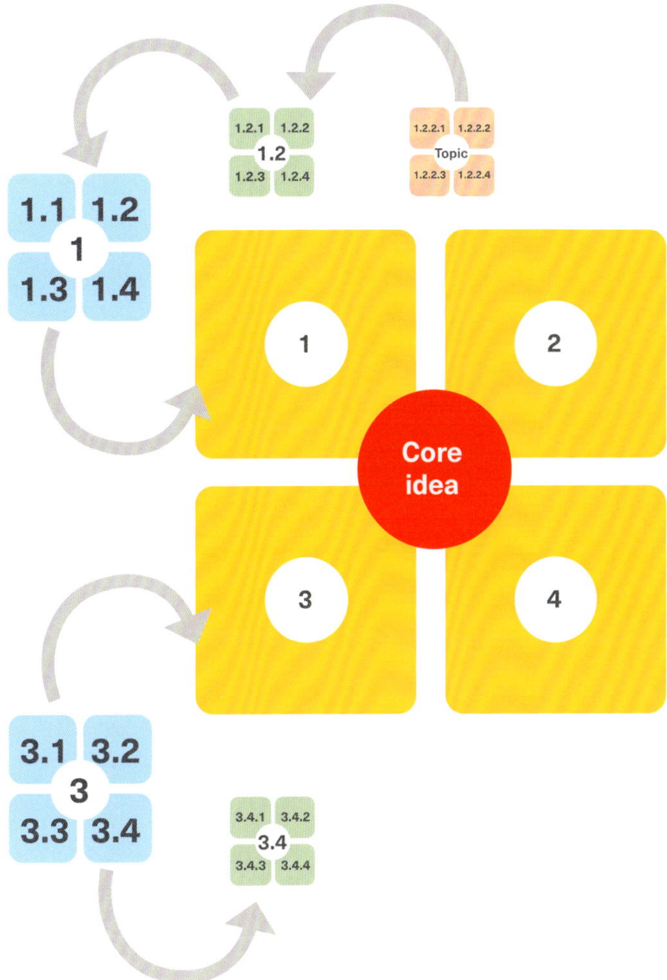

While many museum practitioners express the concept and its logic in a text-based format, it is strongly suggested here that it also be set out as a schematic framework. A schematic, figurative structure is more rigorous and unforgiving in its logic than a text-based format. A subtopic has 'to fit in'. Defining this underlying structure - 'boxes in boxes' - will then allow further work to sustain and expand on the same logic and avoid content inconsistency. As well, a schematic construct is much easier to translate into space and spatial relationships. It will be a great tool for the next phases, as design and text development.

The analysis grid above is a schematic representation of a concept, which consists of a core idea and its underlying logical structure of themes, topics, and subtopics. It represents a grouping of the components into logically aligned modules. While these modules are not directly linked to a space, there is the underlying implication that they would become thematic spatial groupings.

Framing modules as a starting point

The coloured squares in the middle represent the thematic (sub)topic, which can be further refined. Each coloured central square thus represents a framing topic, theme or whatever name we use. It defines the underlying content matter. It can be thought of as a 'flag' too. What visual representation or key object may represent this framing module?

The framing of the core idea is central. It is the starting point, and thus guiding the analysis. Work iterative. Do reframe the core idea if it turns out not quite right?

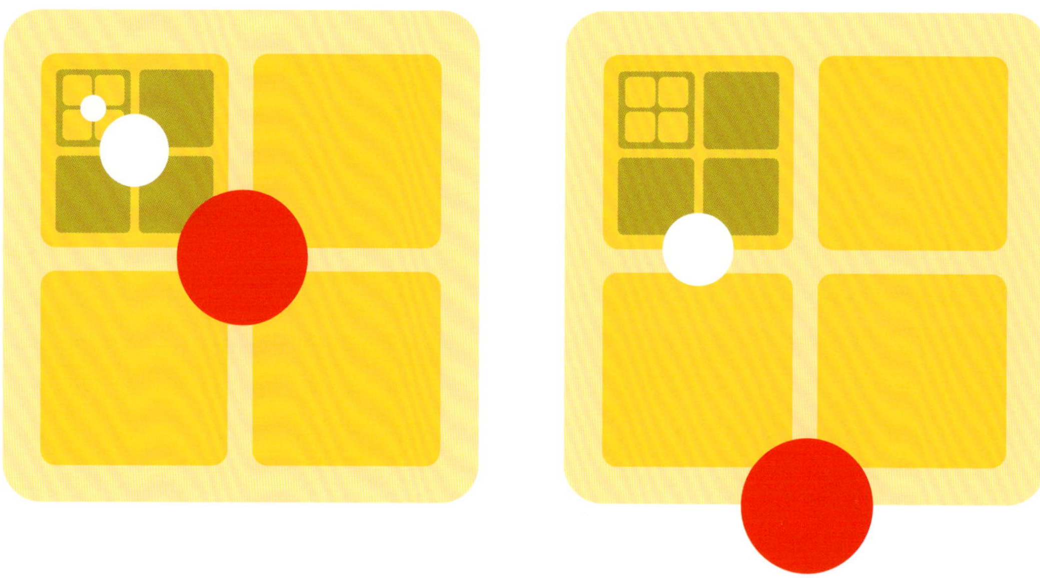

Core or entrance?

The coloured boxes 'in the middle' can be seen as the core – as you like the heart – of a specific topic or type of subject matter. We put it in the middle, arranging the deepening modules around it. However, you could also take a different (visual) viewpoint and regard it as the entrance topic to the same set of modules. The models do differ but are both justifiable. What to choose is up to preferences of your team and what you see as easiest in explaining it to your team members and stakeholders.

Uniform sizes to acknowledge equal value (for the time being)

In the figure all components of the spatial form are uniform, so as to make explicitly clear that there is no judgement involved on how important or, for that matter, how large various (sub) modules will become. It is no more or less than what belongs together. It does not encompass the (relative) content or spatial importance of any theme.

Differentiation in detailing

In practice there will, of course, not always be a neat 4*4*4 etc scheme. Just as well, some modules need a further differentiation or deepening than others do. What is important though is to have all major subjects aligned and put in their proper place.

It is wise too to have it accompanied by a list of some subject matter or key objects which is considered of importance by the museum staff, its opinion leaders and decision makers. In which box will this .... fit?

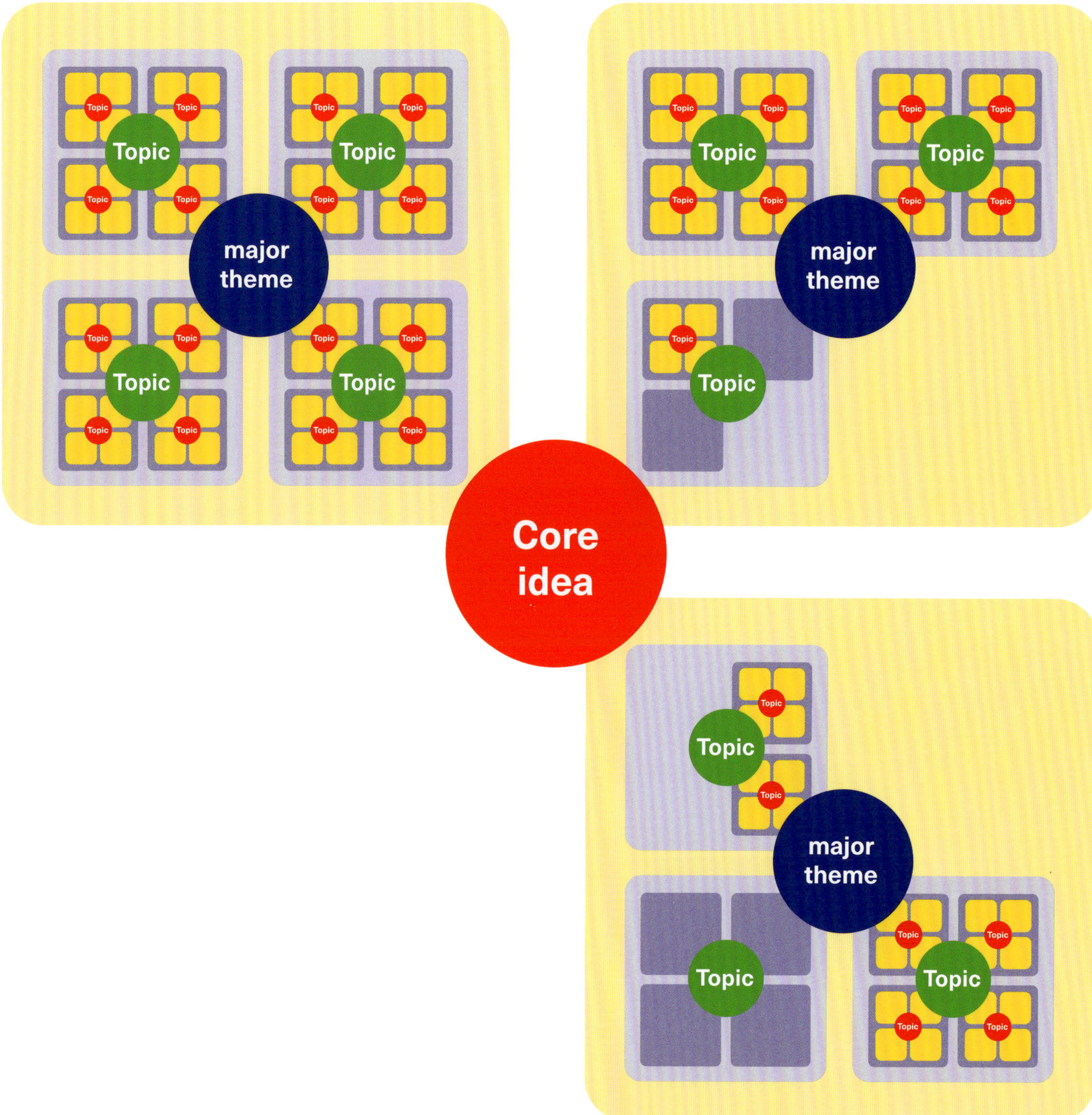
Core idea
major theme
Topic

The value of an analysis grid for building the storyline and the spatial arrangement in the design phase

This strict and unforgiving modular organization is essential to facilitate a later translation of content into a storyline and into space. They are needed to explicate the logical structure of the components. What belongs spatially to what?

When a visitor enters a specific part of an exhibition, let's say a 'green topic' part of the exhibit, he or she will consciously and unconsciously recognize the spatial arrangement. This spatial arrangement does 'tell' what information is connected. It does mean too that the distance between groups of topics should be larger than within a group. When done so, it is clear to the visitor instinctively.

13.3. How to start?

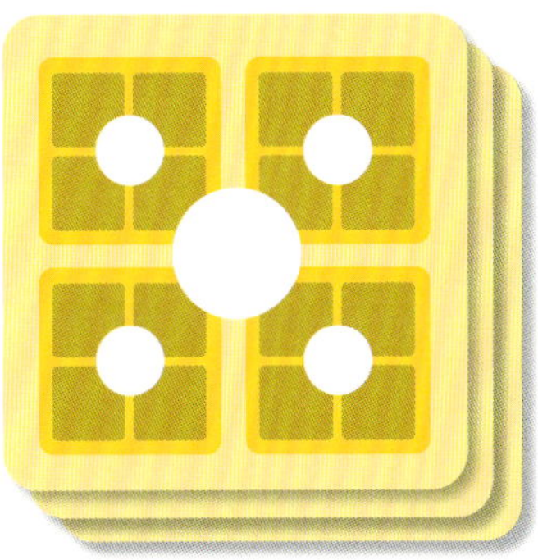

We repeat, to develop an analysis grid - thoroughly thought out, consistent – is time-consuming, not easy and does need more (processing) time than you might expect. Moreover, by just starting and scribbling down your first groupings of subject matter, you will find you often have to redo certain parts. The good thing is, however, the act of doing this often enough re-organizes and sharpens your thinking.

Start with a stack of empty sheets

The analysis is easiest done by hand. So, you need a number of stacks with empty grids, and/or a roll of white paper, as well as robust colour crayons or markers.

There is no fundamental difference if you do it all by hand, using your own sketching skills.

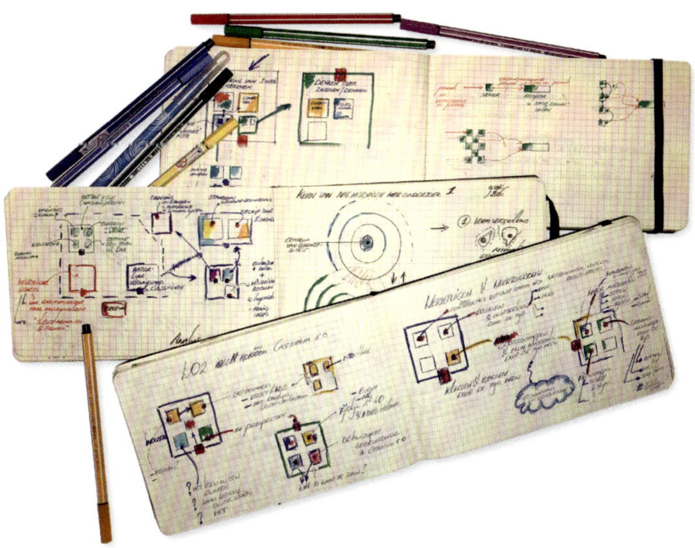

Scribble down all topic headers - and some short tagline.

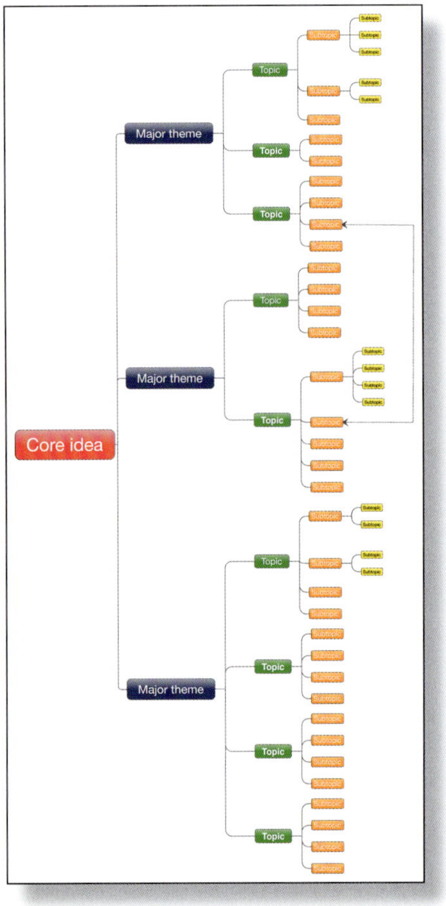

Mind map as an alternative to start

An alternative grouping could be a 'tree' as represented in mind map programmes. There is a reason we do not promote it. A mind map is a format which gets 'polluted' easily. It simply is too easy to 'mess up' – and the logic is a bit harder to grasp for others. Nevertheless, it might work for some of us. And it definitely could be an easy starting point when you start playing around with your first ideas.

13.4. Presenting and reporting the structure

When you have reached a satisfactory level of breaking down the core idea into its subsequent units of content, there is the phase to discuss it with your peers.

It will be almost impossible to have your preliminary breakdown represented in one slide or one picture. It is simply too complicated, with all the additional, descriptive taglines needed. Besides, it would be confusing too. A stepwise breakdown, showing the larger structure first, will be much easier for any audience.

There is therefore a necessity to number the different modules, to communicate the structure in a slide show or text document, and in a later phase to start working on text blocks. It takes a numbering like 1.1.1 and 1.1.2 in module 1.1. And so on.
When all is done, you might want to redraw it into slides. You then might consider programmes like PowerPoint and the like, Prezi or a professional (more adaptable) mind map application.

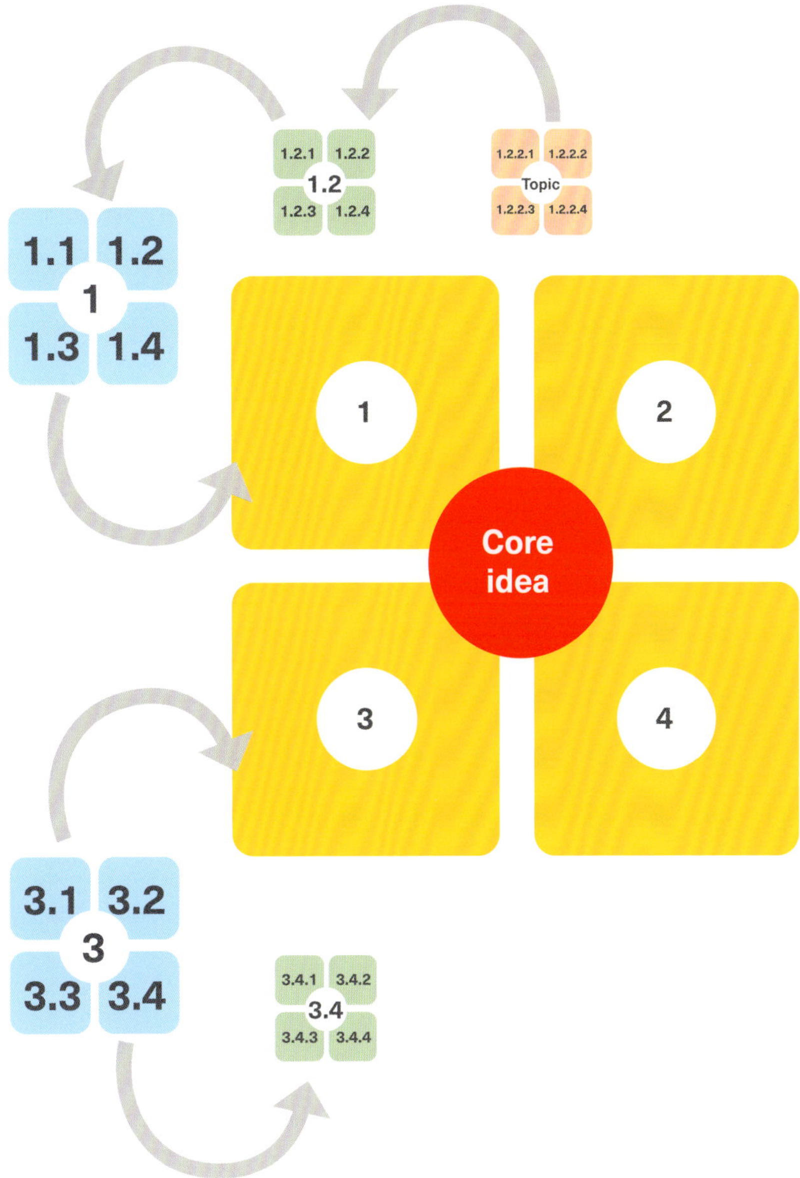

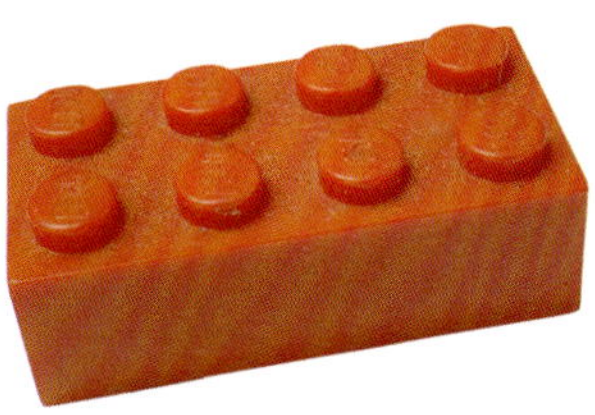

Think modular, think building blocks.

Conversion into text blocks

Again, the structure of the boxes-in-boxes thinking is a visual way of structuring.

If you also need to have it text-based, just add a table like the one below. It will be needed anyway at a later stage of the content development – though then aimed at content developers and experts.

Number	Descriptive title	Short description	Key message and (first ideas)	Possible key examples and objects (first ideas)
1				
1.1				
1.1.1				
1.1.1.1				
1.1.1.2				
1.1.1.3				
1.1.2				
1.1.2.1				
1.1.2.2				
1.1.2.3				
1.1.2.4				
1.1.3				
1.1.3.1				
etc.				

You need to go in-depth. Beware, however. When presenting this kind of detail to designers for example, they easily get lost. The amount of detail could be geared to the needs of the phase and the person.

In addition: key symbols, pictures and taglines

Each framing module is, as the word indicates, a framing of the group of modules it stands for. It is thus helpful to think of a tagline and/or visuals or objects which can easily convey this core idea.
Though a chosen object or tagline might lead to a discussion in itself, it could be a helpful way for the explanation of a certain grouping to your peers - and in a later stage to the visitors. It works when the visuals / object / tagline is clear enough to 'convey' automatically what this specific groups of modules stands for.

This procedure can be repeated for all framing modules, on all levels.

13.5. From concept and analysis grid to global storyline

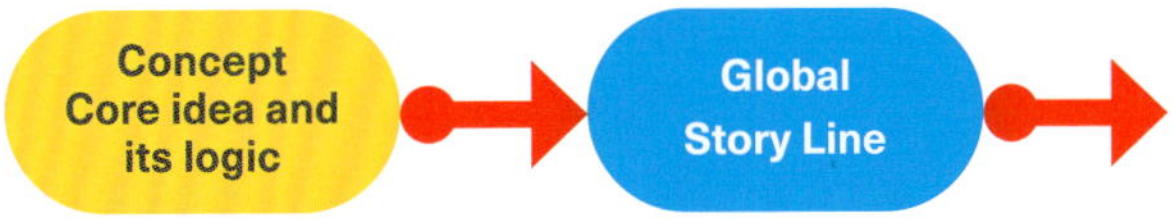

The organization of a concept and its core components is followed by the development of a storyline. In the next chapter we will get into how to develop a storyline. For now, it is important to note the value of an analysis grid as a base for building a storyline.

The storyline mainly describes the spatial arrangement of the different modules and the interconnectedness. It conveys a story. Where to begin? What lines are there to be drawn between them? Who are the 'actors'? What is the 'play' to convey. Is there a chronological or otherwise a line to be followed or can it be independent sub-stories, scattered in the space(s)?

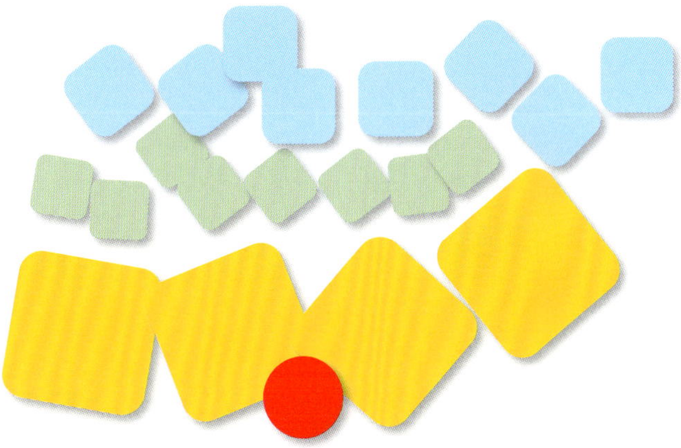

14. Storyline

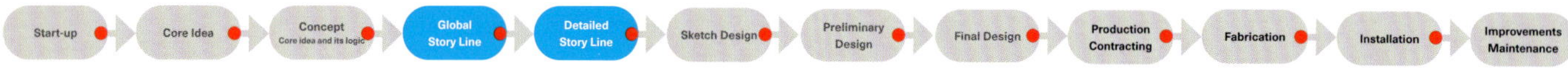

In the order of things, the organization of a concept and its core components is followed by the development of a storyline. The storyline first and foremost describes the spatial arrangement of the different content matter (modules) and the interconnected 'thread' of the story, i.e. the components in a line of telling and /or experiencing. Also, the storyline gives an idea of the experience you have in mind, as a prelude for the instruction to the designers in a later phase.

For quite some museums and countries it is the global storyline that is the crucial decision-making relevant document, either within the museum or to external stakeholders. It is for example often used to decide if the museum is to finance a specific exhibition. It often is used too as a first proposal to potential sponsors.

So, a storyline often is more than just a storyline. When this is the case, this particular version of the global storyline is a more extended version than we would originally propose in our methodology. But as life fortunately cannot be modelled as we please, we include in this phase a visual representation of the kind of experience we have in mind.

14.1. An exhibition is a story and an experience in one

An exhibition conveys a story and an experience. The storyline basically deals with the story in itself, and touches upon the experience you have in mind. This is needed for communication purposes to stakeholders and peers, as a guideline to the designers who will design the experience you want and not in the least, it sometimes helps you rethink your story.

As we argued before, museums are commentators. Storytellers. We reflect on society, on particular parts of its history and its 'Umwelt'. Our essential 'language' is primarily visual and organized in exhibitions, a three-dimensional story with objects, and much more. All these elements, and their overall effect, are vital visual components. They are to engage visitors in a particular story, a concept, or extended information on a particular subject. The difficulty is: visitors almost never follow prescribed paths. They 'read' the narrative while wandering through the space, picking up the clues as they come along. We also have to acknowledge that it is difficult for anyone to keep track of the essentials while being lured many times by objects and experiences into interesting side-lines and details.

There are several questions to be asked, when you start developing your story. And we assume you have your analysis grid done properly, i.e. you feel confident to have all relevant, major topics in position. The information components are there, ready to be organized into a line, so to say.

Core idea as a leading factor

We assume you have set the tone already in the formulation of your core idea. There is stated what it is essentially you want to convey. This being done, this messaging automatically (should be) followed through in the differentiated building blocks – all content components - of the analysis grid. The consistency will become even more clear when all blocks are lined up in the storyline.

When the previous permanent exhibition of Naturalis (Leiden, The Netherlands) was developed (in place from 1998 to 2017), its core idea was to explain how *System Earth, the machinery of the earth system, with its driving energy forces, lead to a permanent and continuously changing geo- and biodiversity*.

Diversity as an outcome of the 'Earth machinery'. Geological and life forces shaping the earth and the ecological and economic system which life has to deal with. All exhibitions were substantiating and deepening this content base, placed in a strong scenography. For example, the 'machinery of life' (eat and not being eaten = survive, live on through children) exhibition showed the resulting diversity (in types of solutions) as well as explaining the driving principles behind it.

Questions with regard to the story itself

Where to begin? If you have to explain it to someone in the so-called elevator pitch, what would you say? What is the main backbone of your story, i.e. the short summary? How would you start, and how would it end? What is the key message (content) and emotions (experience) to be transmitted? What are the 'building blocks' and who are the 'actors'? What is the 'play' to convey? Is there a chronological or otherwise a line to be followed or can it be independent sub-stories, scattered in space(s)?

Adapt to visitor behaviour

A lot has been said and written about the way we walk around in exhibitions. We wander around, get involved with some particular parts while neglecting others, and getting tired quite soon. And we should not forget the influence when members of our group need to go to the bathroom, or when the need for coffee gets strong.

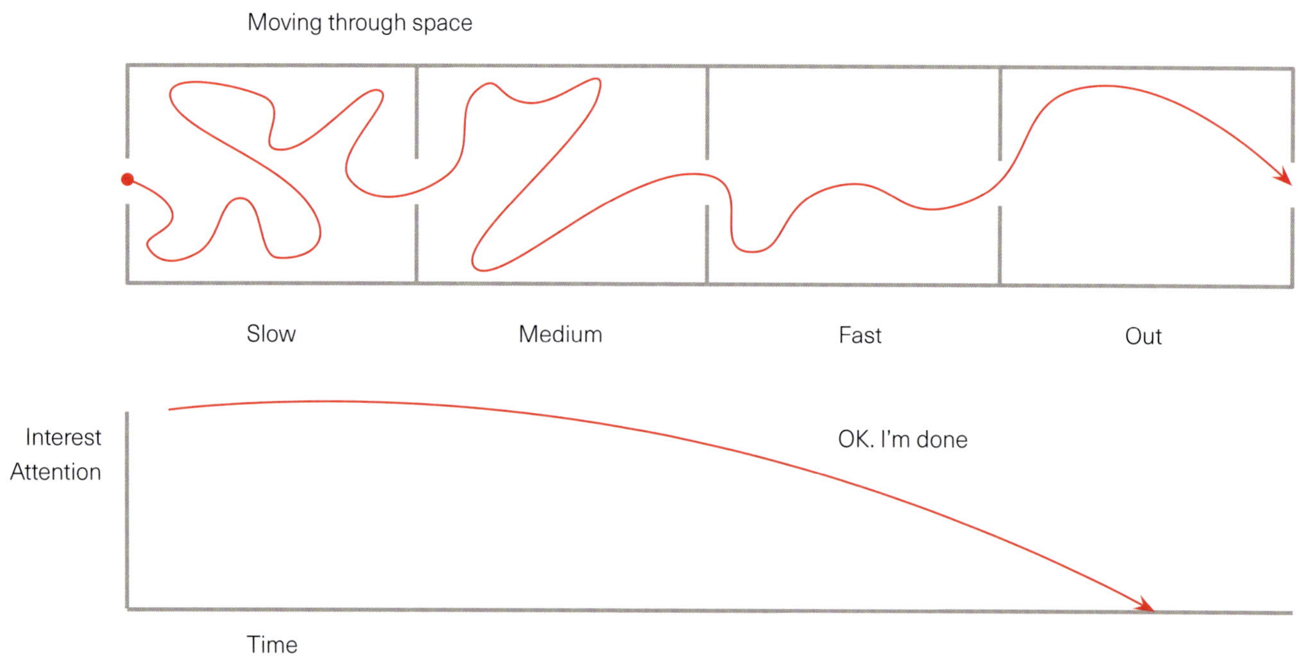

14.2. Principles of interpretation

There are different words in different countries for what we call storytelling. Interpretation is one of them, and as far as we know most common in English-speaking countries. There is a slightly different meaning attached to it though. It does signify the process of transmitting meanings and meaningful relationships to our visitors, but there is also an element involved of deliberately choosing what meaning you want to transmit. The angle of looking. In a sense this is always the case when designing stories, it is just that the word interpretation emphasizes it.

The aim of interpretation is not instruction, or providing information, but insight on an emotional and conceptual level. It aims at a revelation based upon information.

Doing so, choosing and transmitting content and emotions/ experiences, you have to acknowledge there is no such thing as 'the visitor'. We all have our different backgrounds, preconceived ideas, knowledge-base and learning styles. So, as any storyteller knows, you must adapt your story to your audience, as well as it can reasonably be done. Therefore, you have to know who you are talking to.

Interpretation must be related to something in the personality or the experience of the visitor

Any story told – verbally, in a movie, book or exhibition – will stuck only if you are able to connect. It has to 'touch' a point in the mind of your visitor, to get him or her 'moved', and to have a little change in his or her emotional and conceptual settings. Put it on a more transactional viewpoint: what is 'in it' for them – on a personal level and on a more social level. So, you have to know what is in the mind of your visiting groups. What do they know, assume, are interested in. Easier said than done of course.

To get to know your visitors – you might call them target groups, though a better name probably is user-groups – you need to have some visitor research and the actual day-to-day experience in your place. This leads up to a small list of preconceptions in the broadest sense of the word. Thus, before starting the storyline, just write out the major conceptions you might encounter and which you have to tune into.

For example: some perspectives on history and our predecessors
When watching the current television series on major historic personalities (the young Victoria, Louis XIV in Versailles, Medici) it is interesting to see how 'nowadays' they are portrayed. There might be quite some current knowledge missing, some morals definitely different (the use of violence) – but they could have been people of today. You could step into their shoes.

From visitor research it is known, however, that this view is not shared by everyone. Many parts of our society believe life was really different before us, much harder and people were not as knowledgeable and smart as they are today. Primitive life, primitive people. There are others who think life and man actually were more authentic and people more social.

Though the above is put too harshly, too black and white, it does pay out to really know what the conceptions are when you develop an exhibition with a historical viewpoint. If presenting facts, figures and explanations, they are to be seen in the context you want them to be seen. In that sense, the facts are a means to an end, not an end in itself.

14.3. Routing: unfreezing (transition), moving, refreezing

Anyone entering an exhibition – or museum for that matter – needs some time to acclimatise. Where am I? How is the spatial alignment, what is the atmosphere of the place? What am I going to see?

In the literature it is called 'unfreezing'. Opening up to new information, experiences, insights. Getting their attention. The entrance area is where this has to happen and thus an independent area within an exhibition where you want to stand still, look around, read the introduction and so on. And as a visitor do not want to feel uncomfortable because new

visitors are breathing down your neck. So, some space, out of the way of new entrants, is needed.
We would call it the transition zone. It is needed in the museum as well as in each exhibition. When actually moving through the exhibitions, visitors are engaged. Their conceptions and feelings are touched, adaptable, 'moving'. Elements of the story, contents and images, are entering and (re)configured in the cognitive and emotional setup of each of us.

At the end of the exhibition there should be a wrap-up, if not literally then at least metaphorically and emotionally. This would be called the 'refreezing' part. It means that there is no sudden end to an exhibit, but as in any story some summative end, with a glance ahead (and they lived long and happily). When some reconfiguring in the mind of a visitor has taken place, you want it to sink in. This preferably takes place in between different galleries, as well as when leaving the museum.

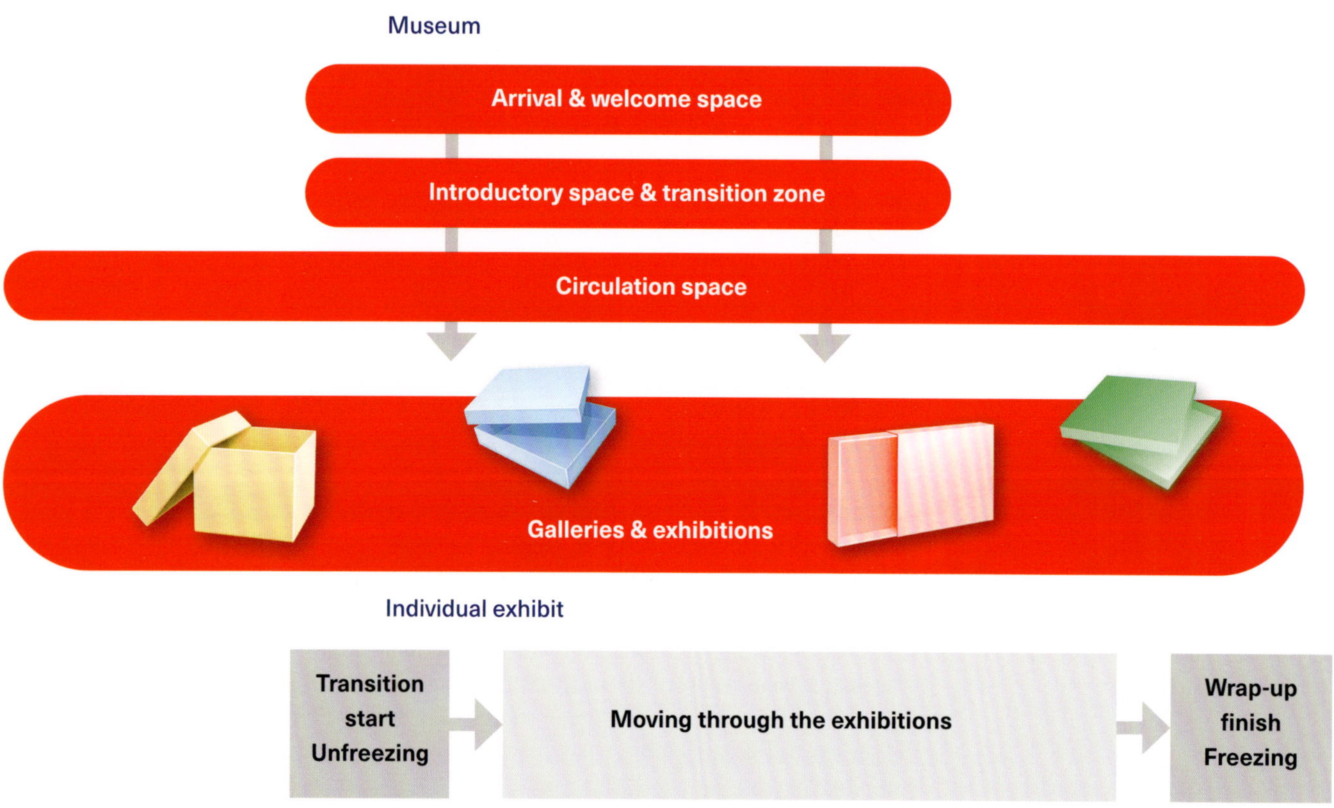

Some examples of un-structuring preconceptions

All in all, any exhibition on a subject should work with unravelling and showing the major (mis)(pre)conceptions on any subject, and hence opening up to building up new insights with their visitors. Unfreezing – moving – and freezing.

For example, when visiting churches – or having them in stories in exhibitions – this usually starts with building styles. However, a church is first of all a place of worship, of a designed spot for the rituals of the Christian belief. Thus, in any explanation on architectural styles of churches, there needs to be understanding of whatever is behind the general design of a place of worship. What ideas were behind the rituals that shaped the general form and formula of churches? What were the ideas and emotions to be provoked in the attendees? And what are the differences within the different Christian faiths?

It is from this generalized preview you might start to understand specific building innovations, leading to new forms and constructions. And the same kind of reasoning holds true when entering the many museums with religion-inspired paintings. In those there is much more to the table, however. What symbols were incorporated, as being part of society at the time?

Another example is the preconception we have in Europe of the native Americans – Indians – as most of our ingrained conceptions and images are based on the novels of Karl May and the Hollywood westerns. These are generally those of the Sioux of the Great Plains, during the colonisation and the times of Buffalo Bill. There were literally hundreds of tribes however, with massive differences in lifestyle, social organisation and so on.

For almost any subject there is this kind of reasoning possible. It all starts with knowing what the major conceptions are in the mind of visitors, before moving over to the story you want to get across.

Pacing

No one walks in a straight line and at a continuous speed through an exhibition. The variations are partly due to individual preferences, interests and temperaments. The design of the space, the exhibition and the story are major factors. So, building a storyline structure, you could already think of the design of where you think / want people to linger and experience. Anyway, keep variations in pace in your mind designing your structure.

14.4. Building the global storyline, using your analysis grid

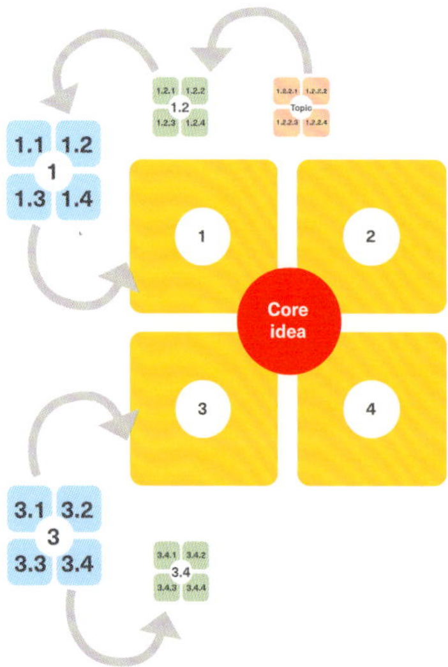

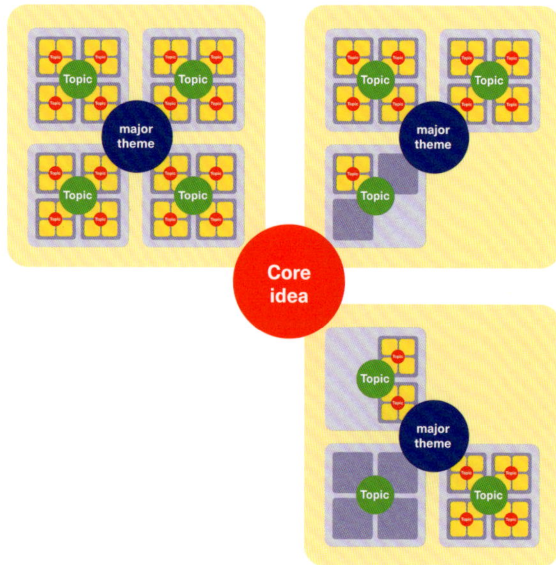

As visitors can only be guided up to a certain level, their understanding of the spatial and logical arrangement is of utmost importance. This is not only the logical line of content elements, placed in a linear or modular organization, but also a very clear 'signing' for each major building block, module, which you as a visitor are to encounter. The subject and preferably conclusive tagline should ideally be clear before you enter a specific (sub)topic.

For each and every larger grouping of visual components it has to be clear what it is about, why they are there together and how this fit in the larger scheme of the story. The (sub) heading is a kind of comprehensive conclusion of what the forthcoming. Think of it like a writer of non-fiction books, or science writer or a journalist. Think in 'building blocks'.

Global storyline

We are discussing the major arrangement, i.e. the global storyline. Which of these major parts should be sequenced? Which can be regarded as more or less independent modules, or even a mini-exhibition on its own? Is there a kind of logic needed?
Adapt the size of the modules to the relative space you think is needed for each. So, in this phase you are allowed to let go of the uniformity of sizes.

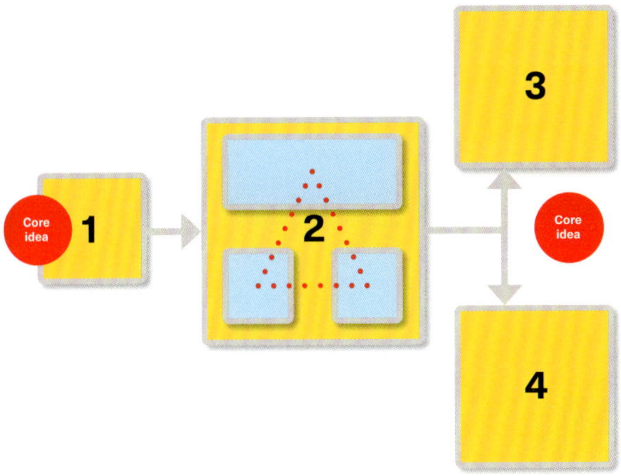

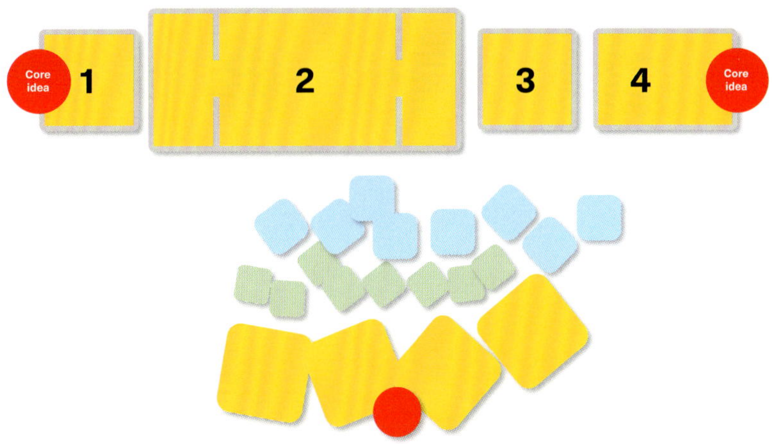

And of course, when you are bound to specific gallery spaces, you have to organize your modules as you think it logically fitting your floor spaces.

Using sketches to outline your ideas for the experience

As mentioned before, the storyline often is used for communication to stakeholders and an outline of the experience is needed. This might be in more or less detail. It is a matter of taste how you do it, in words or in preliminary sketches.

The sketches as shown – on the geological forces, creating the face of the Earth - were used as such in the former Naturalis. They were later on in the process of crucial importance in guiding the design companies in our thinking. To the designers a strict storyline is of crucial importance, as it guides them to the relevant design questions to solve. It will be in the design phase where the storyline will be transmitted into a real story and a kind of scenography. It is this outline that provides the museum and the exhibition designer with indications of possible or best methods for capturing and communicating the essence of a story.

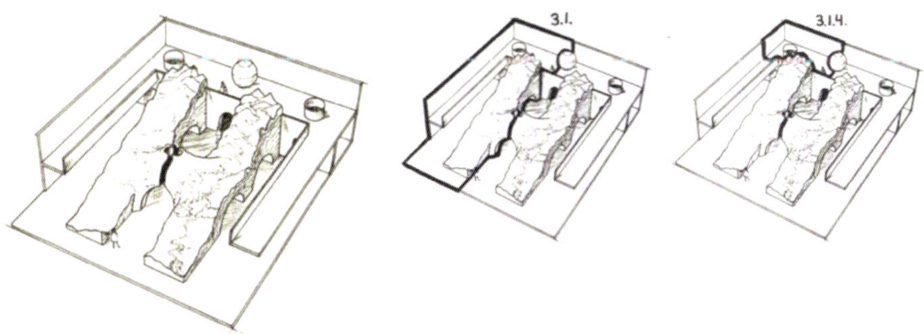

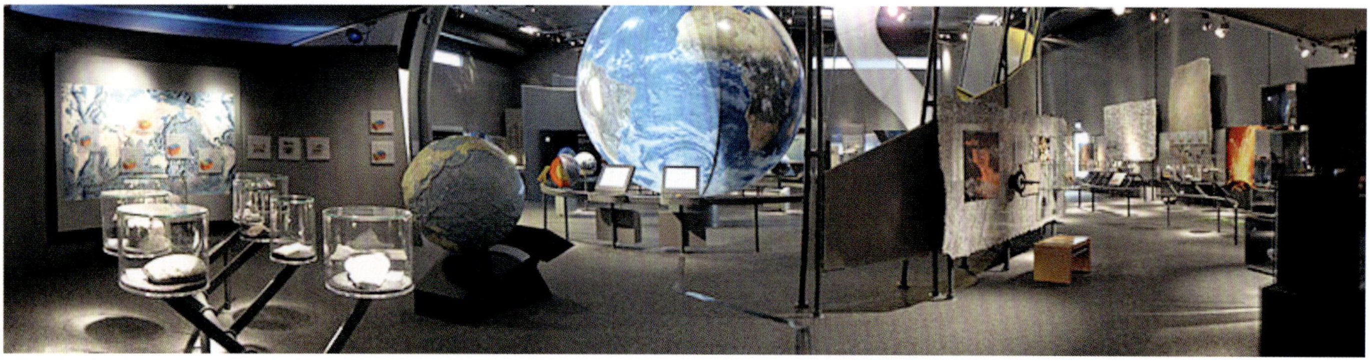

To make it very clear that the sketches are more for instruction and sales purposes, you'll find an impression of what the real exhibition had become later on. Much different from its first impression, though the content modules were relatively positioned exactly as wished, and the actual experience had essential experience elements in common with the sketches. So, the sketches were very functional.

14.5. Do write a visitor journey

As a story is often the easiest and most persuasive way of transferring what you want to get across, it might be very helpful to practise in shorter and longer presentations the story you want to get across. It is the story of a visitor (visitor journey) as well as an overview by a narrator. Keep one version simple and short ('elevator pitch'), while having a longer version (several minutes presentation) available too.

To get your story straight and have everyone on the same track, writing down the visitor journey is most helpful. This has to be done by the content developer and the designer. No better way to check the consistency in the line of thinking.

14.6. The *detailed* storyline

Once the global storyline is set, and agreed on, there is the need for detailing it. Basically, it requires putting all submodules in position, and describing its key content. This might be done in words and tables, and once in a while a sketch or a mood board type of impression.

You have to have a preliminary selection of key objects, including missing collection objects or specimens not in the collection. They serve to illuminate specific components in the story for consulting the content specialists and collection people, so they know what message you want to get across, and thus for them to come up with further suggestions.

There is no uniform, agreed way (yet) to describe this detailed storyline. Pick your choice then. We would suggest though to use the table you started while building the analysis grid.

Do further increase the depth and breadth of it, where it serves as a table of contents for the report, you'll have to come up with finishing this phase (having a separate chapter for each submodule).

Number	Descriptive title	Short description	Key message and (first ideas)	Possible key examples and objects (first ideas)
1				
1.1				
1.1.1				
1.1.1.1				
1.1.1.2				
1.1.1.3				
1.1.2				
1.1.2.1				
1.1.2.2				
1.1.2.3				
1.1.2.4				
1.1.3				
1.1.3.1				
etc.				

The report does not need to be too complicated. On the contrary, you might say a simple but well-structured booklet would be best. As each and every module gets its position within the imagined experience, a descriptive list of the set-up, the proposed key objects, the key knowledge needed and such.

A page of this kind might look like this

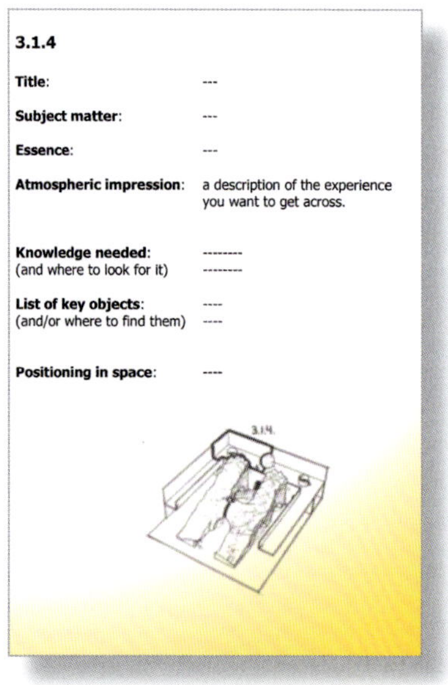

3.1.4

Title: ---

Subject matter: ---

Essence: ---

Atmospheric impression: a description of the experience you want to get across.

Knowledge needed: --------
(and where to look for it) --------

List of key objects: ----
(and/or where to find them) ----

Positioning in space: ----

Besides, it has to fit the communication and sales purposes within your museum. Whether this purpose requires some adaptation of the structured booklet, which we would prefer, or some added or separate 'glossy' is to be decided within the museum.

Administration

As these are 'living' documents', do keep a thorough administration. Include dates of creation, changes, version numbers. All to avoid the all too easily generated chaos.

15. Sites and storylines

Heritage sites are not that different from museums. A heritage site could be regarded as one large exhibition in itself. You are entering a story, from the parking place, the actual visit, the restaurant, and back. You might see some additional exhibitions, even an additional museum, but most surely there will be exhibition elements on the site. Sometimes it is the other way around, when a museum is housed and connected to a site of memory as with Chaplin's World, a museum within his former home.
So, our methodology with respect to content development, storytelling and design can be extended to heritage sites. There is one extra factor though, which we will call *the spirit of the place*.

The 'spirit of the place'

The major, huge difference between a 'clean' museum and a heritage site is what we would call the 'spirit of the place'. What is it this place stood for? What happened? What was the deeper value in the light of history? Or at least what do we think it to be nowadays? What is essentially the core, the essence or, in other words, the spirit of the place?

The need for interpretation

History does not spring up spontaneously from the remains of the past. Heritage sites can only be enjoyed by virtue of interpretation. The art of interpretation is to navigate between scientific evidence and attractiveness. The more so because nowadays there is an increasing emphasis in the heritage industry on experience. If we fail to provide adequate interpretation, the visitors will do so for themselves, based on their own ideas, misconceptions and prejudgements. They have to be assisted. Interpretation is the art that makes history 'real'. Artists, and especially painters have known this for ages, as Degas stated: 'As a painter you have to transfer the idea of the truth by means of the untrue'. Picasso said it even more precisely: 'Art is a lie that convinces us of the truth'.

Interpretation through storyline development

The emphasis of our efforts to help visitors to understand the past is on storyline development. A simple trail through the site and a few panels with information is really not sufficient for visitors to appreciate what they are looking at.

In the development of visitor attractions, a good storyline is of vital importance. Canadian Heritage starts every development of a site – whether it a cultural or natural site – with the question "What is the spirit of the place?" and secondly "How do we get that across to the visitors?". This may sound obscure, but it is not. It is the prime task for the management and experts of a heritage site to answer these questions.

Step into the shoes of the visitor

Visitors are looking for a ***UNIQUE*** experience. In visiting a heritage site, they expect these elements:

- **U**ncommon, it will be out of the ordinary, visit the site is in leisure time;
- **N**ovelty, it will raise curiosity, provide a new experience, a new insight;
- **I**nspiring, it will be provocative and stimulate;
- **Q**uality, it will be customer- and service oriented;
- **U**nderstanding, it will lead to a profound understanding of the phenomena;
- **E**motions, it could evoke emotions and be a touching experience.

What the visitor wants and need	What the expert thinks the visitor wants
Interesting	Important
Meaningful	Significant
Revelation	Relevance
Interpretation	Information
Imagination	Facts
Story (narration)	History

Choosing

The physical remains of the past, whether landscapes, sites, or objects, have many layers of significance, which can be important to present to the visitors. As there are many stories to tell, one should make a choice based on the identity of the region, its markers and is depending upon the objectives and the customer profile.

For example, a building or an artefact is always more than it seems to be. A palace is not only the dwelling place of a monarch but is also meant to impress. A palace is to take care that the subjects are duly impressed and have to look (literally) up to their king. The layout expresses the differences in status of the activities to be performed in and around the palace. The interior and decorations tell us something about the relationship between the monarch, his court and his subjects.

So, bear in mind what the visitor wants and need, see the table, when you write down your storyline. Take a bigger perspective and context.

All these different aspects can offer a clue for the development of a storyline. The 'story' is much more than merely making the information available. It essentially is about the possibility for visitors to identify with the site and what is offered to them. Some 50 years ago Freeman Tilden, one of the first people to set down the principles and theories of Heritage Interpretation, already stated that *interpretation is not the same as the provision of information, but is a revelation based on information*. The facts are a mean to an end, not and end in themselves.

Storylines can for example be developed diachronically, through time on one location. What happened here through time. The emphasis will in those cases be on the different layers of habitation of a site, a biography of the landscape if you like. This is what you see most, at current sites. The story unfolds at the spot.

It becomes more difficult when storylines, for example, diversify one historical period in geographically different locations. Or when your site is one of more 'markers' in a larger story, but as such is not a spectacular site in itself. In the appendix we discuss an example of the latter, a storyline developed for an archaeological-tourism project around the Limes, the frontier of the Roman Empire. In this example understanding and *feeling* the larger story is of major importance to appreciate a reminiscence or object which in itself is not in any way spectacular, beautiful or impressive.

An interesting project, worth naming here, is a project called Street Values by the Reinwardt Academy, which explores how the everyday environment could be using some of its roots, and thus integrating and embedding history and heritage into daily life. You are not visiting the place, 'doing an exhibit'. It is the story presented to you in your daily life, where you live, walking the dog, do your shopping, live your life. The emphasis is put on how heritage can be perceived as a social design challenge rather than an object or location to be preserved. It is the practice of heritage-making visible and worthwhile in the daily living environment. In this it is more interconnected to social actors and is more closely attuned to the values of local communities. This takes us too far from our methodology though.

When starting your writing

Heritage and thus also heritage sites are the outcome of a melting pot of value systems. Think of it as belief systems, traditions, ethnicity, and so on. There is no objective, clear-cut 'true' story. What we feel as we enter a place, what we think of what has happened there, where it stands for, and how we interpret it today, this full set of feelings and knowledge is a matter of interpretation.

Before going into describing, explaining, building an experience on a heritage site, you have to be clear-cut on what you essentially think the place stands for, i.e. what the spirit is. What

is it you want to transmit? What is the story, the core idea, the insight and experience, you essentially want to get across?
Having done so, you then enter the content development phase, as described before. If this is carved out, there is the concept of authenticity too. Whether it is material (the real thing?), contextual (the proper context?), conceptual (what is behind it?) or functional (does it still do what it was meant for?).

In the storyline phase you then have to step into the shoes of a visitor and weave the story you have in mind, using the building blocks developed. In doing this, you can use the toolsets presented in this book. There is however the fact that the *spirit* is an essential to be written into the core idea and its elaboration.

16. The use of an educational model

There is always an educational framework at the base of our reasoning. It might not be that outspoken or consciousness when you develop your ideas, but there is. We have it too, and it was implicitly used in the development of the storyline. So, it is fair to make it explicit.

The model we present here is not *the* model. You might have your own version. This one does have some advantages though when developing your storyline.

16.1. An educational model in the exhibition story telling

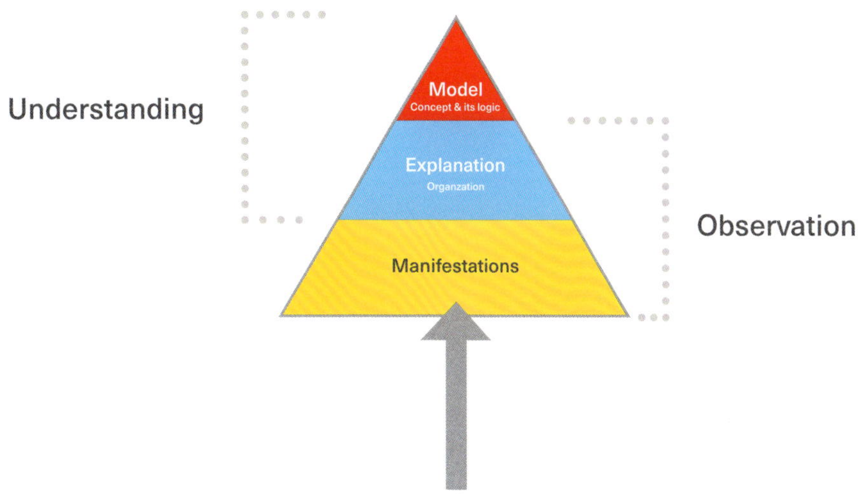

We see and experience a setting, a context, an object, an event – and then try to interpret it. We 'see' a manifestation, an outcome, a result, and then try to explain it using our observations and basic knowledge.

On a deeper level there is the underlying root cause. An earthquake is happening because the earth beneath our feet is resetting itself. We know of moving plates and the building of strain or tension in the earth beneath our feet.
On the deepest level, the underlying model of understanding is understanding how the inner fluids and (nuclear) energy inside our earth sets the plates in motion and causes its traction and 'bumping'.

So, we consider three phases: what we see (manifestation), what we nearly immediately understand (explanation), and what is the root behind it all (model).

Exhibiting manifestations

Entering an exhibit, you see – at eye-level – objects, experiences, all in a scenography with accompanying explanatory infographics, movies and text usually added
As quite some manifestations can be organized around one cause, there will be logical groupings. And many of such groupings can be, in turn, organized around one underlying model. In the example of the earth system: the inner energy and movements in the earth core are also at the root of volcanoes.

Spatial organization and connection to the analysis grid and storyline

As the figure shows, you can imagine how this educational framework has its implications for the way we spatially and visually organize our contents and tell our story.

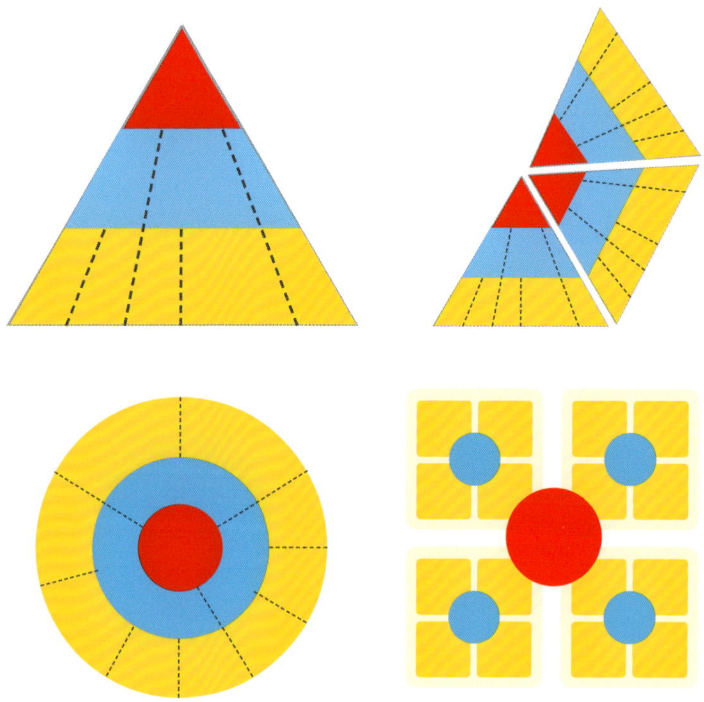

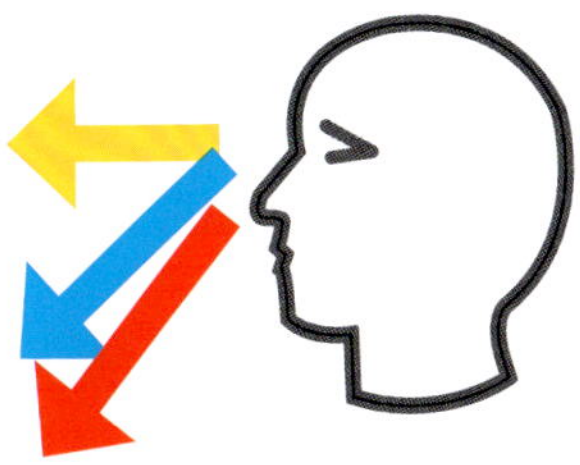

Manifestations at eye-level

There is a case to be made to have as much overview for visitors as possible, to get the big picture easily so to say. To see where what kind of topic is. Additionally, you could argue too that it fits a learning style to see at eye level the 'real thing' and have the explanations at a more 'studious' level.

There are many other possibilities to consider. To describe your own, specific idea on how to present the different levels of information is an additional feature of an educational model.

16.2. A methodology – and a book - on its own

Though the educational model presented here, is meant for exhibiting purposes, it is a logical expectation that the educational framework used – the kind of thinking and the content - should be used in the development of educational programmes too.

There is hardly an exhibition which is not accompanied with at least several educational programmes. And it should. Being guided by educational programmes can bring new and lasting experiences too. Building on what the exhibition shows, there can be new layers of stories and insights.

Developing an educational programme therefore is a major enterprise on its own. Many of the steps taken in this exhibition methodology are of use in developing the programmes, but of course there is a major shift in approach and there are also some additional tools needed. Developing an educational programme requires a methodology – and a book - on its own. We think.

16.3. In concordance with the exhibition development

As we stated before, it is absolute necessary to have the educational officer, the one responsible for developing the programme, on board in the developing team of any exhibition. In the stage where the content is defined and structured. It is this phase where most or all options for programmes are set.

Some questions:

- Which groups?
  - If schools: what levels?
  - What is the curriculum – and what can be addressed by this particular exhibition / programme? NB. What can be done for individual groups of adults, or for adult education for that matter?

• Which themes? There are programmes 'following' the exhibition themes, and there might be ones which addresses some new angles and/or additional storylines. (It can have real added value to come up with new story lines taken elements from the exhibitions)

These questions can be addressed in a cross-reference table.

	Theme 1	Theme 2	Theme 3	etcetera
Group 1				
Group 2				
Group 3				
etcetera				

'Plotted' in the exhibition development

In the development of an exhibit, it is of great help to have materials made, as infographics and such, to be ready for re-use in other contexts. So, the concept and analytic structure of an exhibition has to be developed in concordance with the development of the concept and content of educational programmes.

17. Text writing, content development continued

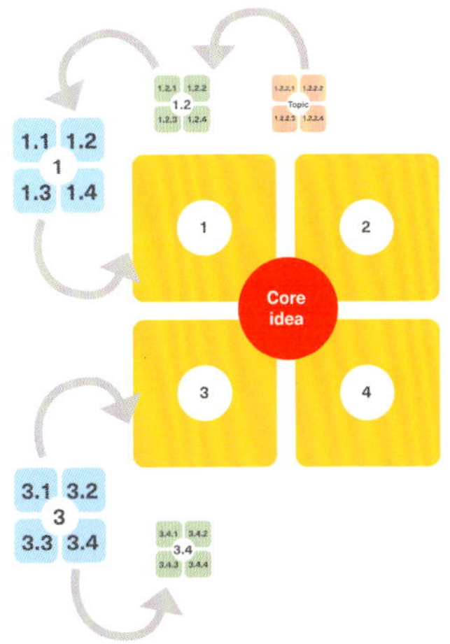

Content description – elaborated description of the analysis grid

Number	Descriptive title	Short description	Key message and (first ideas)	Possible key examples and objects (first ideas)
1				
1.1				
1.1.1				
1.1.1.1				
1.1.1.2				
1.1.1.3				
1.1.2				
1.1.2.1				
1.1.2.2				
1.1.2.3				
1.1.2.4				
1.1.3				
1.1.3.1				
etc.				

Determining principal text messages

Number	4.3.2.2.2.4	
Short description of the module content		
Description of objects, infographics and AV elements		
Key text messages	**Text messages of secondary importance**	**Text messages of tertiary importance (and nice facts)**
1.		
2.		
3.		
4.		

Reasoning or Argumentation schemes

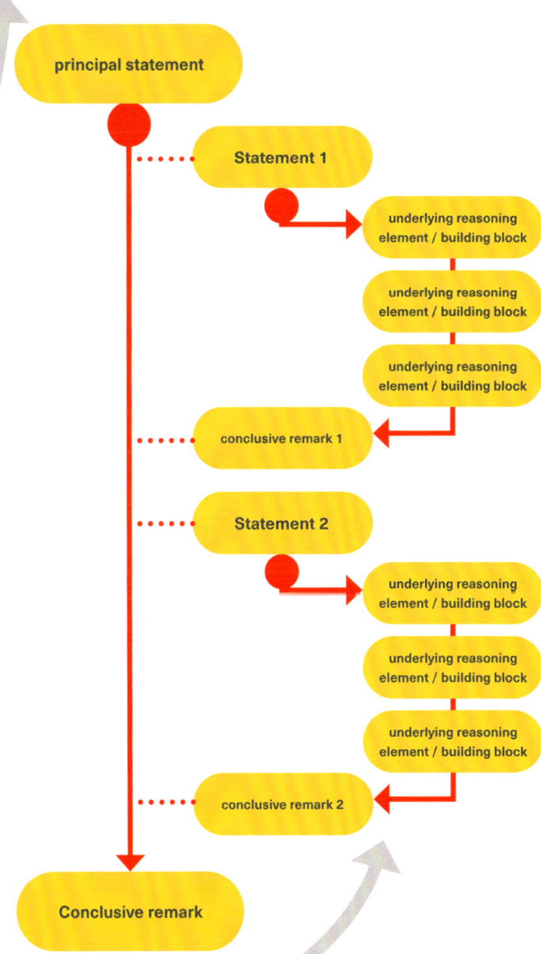

17.1. Research

There is substantial time needed for research into the subject of your exhibition. That will continue and is included throughout most of the content development and storyline phases. It therefore is not logic to describe research as a separate phase, which is to be checked as 'done'. Nevertheless, we just did so, also to make clear it needs time and often some break in process.

The informal rule of thumb says you need to master a subject in-depth, just to tell the 5% which is the essence told in the exhibition. To be able to decide on the essence, to know what really matters and how the story should be told, you need to know an awful lot. Better said you need to have a helicopter (over)view on the content matter before starting to develop an exhibition. You might argue that you have the experts to take that role, but we think that is not the case. As a content developer you basically are a science journalist. You need to grasp not only the structure, but really do need detailed knowledge of important cause-effect relationships just to be able to tell a structured story. As a science journalist does indeed.

17.2. Getting step by step to texts and other interpretive contextual information

The writing and development of supporting texts, labels, and other interpretive information, such as video segments or infographics, usually is not as straightforward a process as it is often imagined to be by outsiders. Especially so when it is the type of content in which nuances are of crucial importance, as in the explanation of complex scientific processes or when presumed historic patterns are revealed. As there is almost always a trade-off between scientific prudence and clear writing, text writing can become alike a battlefield with the experts.

There are some tools to avoid heated arguments on texts. Better said: to have the discussions on content before they get written down as texts. The methodology basically works by deconstructing key messages, reasoning schemes and logic first. It works stepwise, starting by building (1) a detailed content description for each and every module on the basis of the analysis scheme or grid. This overview subsequently leads to (2) a detailing on the key messages, the principal text messages, and where needed accompanied by (3) reasoning and argumentation schemes.

Determining principal text messages

Number		4.3.2.2.2.4
Short description of the module content		
Description of objects, infographics and AV elements		
Key text messages	**Text messages of secondary importance**	**Text messages of tertiary importance (and nice facts)**
1.		
2.		
3.		
4.		

Once the overall argument for each display and its components is defined, as elaborated in the table on the previous page, the development of text messages normally would start. We propose however to use two intermediate steps.

The first step is to define for each module – and mind you, there can be many – a separate table (or index card or ..) in which the key sentences are noted. They are written as clearly as possible and will be accompanied by statements which might be of interest but are not of key importance. This way it is easy to understand what the text should convey, without having discussions on how it is said or if it is said correctly. They function as a checklist with scientists and curators and are as well helpful when text writing is outsourced.

Argumentation and reasoning schemes as a help

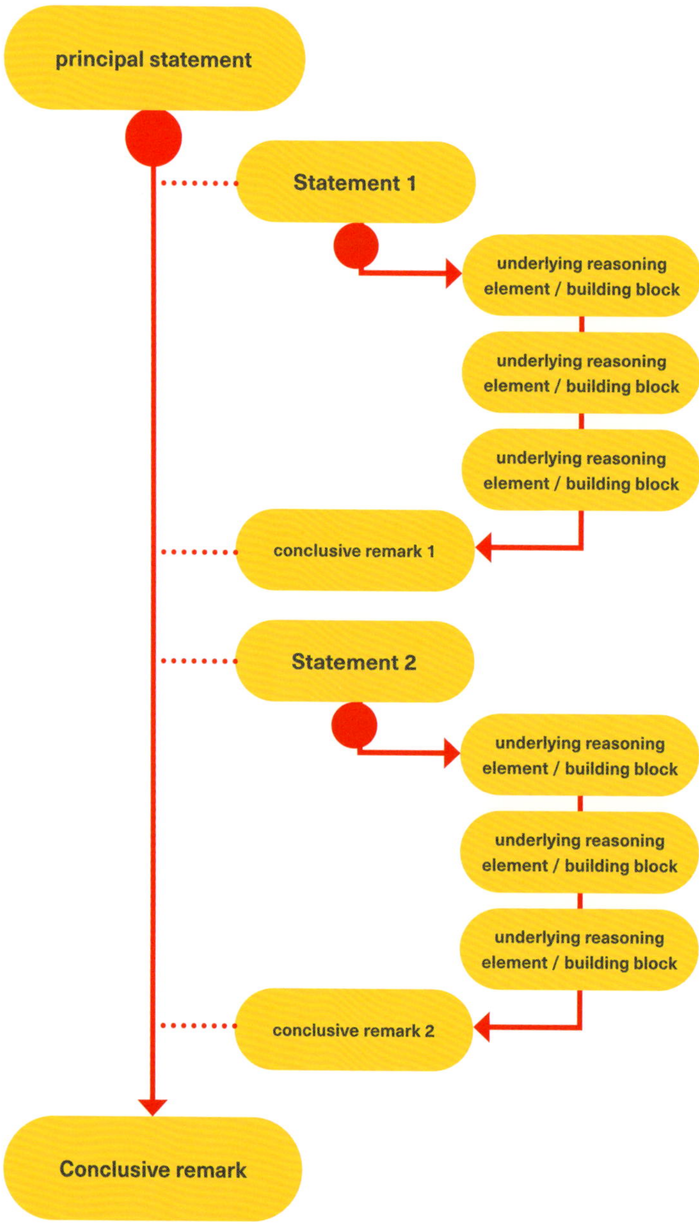

The second optional step is to come up with reasoning schemes. These are ways of checking whether the reasoning, the explicit or implied logic, is correct.

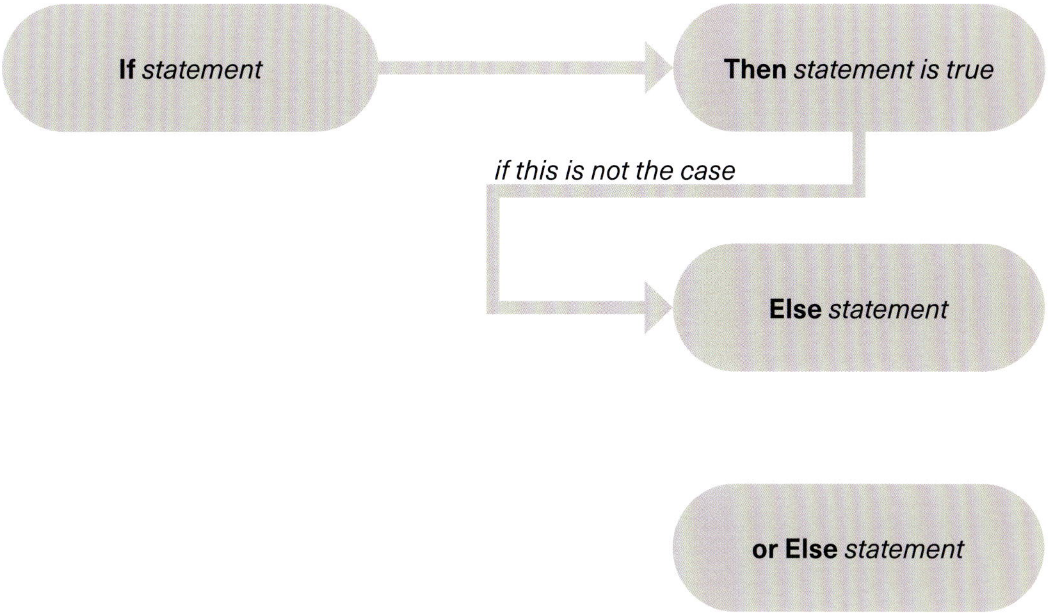

This process of building the basic argumentation or reasoning scheme for a concept is particularly important when describing complex social, historical, creative, or scientific processes. It also assures that the experts who supply or contribute to this information (scientists, curators or guest curators in most cases) and the exhibition content developers, as well as the designers, educators, and other involved parties who might provide or use the content, will have a common understanding of the message as it is being developed. This helps to ensure that the message is clear to the ones who do the actual text writing.

The principal objective for setting out the argumentation for any scheme is to see if the underlying insights into its content are thoroughly understood. If a reasoning scheme is well built, it can be verified by those with the necessary expertise and, eventually, enhance understanding of the content by the museum staff, its stakeholders, and its visitors. It accommodates questions such as 'Is this how it works?' or 'Where is this wrong?' A reasoning scheme is a valuable instrument to assure the clarity of the content. It serves as a starting point for drafting texts and for checking those draft texts.

A major type of scheme is the 'if than else' reasoning. There are other though. Examples use words like *While ...then...*or *As long as ... then .... else ...*

Mind you: a reasoning scheme can in principle be read without using the underlying, explanatory reasonings. First of all it is concerned with deciphering the logic, the structure.

> *As an example of a reasoning – which can be checked against scientist's knowledge: A frog cannot actively regulate its temperature. If the outside temperature drops, then the inner temperature of a frog drops too. If temperatures drop below zero, and the water freezes, then the water inside the frog's cells freezes too, which will in turn lead to the death of the frog. So, frogs will die when it freezes.*

17.3. A manual on some principles

After there is an agreement on the principal messages, the actual text writing is to start. A manual will be helpful, like a brand guide for writing. It includes the degree of detail in the various texts, its style, its tone-of-voice, factual or more story-telling techniques, and more. So, do develop a manual on the text writing itself, as well as on infographics and other interpretive materials.

There is quite some differentiation to be considered. Will it be an adjacent text? A text which is to be shown on a mobile device? Whatever way(s) you choose, have it outlined and described before starting. We discuss some key points which we think are basic.

Start with the conclusion

Museum texts need to adopt the famous 'inverted pyramid' or journalistic form, with the conclusion preceding the argumentation. This has a reason. For only 5-15% of visitors read the whole text, so you be sure that at least the essence is read. More important however, when starting with the conclusive statement, the thing which is the essential core, the logic of the following text often is much easier to write. You will stick to what really is there to be said.

Ideally the title should contain the principal message, in a more or less catchy or memorable one-liner. A tagline.

Each and every paragraph starts again with a conclusive statement, then followed by some small explanatory text. Ideally, all 'first lines' should tell the story.

In other words, text titles should contain the essence of a display's contents. If that is difficult, a smaller visually outstanding paragraph can be introduced directly following the title. In previous methodologies this was often referred as B-texts.

Some additional rules

There are some acknowledged rules in science writing. For example, stick to one message in every sentence. Do vary in longer and shorter sentences and restrict yourself anyway in the number of long sentences. Have empty spaces, blank lines, between the paragraphs to enhance a quick overview.

There are some discussions on putting (provoking) questions as a starting point, to arouse interest. We do think this is not necessary as we are promoting very concise texts. Putting questions into texts fits more in an entertaining way of writing. Whichever way you choose, be careful to avoid the 'childish tone' as, for example, the 'did you know' type of approaches.

Infographics and instructional films

Depending on the objectives of a display, this phase can also lead to the design and creation of infographics or other interpretive materials (films, cartoons, etc.), which may be more appropriate devices for effectively communicating principal messages. The creation, design, and production of these additional interpretive materials also require planning and development, which will for example use additional explanatory sketches and storyboards.

The importance of infographics in museums is not fully recognized. The importance of visuals is nowadays everywhere, in newspapers, schoolbooks and such. But not so much in museums yet.

There is a reason of course. Most curators are historically more text based scholars for one. But the development of infographics is costly and time-consuming too, especially when the preparations are not thoroughly done. To have them developed, you have to hire specialists, to give clear instructions on style, messages – and not at last, you have to prototype them yourself. This is all more than is normally within the competence of museum staff.

The same holds true for the development of instructional films. The way to develop them is really not very different.

The art of leaving out

Whatever the form, concise and clear writing and drawing (when infographics are used) is very helpful. The use of other journalistic principles is needed too. That is, for example, to structure longer texts in small building blocks, with headers which describe the (sub) conclusions, and have the most important statements first.

Be however strict on what the essences are. Interesting sidelines tend to distract the readers and hamper the understanding on what are the essentials. Most readers do not complete reading the whole text. As a generalisation one could say that a visitor reads until he thinks he has got the message. A sideline in the story thus often leads to pull out, to 'zap' so to speak.

For consistency reasons as well as easing the writing, it does help to have a specific, overall writing style for the museum's communication with the public and for strengthening the museum's brand. A museum thus is to develop a manual regarding its writing style and 'tone' for all its information.

The developed texts are carefully reviewed from a number of perspectives: scientific accuracy, educational validity, writing style, voice, copyediting, and so on. The result of this review process and subsequent corrections is a text that is accurate and agreed upon and that encompasses all the textual components of an exhibition so that they can be cross-referenced to avoid repetition before being printed.

A reviewing committee (text writers, communication professionals and/or general as well as science journalists) can be helpful – for example to read all text in a one- to two-week time period for complete batches of text. The same committee can be responsible for reading the exhibition texts as well as all marketing and communication material. A community consultations advisory may also be very useful in providing input at this point and help the museum steer clear of unintentional misstatements. Testing with adolescents might work very well too.

17.4. Reflection on the earlier presented educational model

There is always a trade off between having a quick overview and more in depth information. What is it that should be immediately clear and what is additional, deepening or more explanatory information. Usually, in the 'old' text based world, this is distinguished by developing A, B and C texts. In the new world, with infographics and digital extensions, this will call for a slightly different approach.

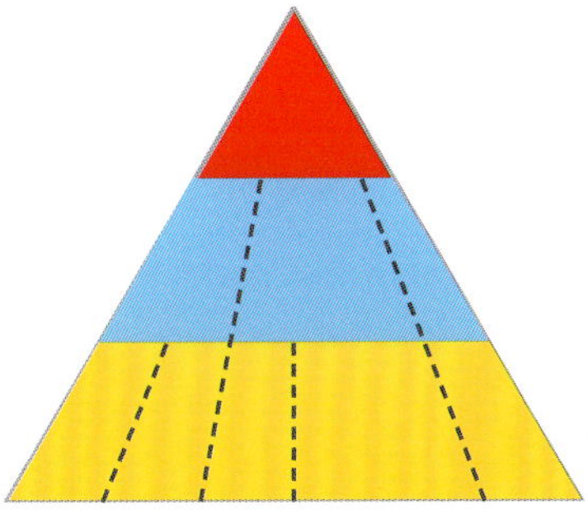

The more effort something takes from a visitor, the less it is going to be used. For text, this is easy to observe in galleries. As soon as a visitor understands what he is looking at, he moves on. Most of them do. And the use of digital text does not seem an improvement. The use of QR coding and digital labels does not seems to reach many visitors for example, whereas informative graphics – easy to grasp – do. And it is all to human to move on, have a quick glimpse at most when you are already in the exhibition for quite a long time.

This said, that does not mean it should not be done. There are different levels of information to be offered. It leads however to acknowledge a strict distinction between what information is needed with an observation or manifestation (something you see) and what is needed to *understand* (*explanation*). And there is the underlying model, a deeper and more descriptive insights in the machinery. driving many groupings of manifestations, each with its own intermediate explanatory forces.

So, for any text writer, to inform visitors at different levels and to have the essential explanations clear in a short notice too, it is worthwhile to think carefully about the groundplan of your information and in which ways to deliver it. What kind of message fits into the educational context – and how is it related to adjacent texts?

We therefore return to designing an exhibition around the core contents and essentials. Having done so, the next step is to structure the delivery around what it is all about and which 'technology' to use. In more historic or scientific subjects, the use of infographics maybe more appropriate than in art exhibitions.

18. Design

Today more than ever, visitors judge a museum by the quality of the visual presentations, the experience they encounter. It is a package consisting of the overall 'look' of the installation spaces, as well as the content of the displays and the design of the scenography, texts, lighting, audio-visuals, and other complementary components. These are the elements of the communication language that characterizes modern exhibition presentation.

Where content meets design

While the sets or display backdrops, lighting, audio-visual effects, and other installation features are usually perceived as the principal aspects of design, it is the spatial organization and overall structuring of the galleries which are essential to the effective communication of the content. This is where content meets design, where they must logically and visually connect and convey the intended messages and experiences. The quality and consequence of a visit are very much influenced by the overall spatial organization of the content, as much as by the scenography, lighting, texts, and audio-visual support for the individual displays.

Museum displays are most effective when content and design are closely related, with design being a function of the narrative and the accompanying objects on display. Structuring the content and organizing the design process are particularly important when dealing with designers from outside the museum. As this is frequently the case today, the museum must carefully and thoroughly articulate the details of the storyline and content that it has developed and expects to communicate. You want the design process to enforce rather than overtaking the essential storytelling.

The next section therefore addresses the spatial organization of display content, both throughout the museum and within a single exhibition or gallery space.

18.1. Content and Space

Once work on the content of an installation has been established – the substance of an overall concept-including its core display elements, their logical organization, and the resulting storyline – there is a need to 'translate' the developed scenario into a visitor experience. A properly translated scenario with a sequence and hierarchy of encounters helps an audience to 'read' the museum's stories throughout the galleries in such a way that they can take greater advantage of the various offerings and experiences of a visit.

For example, a museum visit begins with an entry space that caters to the arrival experience itself, providing reception information and a degree of release from pent-up emotions for

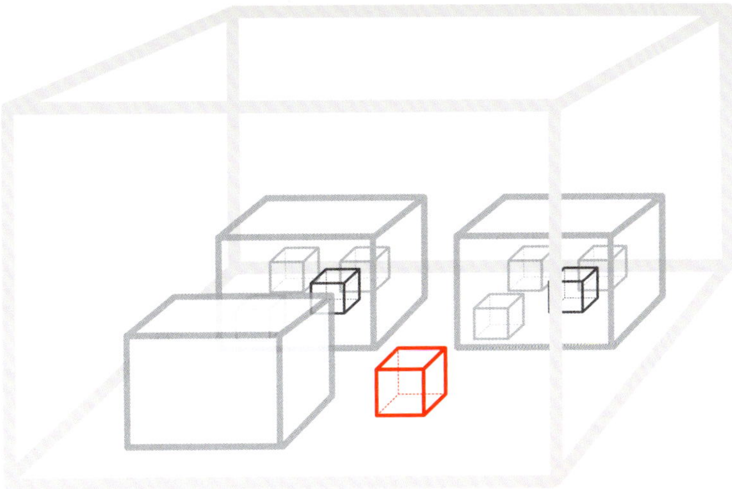

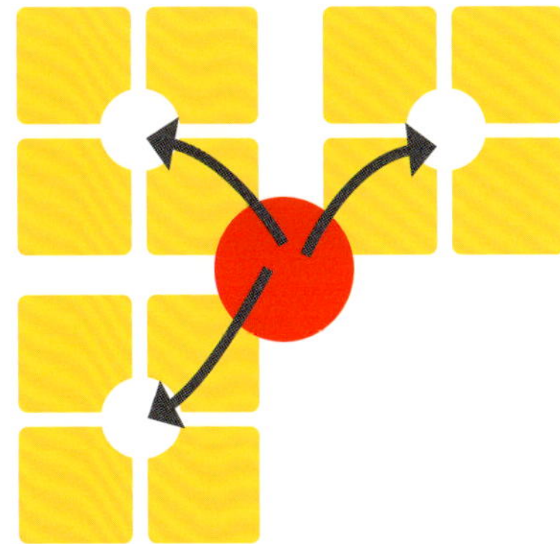

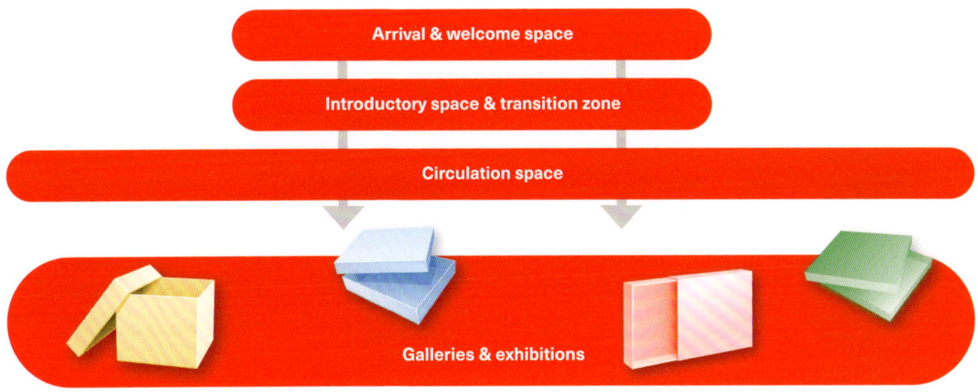

weary or excited visitors. This is a transition area where visitors come in from the street and get ready for the museum experience.
The same holds true when you enter an exhibition or a specific gallery. There always is a need for some transition area, for orientation, for getting a good insight on what you are going to encounter. In effect, this area should hint at the underlying structure and content of the intellectual and material resources that will inform the rest of the institution's displays.

As they move on, visitors will encounter more specific, theme-oriented spaces, each of which presents one of the main ideas or stories that the museum has decided to use in order to characterize significant aspects of its collections and intellectual resources. These spaces might include a cluster of exhibitions or displays in which a particular theme is explored more fully, and visitors might discover links to other display modules.

Hence it is worthwhile to try to put the storyline, including all groups of modules – as depicted by the analysis grid – in a logical spatial arrangement. It is setting the core messages in such a way they are easily recognized as such. Based on the developed storyline, the principal thematic content modules are 'placed' in the main spatial units, followed by the development of three-dimensional 'sets'. The placement of sets representing thematic units again follows a 'map' similar to that with a somewhat different focus.

When designing sets, the following four basic guidelines are suggested:

1. The individual sets, as well as the entire space, need to be aesthetically appealing and stimulate the imagination.
2. Each section of the storyline, particularly if one is working with an entire museum or a gallery, needs to have a distinct design character.
3. Each 'chapter' of the storyline usually needs a visual icon that stands for the central idea. Using visual icons as metaphors for different topics is a very powerful visual communication device.
4. Different galleries and spaces need to have a different feel and appeal. As with music, varying rhythms, from dynamic to contemplative, add to a visitor's experience. Also, different members of the audience have different learning styles (have a look of those of David Kolb for example) and respond to different approaches to design.

With already established buildings, there may be less flexibility to create new visitor pathways. What is important to note is that the content and spatial relationships of thematic modules established during the content development phase still remain the same. The general nature of the approach described here is thus valid for any museum.

18.2. Visual literacy and Wikipedia

There have been some buzzwords and developments around for a while, such as experiences, edutainment, authenticity and virtual reality. Nothing wrong there. They do bring new ways of how storytelling can be done. It does also acknowledge that we have entered a new era of possibilities and of changing ways we learn and look.

Most interesting and in certain ways compelling, is how the IT-revolution shapes our visual literacy. We will call it IT, but it definitely stretches all the way – from movies to the way our schoolbooks are organized. There is more to it than just visuals taking over. It is also about interpreting sequences in scenography. For example - just to compare the sequences of scenes in older movies to modern ones; many in-between scenes have been skipped nowadays as we have internalized the logic during the last decades.

In certain ways there is a parallel in how we absorb information. We are getting used to a fast uptake of short pieces of information, embedded in larger frames of knowledge. There is the old sequence of information – knowledge – understanding – wisdom. This Wikipedia era, however, brought us a much quicker and in-depth way of acquiring information. The building up process of information to knowledge and understanding has changed.

As exhibitions are story-transmitting media, this grown capacity and enhanced possibilities, is a major influence on designing content and space in exhibitions. There is a higher expectancy of the way information and visuals are incorporated in the design.

18.3. A bouquet of approaches

The design is – broadly speaking – meant to put your concept turned into a storyline into a comprehensible, consistent and 'beautiful' experience. We used the metaphor before, but it is like a scenography in a movie or opera, you are taken on a journey of content and experiences. There are many ways to do so, and they can be a 'bouquet' as well. We can distinguish these five possible mental and operational attitudes:

- Conceptual approach
- Metaphoric approach
- Informative approach
- Emotional approach
- Aesthetic approach

The approaches speak for themselves. In the context of this methodology it is important to recognize the approaches, make sure you have your reference(s) stated clearly enough, and translate them into clear and substantiated guidelines in the design manuals.

The five senses.

Before, in the 'old days', a museum was about looking at objects and reading texts. Those days are gone. Nowadays, with the 'bouquet of approaches', 'scenographic thinking' is taking over. There is a growing awareness of the global physical dimension of the museum visit. Walking an exhibition space, a visitor's experience is to be dissected into its intellectual components made of rationality and emotion, of sensuality even, and the related physical components: movement in space, listening, sight, touch, smell, and taste.

Including all senses is difficult, especially when it comes down to taste and smell, and for obvious reasons. However, entering the design phase you do choose types of approaches and you have to take care of thinking how to include the five senses.

Sounds in Museums

In the public imagination the museum visit has been for a long time associated with silence and whispering. Besides the walking and talking of visitors, individuals listening to the still popular audio guides, guided tours were the other prevalent 'sound event'.

Sometimes lectures in the exhibition space took place or - especially in museums dedicated to musical instruments or a musician - musical performances.

To simplify we could point out different ways of listening in the context of the exhibition environment: as a soundtrack (music, poems, noises, nature) addressed to the public as whole in the galleries, or addressed to individuals via different devices and/or addressed to small groups via directional digital microphones.

The potential of sounds in museums as a tool in the development of an exhibition scenography, is not to be underestimated. The menu is rich. Words, sounds, music: these are narrative tools. They have a great potential and multiple applications. The association of an exhibit or a group of objects with 'iconic sounds' (the whistle of a train, the blast of an explosion, the opening of the Fifth Symphony by Beethoven) can totally change the perception of the visitors, similar to what happens with lighting, for instance. However, this requires additional skills, for example a sound engineer and some thorough knowledge with the content developers and curatorial staff.

Taste?

In some cases, the experience of taste is an element introduced into the exhibition, that is to say a specific dimension of the museum environment. For obvious practical reasons the case is rare in which everyone can always offer the opportunity for a taste, but we can offer the smell that is so closely intertwined with taste and the tactile element which is also important in the act of consumption of certain foods. Increasingly widespread in some types of museums are 'community' occasions in which the museum is home to experiences not so much as just gastronomy, but as cultural communication through food. All this regardless of the disciplinary scope of the museum: it can happen to illustrate some aspects of ancient civilizations (the kitchen of the Romans), or in industrial museums (a miner's lunchbox), or in art museums (between subjects of still life and preparations of the kitchen of the past), and so on.

All these activities can be better performed if the functional planning of the museum includes them as part of the exhibition strategy. That means it is part of the setup in the design phase.

18.4. Design phases

The design stage has three phases of development:

1. a sketch design phase,
2. a preliminary design phase, and
3. a final design phase.

A sketch design conveys the central idea and captures the overall atmosphere of a space. It also provides the basic spatial arrangement of the exhibition modules. The sketch design is sometimes accompanied by a model constructed to scale. The sketch design and the scale model are usually presented to stakeholders and other evaluation groups.

The preliminary design conveys all the constructed elements of an exhibition and outlines the major choices that need to be made. It is the transformation of the accepted outline in the sketch design into a realistic design. It encompasses all major elements in a more detailed form and structure.
The final design renders all the installation details, accompanied by precise measurements and cost assessments, ready for fabrication considerations. If cost adjustments need to be made, it is easier and more efficient to make those adjustments as early as possible. Cost cutting in the final design phase is very difficult and usually not very successful in modifying the design.

More detail in the actual planning

When you work on your overall timeline, there is much more detail to be added, as you see in the example. Do not take this example too literally, as it is a detail of one of the exhibitions in

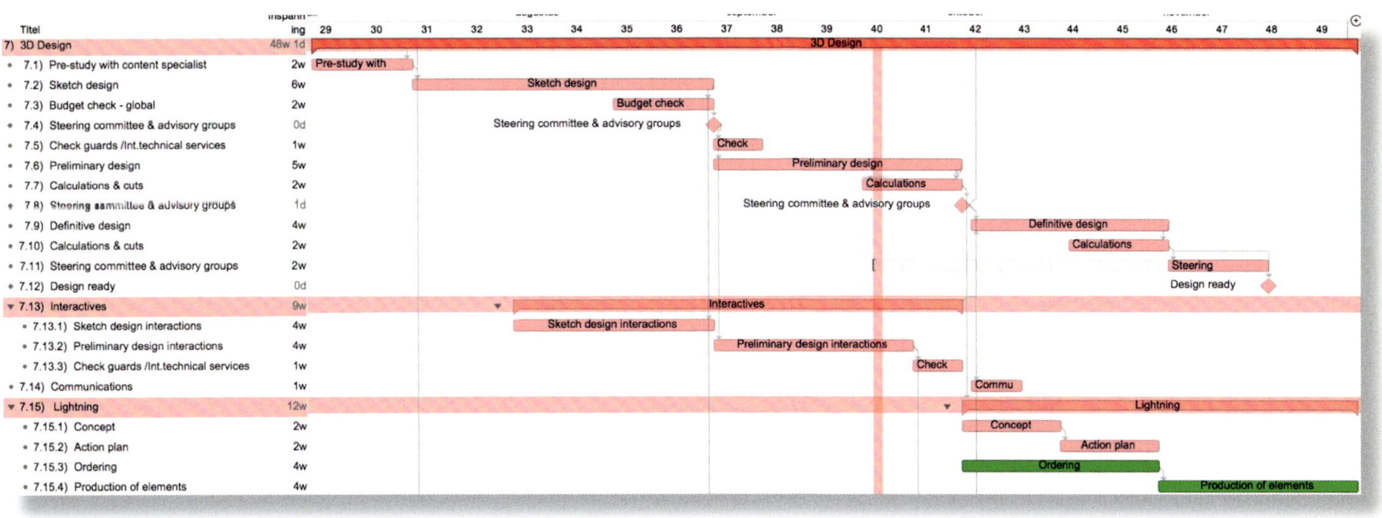

our museum. In this one there are separate lines added for lighting and interactives and for checks to the guards and technical services on feasibility for instance. And you have to add the time needed for the decisionmakers.

This is a general remark, as it is true for all planning phases.

18.5. Design manuals to organize the consistency of the exhibition 'language'

Much of what we think and feel has a largely unconscious aspect. We feel an exhibition is 'beautiful' or 'well done' without exactly knowing why. It means for example in exhibitions that you will often not recognize the quality of the details until there are some minor irregularities. You will often notice them unconsciously, which adds to your overall feeling about an exhibition.

One very important aspect is the consistency of the 'language' used. The signage, the fonts, the colours used, the way objects are shown, the lighting, and so on. It is a pleasure to everyone if the museum as a whole has a consistent and well-detailed use of the way it speaks to visitors. But if this, for whatever reason, is a bridge too far, then please make sure you have consistency organized within the exhibition you are developing.

Manual(s) more of a (brand) law book than a guideline

The surest way to consistency is a rulebook on the design principles in your museum and / or exhibitions. As there is a broad range of topics addressed, they can also be divided, for example into two different sets such as a 2D and a 3D one. Any other division would do too, as well as one manual with clear chapters.

The manuals describe the use of design elements, sometimes clear and directive, sometimes offering a range. There should preferably be some examples. It also offers what is your 'brand', the way you address the audience and so on.

One thing should be clear: we do not mean in any way that all exhibitions should be alike. On the contrary. We like diversity. There however is a big 'but'. We like diversity within an accepted range. We even prefer to have different design companies for the different exhibitions to stimulate diversity, but clearly within the predefined range. The 'one guiding hand' is to be delivered by the manual(s).

A manual does not restrict itself to the obvious. You can (and we think should) extend it to text writing style, lighting, objects used and positioned and much more. The type of elements addressed could be for example:

Fonts	What is or are the font(s) used? What sizes? What spacing? Eventually: colours of the texts.
Graphics	Placing. Style of drawings (clear lines and functional for example). Sizes and proportioning.
Text signs and name plates	Sizes & proportions. Material. Placing. Colours.
Writing style	Style. Approach (for example: start with conclusion = science journalism) Amount of words used in sentences. Forbidden words. Maximum size.
Arrangement of text blocks	In concordance with the style: the use of paragraphs. Divisioning by white spaces. Subheadings.
Spacing of exhibition modules	Preferred spatial organization of independent units described in relative positions. Regular or irregular. Patterns?
Organization and width of passages	Traffic guidelines (straight flow, spiderweb, hidden corners)? Minimum width of pathways? (passing wheelchairs).
Colours and ranges	A colour chart, i.e. main and supporting colours - and for different uses. Brightness. Acceptable ranges.
Lighting and general atmosphere	Type of lighting; profiles. Atmospheric guidelines.
Object presentation	Objects within context or stand-alone? Real life or as collection pieces (example natural history).
And so on	

Have manuals before choosing a design company; the design director in charge

If you have design manual(s): great. If you have not: start working on them right away. It pays off to have your manual(s) ready and established before you do choose design companies. That way you have your consistency and unity organized as well as better checks and balances in your process.

A design manual first and foremost is the competency of the design director. As no one is knowledgeable regarding the full range, some helping hands are needed. This is best done to hire a company you really do trust and can fulfil a role as supervisor. It would even be better – especially when you do not have a design director as most of us have not - to find a senior designer who wants to act as your 'check' and sparring partner to do so. One condition: all effort is to support the designers, so the ego('s) and strong personal opinions should be subordinate.

There is a reason to go to all this trouble. We think it wise to have someone once in a while to check on what is proposed. And it then makes sense to have an independent person or company to do so. You are easily taken in by the daily business and proposals. And be assured: design companies do try to overstep your boundaries. And that should not happen.

The use of mood boards as a starter

We all know mood boards. Although they might look a little 'simple' or childish', it actually is a good tool to understand the preferences and ideas within the team. It helps to compare and discuss different mood boards by the different individuals in the exhibition team. Even more important, it can be used as a starter of composing the design manual and an additional paragraph to it.

18.6. Working with design companies

Design companies and designers have their strong points and weaknesses. Some, for example, excel in their knowledge and capacity to structure space, to build a content mapping, while others have highly imaginative approaches to exhibition scenography, defining a context and creating or accommodating audio-visual and atmospheric effects. A consideration of a designer's strong points or particular interests will be very important when choosing an individual or firm for required tasks. For instance, when developing an overall master plan, the first type of designer or design group with a particular sensitivity to the intellectual structuring of space, might be preferable to the second type.

In any case, if and when a museum may choose to work with an outside designer, the selection of designers has to be made on the basis of their affinities for the task, the subject matter, and the overall team dynamic. Design charettes, for example, allow an assessment of the working methods of different designers, their listening capacity, and inclination for teamwork. It is not unusual for a museum to consider many designers for a large master-planning project before short-listing or choosing only a few (for example, we once interviewed thirty designers before selecting only seven). If a RFP (Request for Proposal) is used to choose a designer, that document should carefully articulate the museum's content intentions.

An independent lighting designer

A good lighting plan has an enormous effect on any exhibition. Light is one of the most influential atmospheric tools you have, and it is a fundamental tool in interpretation. As lighting design is a profession in itself, we therefore are convinced that if it can be afforded, it pays to have a separate lighting designer, equally positioned to the general exhibition designer. Thus, he or she is not a subordinate. The effect though will be some added complexity in the management, so you have to experience for yourself how it works out.
A lighting designer should of course take into account maintenance, conservation issues, energy saving, and updating of the systems adopted. A plan needs to address these issues explicitly.

The design manual

In addition, when renovating an entire museum, there is a particular choice to be made between having a single designer direct the overall approach or assigning different galleries to different designers. The first approach may give a more unified overall appearance to the institution, while the second approach can provide a more diverse and tailored expression for each gallery and individual subject. If the second approach is adopted, then it is important to have a design director and a good design manual to harmonize the 'look and feel' of the different galleries and spaces, as well as a strong content director to ensure that the messages remain consistent with the museum's overall intentions.

See the part on the design manual earlier in this chapter.

Decisions organized in the contract

Most design companies are used to making decisions along the way. When for example during the sketch design some choices are proposed and a route chosen, it will normally be seen as a final decision. So, when the steering committee decides otherwise and adjustments have to be made, this could be regarded as supplementary work requiring the museum to pay an additional fee.

This situation can be mentioned explicitly in the contract. Do state 'whatever we choose within a design phase, the final decision will be made in the steering committee and hence adjustments do fall within the accorded fee'.

When a design contract is put together, it is also very helpful to have a concrete fee (or percentage of the fee) assigned to each of the three phases. That puts a 'reward' on finishing a phase as it is supposed to be done. Let's for example assume that the fee is 20% of the total exhibition budget. Then it could be something like 5% for the sketch design, 5% for the preliminary design and 10% for the final design, including all instructions for the building companies. Only the final agreement of the steering committee for a certain phase, the fee is paid.

Then, sometimes the work is not satisfying. It therefore is wise to put in a paragraph stating that a museum may stop working with the external designer, who will be paid then only for the current phase. This way it will be much easier to dissolve the contract and move on with another company.

Do not forget to state explicitly that all work done and agreed upon by the steering committee has full copyright for the museum and can be re-used with another design company.

In our experience these conditions are not easily accepted by design companies. Do withstand their pressures though. It is common practice in all kinds of work and thus there could not be a reason to do otherwise. And it makes the work far more straightforward as we know from experience.

Some options for design companies and contractors

In many cases the design company is also the appointed party responsible for actually building the exhibition. That is for a reason. It takes a larger museum to have their own production manager, with the skills to direct the actual building process, based on the working papers of the design company.

However, when you have the option available, just do use your own production manager. It normally saves you quite a lot of money as there are often some hidden rewards in the contracts between designers and contractors. And it will help you to master the process significantly.
If you do not have such a production manager, you might consider hiring an independent one, thus guarding your independence.

There can be a reward in it for the design companies too. If the end result stays within the allocated budget you might consider an extra fee, recorded in the contract. And for sure, if the delivered design can be realized cheaper, the difference is to be shared, with a significant percentage for the design company.

This way there is a reward for the design company to be effective and stick to the budget. And as we all know, there is an innate tendency for budget overruns. This can be quite effectively countered this way. We had the experience of having saved 10% of the total budget this way for an entire new build permanent museum, which savings were fully due to the measurements as proposed in this paragraph.

19. The digital world included

Museums old-style can be truly boring to families with kids. For most children there is a need to move, to act, to play. Learning by playing. And to be honest, playing is a great help in learning for most adults too, as long as it is smartly done, and the place does not turn into a playground.

Digital tools can be a great help in livening up an exhibition. They come in different grades. It can be an additional tool to enhance visitor information, they can act as modules on their own, and/or they can be 'underwater' and improving a hands-on experience. What we use to call electronics, can be regarded as part of the set of electronic and IT-world of control of lights, games and actions in general. And digital... what is digital? Nowadays almost all audiovisuals are part of a digital 'ecosystem' in an exhibition.

As there are many, many ways to bring life and play into exhibitions, it is a matter of design choices how you are going to bring 'action'. There could be old-fashioned screen-based computer games, theatre-like activities, audiovisuals reacting on visitor behaviour, and so on. You name it. Though, and be aware this is a value judgement, the really interesting use of technology we think, is when it is fully integrated into the physical world and the storytelling of an exhibition.
So, use complex technologies only when needed, when you feel it is the best channel of communication and that there is nothing else that could be adopted for the same purpose. And if possible, integrate technology with the real thing as much as possible.

Not fundamentally different

Anyway, the development of interactives is not fundamentally different from other exhibition elements and thus can be easy incorporated in your planning. Where it differs somewhat is the process of cooperation with the designers of the games or software. However, to add knowledge of digital media / multimedia and the possibilities to your team, find creatives specialized in the field to see what is possible. That is thus not the technical oriented designers, but dedicated developers. However, it all starts with the subject matter and the experiences you want to transmit.

We share some thoughts on this subject matter. As this is a book on exhibition development methodology, we restrict ourselves to the development of virtual, digital components within the material world of an exhibition.

19.1. Additional in-depth information using audio tours and mobile devices

You can accomplish only so much on information using text signs. Especially within art exhibitions, the information displayed can be scarce. There are many ways to add additional information and/or bringing more context to the whole. Besides using infographics or short introductory audiovisuals, most often used are guided tours for the collective or audio tours for the individuals. These are valuable additions, and often used by a substantial part of the visitors.

Within the audio tours there is a tendency to make the choices optional by using numbers or QR-codes. You choose what you want to hear. If you want the visitor to have an additional experience, for example to include music, the audio equipment might react to sensors. An upcoming trend is to use QR-codes and/or apps so visitors can use their own mobile devices. They might be less effective though, as you can experience when just looking at visitor behaviour in exhibitions.

The additional layers of information can thus be generated within the exhibitions on separate devices, and consists of spoken texts, music or other audiovisuals and / or additional texts.

Build upon the developed content grid

Whichever way you choose, the additional information fits within the storyline composed. You will use the content (analytic) grid and the storyline composed, to build upon. This way you'll add an extra layer, but it stays within what you have already developed.

The text producing phase does use the same principles but might follow a different structuring. There is quite a difference listening to a spoken text, without knowing the structuring, or reading one where you can pick out the headlines. The thinking, the structuring, might ask you to develop a slightly different set-up.

Develop new stories on top

In some type of exhibitions there are more alternative stories possible, using certain objects and themes in a fully new order. This is especially the case in object-based exhibitions. The visitor is offered alternative stories and routing. In these examples new, alternative analytic grids and storylines are to be developed. The good thing is, you can use the methodologies as described earlier.

Virtual reality

An (still) expensive option is the use of virtual reality 'goggles' to help visitors 'see' and experience something which they could not otherwise. It then adds in-depth insight, you might say. It is a growing business. However, we are still quite sceptical. It is an expensive medium, very solitary, quite unstable (keep maintenance at hand) and becoming obsolete fast. So, it has to show something completely refreshing and/or from a different perspective to use it. And that can be done, but it takes an excellent idea, money and time. So, if you plan to use this technology, make sure you test the experience properly before spending and look at some alternative ways to convey the same content. For the moment.

19.2. Convert your in-depth information to the web

For many educational purposes, schools and interested layman alike, it is very useful to find the (in-depth) information you structured for the exhibitions on the web. This way there is a second life to your exhibitions, and it is a great help for educational programmes. Do not underestimate the 'positioning power' of such a web-based addendum. It might not attract many new visitors, though a trailer never hurts, it does signal the content power of your institute as well as substantially broadening your audience.
It does require some additional work of course. There should be a grid, a way of organizing your museum's informational structure. There should be some regrouping and a re-design of your material as web-based information is of a completely different order. And often users do search more dedicated, focused on structured, concrete information.

Again, the use of infographics

As the importance of infographics cannot be stressed enough, we write it again: do use infographics and do use the ones you developed for the exhibitions. There is some extra layer possible, as in web solutions you might often use infographics in a time sequence. They 'act' as a mini-video instruction so to say. So, when developing infographics, keep in mind this kind of multiple applications.

19.3. Screen games, IT-supported interactives and quizzes

For a family there can be much fun in being submerged in a game or quiz in which you have to accomplish something, which at the same time raises curiosity. Our experience is that the simple, ingenious game is the most successful. However, when the first games entered the exhibitions, there were quite a few remarks that museums were turning into a children's playground or a 'museum of buttons'. This was rather logical, as the first games were purely screen-based, often not really integrated in the storyline and not high-end. It is associated with running children, not really interested in what they were doing.

Where it gets interesting though, is when interactives – IT-based or not – are fully integrated. It asks some more intelligent thinking on what the game is about, how it fits into the storyline and what it does to the experience of non-users the overall exhibition.

One key issue: a game with no real 'end' will add to the visitor's satisfaction. For example, a game in which you controlled the flight of a swallow, by a joystick as a real pilot, catching insects to survive in a certain timeslot. It could be played endlessly. The example was a screen based, 20 years old and quite simple. However, it would still work today.
Another example is of a restaurant with larger-than-life-size animals which have to be fed. When the right food was served, they opened their mouth and you could put in the food. If not, they were shaking their head. In this example the IT was integrated in the display; you would not even notice it.
Actually, the same holds true for developing quiz-like systems. The most enjoyable for visitors are those which can be played together as a family, and when children have to go around to find the answers.

19.4. A virtual exhibition

The production of a catalogue or book can be done fully online, and beautifully so. There are many examples in which the online version defeats the paper one in quality and definitely in flexibility, as well to the producing experts as to the reading consumer. The same holds true for an online exhibition. It used to be one of the 'angstgegners' of museums when asked to have their collections online, let alone to start having online exhibitions.

In fact, the opposite happened. The more gets online, the more attention it gets and the more visitors we have. In the end online can be seen as a extra information and promotion, but not as a competition. Having said this all so boldly, we think it will take a while before there are interesting online exhibitions, real story-telling ones, not just picture showings. We would like however to see it happen. In fact, the many initiatives in the 2020 lock-down period might guide us to new, fruitful ways. Time will tell.

Methodology could be used for virtual exhibitions

It is necessary - somewhere, some place, sometime - to reflect over digital exhibitions which is a growing activity area. That goes for both art museums, natural and cultural history museums. We need to include a discussion about to what extent the presented methodology for analogue presentations works for digital presentations. We think – without having thought in depth about it – that in principle the methodology works independent of chosen media which means it could be used to develop online exhibitions too.

19.5. Keep the development in control

Whatever you choose, do not outsource the IT development head-on. It is an amazingly costly experience when you do not know exactly what you want. First develop a prototype with simple tools – using squares and circles and small text –and have it discussed within the team and have the idea tested. And if it is a little out of your league, hire an intermediate who can do so. The actual programming and designing would be the last stage. When you do hire intermediates, make sure they are not the ones who actually build it. At least, not beforehand. This way you control the costs much more tightly.

Before you are ready for an offer or a tender, make sure you have tested your prototype and have all your expectations and requirements in place. This has a technical side to it, ideas on maintenance and updates if needed, a clear outline on the house-style and not in the least, how you would like the visitors to use it.

The actual 'building' (programming and everything to do with it) can be best done in a three-step phase again: a prototype (sketch), followed by a preliminary version and the definite one. And if possible, make sure in the contract you can drop out if the results are not what you like.

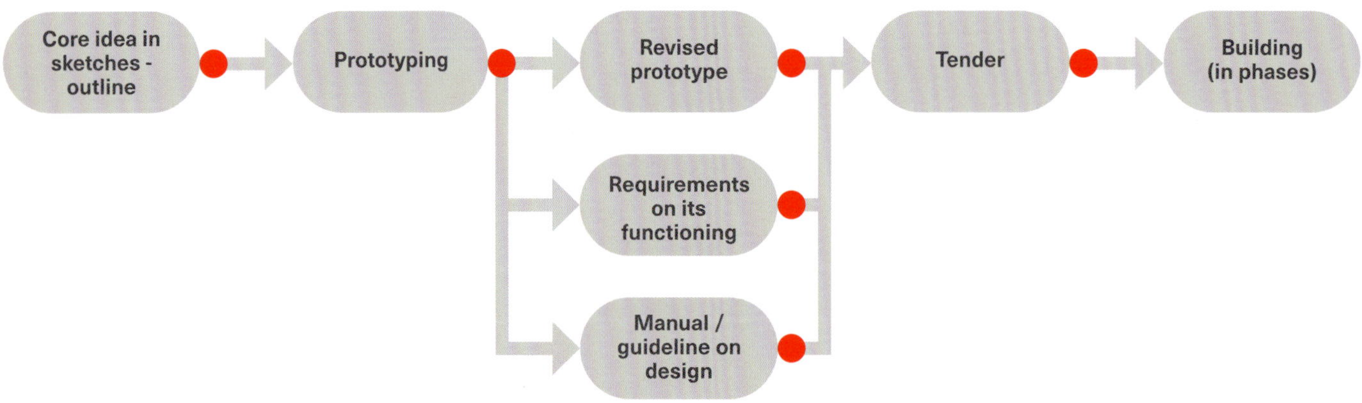

20. A dedicated financial system

Whatever the budget, money often seems to fall short of a project's needs. Like attempts to make up lost time when a project has fallen behind schedule, cost-cutting measures in the later phases of a project are often unproductive. Therefore, it is important to share a few words here on proven ways to master the budget.

As soon as the concept development phase is concluded, a dedicated financial system needs to be put in place, guided by an experienced finance coordinator who is a member of the exhibition development team. It is highly unlikely that a museum's general finance administration has the necessary time and capacity to master a large capital project such as a gallery renovation. Often, they do not also have a satisfactory financial system for fast-moving projects. Therefore, it is important to plan for and include a finance coordinator on the project team and to invest the time to develop an effective financial information system.

A fine-grained spreadsheet

The financial information system template presented essentially is a fine-grained spreadsheet that goes into greater detail and indicates links that may not have always been part of a traditional budget tracking system. The columns list the exhibitions and their modules while the rows list the phases of the project with their specific tasks, divided into an expense for each type of exhibition component. Thus, this spreadsheet is closely related to the timeline and its phases, as well as to the actual exhibition modules.

In this elaborated version of a spread sheet, each of the cells provides a series of budgetary details listing expenses for projected, encumbered, paid, and the remaining unspent expenses for each component of the exhibition. Then there is a certain percentage set aside for real unexpected work or extra costs (contingency).
It works as follows. You expect certain costs and turn them into 'projected', so it distracts immediately from the available budget. When obligations come in, the (changed) amount turn into 'encumbered' until it is 'paid'.

Categories of costs

Building a template like this means to distinguish the types of relevant and significant costs. As framework budgets, or projected budgets, for all exhibitions need to be developed beforehand, you have to have an idea of the types relevant to you.
In practice, some 5 percent of the total budget is usually dedicated to concept and storyline development; 15 to 20 percent to design; 65 to 70 percent to production. The remaining 10 percent should be set aside for post-opening adjustments.

Within production we propose a certain division (construction, AV). See the column in the table.

Automatic (pre-)calculation

The development of a detailed framework budget includes assigning percentage costs for each exhibition and for each of its modules. So make a distinction for each. The resulting fine-grained table / spreadsheet thus have many 'cells', each dedicated to a specific exhibition or exhibition module.
So too, each cell will have its specified budget. It can automatically be calculated on the basis of a dedicated division of type of costs. If for example 20% of the production costs of a certain exhibition is projected for construction purposes, and you have 10 modules, you can assume an automatically division of 2% for each module. And so on.
And then adjustments can be made based on your own experiences, but again, use a systematic approach. Do not do it freehand.

Keep track of all expenses, however minor

Keep track of every expense. So, for each 'cell' there will be a budget allocated – and every expense is noted in separate worksheets in the spreadsheet, finding its expression within the cells by links. Note all projected expenses, all forecasts, all obligations (encumbered), keep 10% contingency – and track of the amount unspent automatically.

This far-reaching methodology thus starts with clear assumptions, to be adjusted for the type of exhibition. It is however the day-to-day administration which is important.

The best practice is never to allow any of the individual expenses to exceed the allotted amounts. This is a crucial step. We do say that you should have a budget restriction for every detailed cell – and that is a far further reaching financial management than usually is the case. Is this hardwired? No. Of course, once in a while you have to make an updated version. But do this at specific moments in time. In this way, certain amounts are kept aside for unexpected expenses, which do arise in large and complex projects.

The advantages of investing in the management of budgets, as well as time to monitor them properly throughout the project, particularly during the content-to-design phase, cannot be overstressed, as this detailed budget allows the project manager, production manager, and financial coordinator to carefully monitor and control expenses.

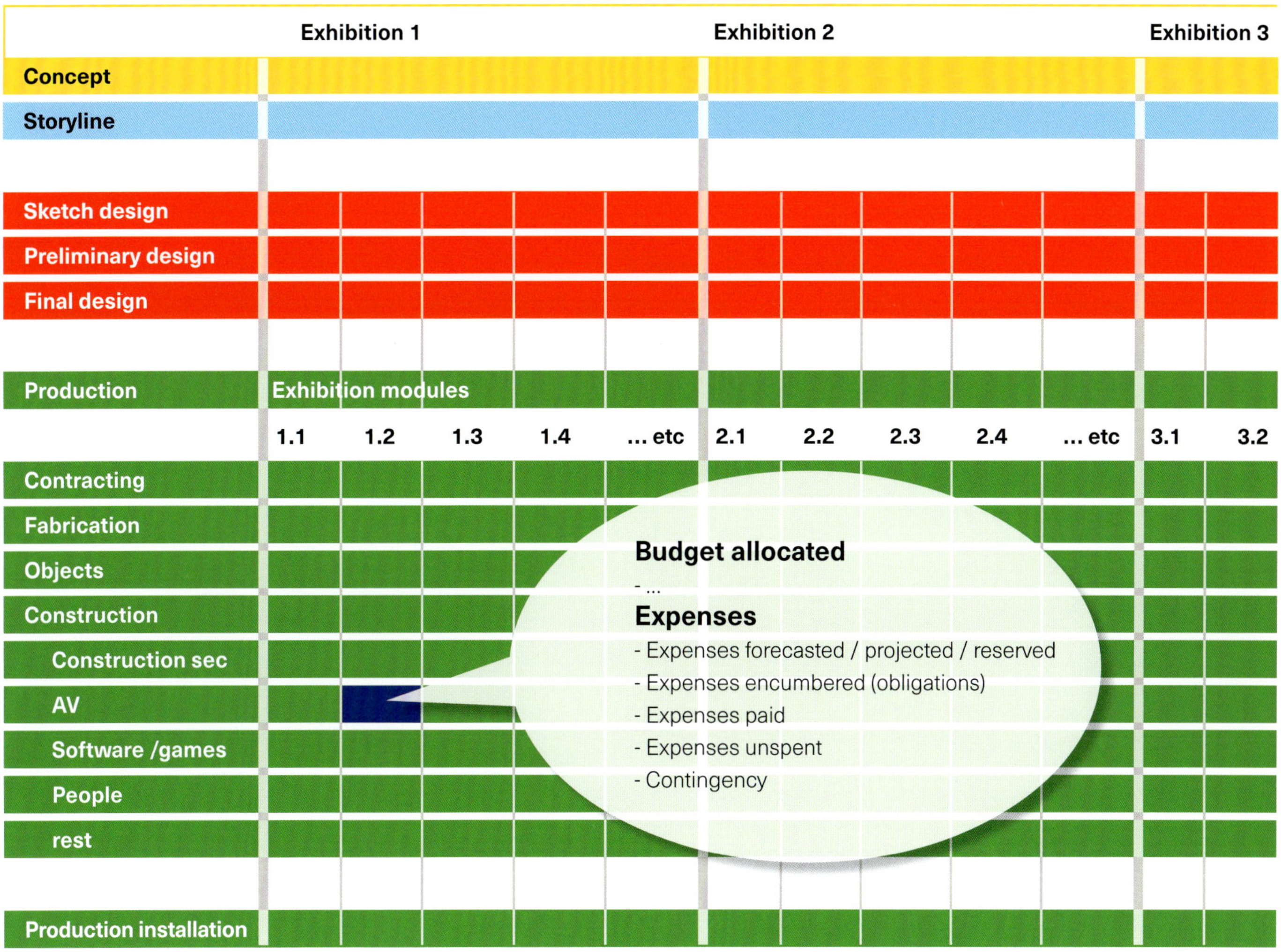
Exhibition 1
Exhibition 2
Exhibition 3
Concept
Storyline
Sketch design
Preliminary design
Final design
Production
Exhibition modules
1.1
1.2
1.3
1.4
... etc
2.1
2.2
2.3
2.4
... etc
3.1
3.2
Contracting
Fabrication
Objects
Construction
Construction sec
AV
Software /games
People
rest
Production installation
Budget allocated
- ...
Expenses
- Expenses forecasted / projected / reserved
- Expenses encumbered (obligations)
- Expenses paid
- Expenses unspent
- Contingency

21. Components in the production process

There is no way you can build an exhibition without a leading production manager. We think. And we do have a picture of the type of person too. We described the role earlier on, in the chapter on the team, but in this part we extend it a bit. We will also make the job more important than it is seen in most museums.

First of all, although production is the last stage in an exhibition development process, it actually is of importance right from the beginning and the more so when the design phase is about to start. It is in the design phase many choices are made for actually building the exhibition.

21.1 Cost management

Keep it realistic

In terms of cost, the designing phase and the actual production take up more than 80% of the costs. And the defining plans mostly are outlined in the designing pase. So, a joint venture between the art-director / project manager and production manager is of crucial importance to have realistic plans and guard the building of mock-ups and prototypes. Testing, discussing options with companies, negotiating, keeping an overview, ... It is a much-needed quality in itself. Without such a person guarding the process head on, costs will easy get out of hand. Even when you are in a (very) small museum, we would still argue you should have a dedicated production manager (as a person or as role). It will pay dividends.

We all know that exhibitions often become more expensive than budgeted and that financial setbacks are common. When this happens, there have to be cuts made in the plans, which again means stressful meetings with the staff. Moreover, budget cuts often take time, increasing the pressure on the building team.

Budget management and a financial system

The proposed financial system of the earlier chapter is to be guarded by the production manager and project manager. Ideally, we would argue for an assistant capable of doing so, including contract management and such and all other systematics needed to keep track.

Tendering

Depending on your country, way of operating and budgets, a system of choosing contractors needs to be in place. Quite often some tenders are involved, which takes time and requires appropriate expertise. Although it is the job of the production manager, it is wise to have a partnership with an assisting bureau and have a very clear knowledge of the process. Whatever you do, make sure your financial administration is tip-top.

21.2. Keeping track of objects, AV and to-do's is essential

Exhibitions usually consists of many objects. When you start the process, you might know many objects you need, but it is during the process you really start building up the full lists of objects needed, including possible alternatives, the state they are in and if some repairs or restoration is necessary. The same holds true for the imagery you want.

Having the databases in place and used has to start as soon as possible and preferably as soon as the concept phase has finished.
It is up to the production manager to build such dedicated databases and make sure they are used.

A dedicated object database is essential

You cannot plan properly if you do not have a proper and full database of what objects are wanted, available, and what has to be searched for. For each and every object there must be a recent picture and the basic information about size, weight, cautions to be taken when moving the item, preservation-requirements, location and the terms of availability (on loan or donated or whatever).

Then there are the necessary actions to be taken. Every object might have its own specific trajectory written down or it can be part of a specific category. Whatever way you choose, this process of acquisition / restauration / storage / transport needs to be thoroughly organized and overviewed and each object is to be positioned in it.

Homemade database at Musil

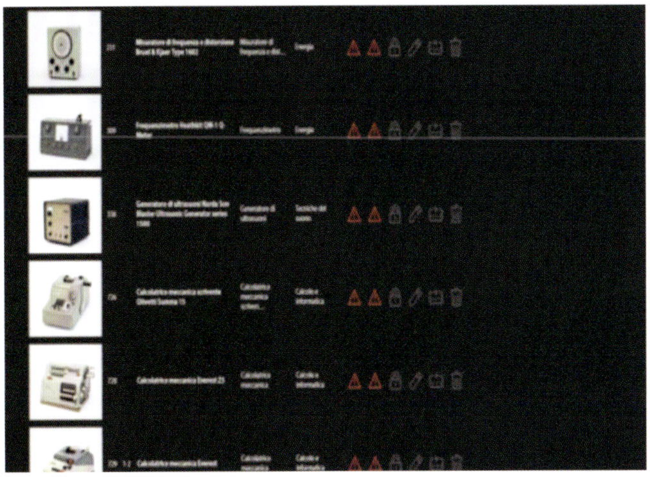

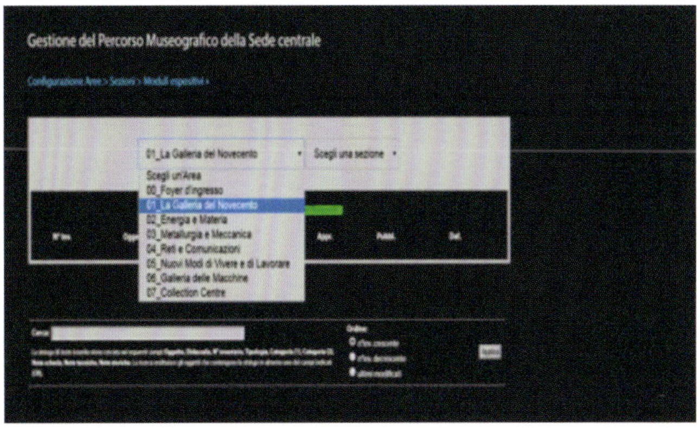

There is a moment when the project team, the curators and the designers must count on a database. As it nowadays more and more frequently designers and graphic designers work at great distance, it is essential to have a digitized inventory to be shared via the Internet. So, if possible, it is recommended that you adopt a simple software which allows an easy collection management specifically in view of the exhibition planning. For example with a drop-down menu that gives access to the different sections (or galleries) of the future museum, so that individual items can be easily allocated to a given sector or deleted or moved to another part without losing time in sending folders of materials to the exhibition developers (architects and or designers, scenographers or multimedia artists) with a timing that frequently leads to chaos. At the same time this system allows all partners to be aligned in real time with the developments of the project as far as the collection use is concerned

Replicas, audio-visuals and installations too

For many exhibition elements there are more options than using unique museum objects. It might include replicas used in installations, educational programmes or representations of a certain process (as in dioramas, sceneries or hands on exhibitions). If this requires additional work on the objects, it also has to be marked in the database.

When it comes down to photographs and other audio-visuals, the same principle of working is to be set in place. There is, however, also the matter of copyrights, as one of the matters to be dealt with – and to be marked and monitored in your dedicated database.

As complete and as early as possible

So, basically we argue a thorough listing of all 'things' is needed. There is no way you can start building your lists too early. It should be there up and running as soon as you have the content structure ready.

21.3. Knowing the climatic conditions needed

You ought to know the range of climatic conditions within the galleries, as well as the range acceptable for the objects used. This information is crucial to the designers before starting. It guides where precautions are needed, either by dedicated showcases for some objects or by regulating the climate in the galleries as a whole.

A yearly update on the measurements in the galleries is not too hard to get done. It is basically one of the standardized processes you ought to have in place. And when troublesome, ask for a one-time audit by a dedicated professional and have measurement procedures installed from then on[4].

Getting an indication of the needs of each object is somewhat more complicated. It is easier to work with some categories. Each object can be classified in a proper category, to be added to the list of objects.

Other risks

Safety is one of the most common issues in exhibits. If there is head-on a list of risks – from fire to theft – with its potential measurements, it eases the design process. Too often it is only put on the table when the designers come up with unacceptable solutions. And to be sure, new requirements do hamper the process considerably.

21.4. Guarantees, service contracts, manuals – as part of the contracts

All things built can and probably will break down, and sometimes even more than occasionally. This also probably happens at moments you are not ready for it. So it is a necessity to include firm and very clear agreements on guarantees, reparations and suchlike in your initial contracting. These agreements contain responsibilities on both sides. If some elements break down, or do not function as proposed, you often have to be prepared yourself for some kind of actions, which should be written in too.

21.5. Archiving all

You cannot overstate the importance of an archive, containing all drawings, photographs, contracts and suchlike. It often happens that after some years almost no one knows any more for sure what was the procedure agreed on. And be honest, when the opening is done, you are happy, very tired, and you do not want to continue with the administrative part of the job. Developers do like to develop, to build, but they are seldom good administrators.

One way of doing it is to be very organized in the production process. An assistant can be of great help here. But if you have not worked in as organized a way as you should, there is no escaping doing it immediately afterwards.

Besides archiving the production part, there is a need for archiving the content matter, the ideas used or explored, texts, audio-visuals, and so on. Have them organized in such a way they are immediately available, ready for use on 'the shelves' so to say.

The making of

In general, there is a limited knowledge with our audience of the process of creating an exhibition, contrary to for example a theatre production or a library. The 'behind the scene of a museum' is still rather mysterious. Some small documentary or exhibition module on the development process will be interesting in itself to many in our audiences. Of course, you have to consider the problems of security, copyright, privacy, etc. but they cannot be seen as insurmountable obstacles.

It need not be a costly process. Use your smartphones to document your work in progress by photos, videos, short interviews, explanations of drawings. The construction phase can be documented by time-lapse recordings and/or webcams. And do not forget the opening of crates, as it can give you entertaining materials.

Such material could be useful also on the social networks, to spread the narrative of the forthcoming exhibition. Do not leave your future audience too long without a clue about what you are working on.

21.6. The organized production manager

Having described just a few of the tasks, it is clear a production manager not only is a businessman, a smart negotiator and someone with a helicopter view, and a slightly pessimistic view on promises, but he or she should also have some traits of an archivist. Of course, there is almost no one so multi-talented and experienced. And some traits are not easily combined. Therefore, it is wise to complement the production manager with some additional assistance. And, when you do have a good production manager, honour him or her.

22. Preventing delays and time pressures

The reason for writing this book was first and foremost to help standardize the development of exhibitions, to ease the process and thus free energy. Much energy often is lost in repairs and overcoming stressful moments. Sticking to the procedures proposed helps. However, to recognize pitfalls and know some 'tricks' to stay away is helpful too.

We describe some common pitfalls in random order.

22.1. Experts not delivering in time

One of the most heard complaints is experts asked to come up with stories, backgrounds and comments, not delivering in time. As this is often early on in the process, there seems to be enough time, so the pressure on them is not too hard. A second reason is some kind of fear. There is often mutual dependency, and that accounts for trying not to anger them and lose them altogether. Besides, these experts most often are curators, who do have a high status in most museums. Whatever the reason, experts / curators are in this process to be seen as part of the production 'machinery', not more or less important than any others involved.

There are some steps possible which can help prevent getting into this situation.

Most important is to help experts to build up a story beforehand. Most helpful is to start their work by handing them a 'bullet list' in concordance with the analysis grid. Every story to be written is started by having your team's interpretation beforehand. Think like a science journalist and come up with a rough – bullet-built – story as a starter. Correcting and supplementing is much easier than starting from scratch. It takes out some of the tendency to be too complete and perfect. An expert does not need to deliver a scientific article. They have to correct what is laid out before them. See the chapters on content development to guide you.

For this reason, we would even recommend having your content developers in your team – and have them in the lead. Keep the role of experts limited to correcting and supplementing.

The second action is to guard their timeslots carefully, by asking for example way ahead what the progress is. If halfway the process there is nothing to show yet, you may presume it will not be in time. In this case you can already start building pressure by asking who can help, to add some extra (writing) work by your team. And it helps to have all delays in the open, so there is some social pressure too.

22.2. Have dedicated intermediates - points of single contact

Another troublesome experience is when a process is on its way and some essential persons are left out and object at a later stage. This often happens for example when outside experts (guest curators) are involved and their content has got directly as an input, without being validated internally.

Whatever reason or phase, it is essential to have dedicated roles in your team. All content passes the content manager and it is his or her duty to oversee that all involved have had their chance to validate. The same holds true for all roles – content, design, production, education. There is one single point of contact whose responsibility is to make sure no choices are made without having all checkboxes filled.

22.3. A list of objects is needed

In the design phase it is not uncommon to have to fit in new pieces, or some do have quite some different measurements as originally provided. This often delays the design process, more often than not already under pressure because of earlier delays. We therefore need to emphasize - again – the importance of an adequate and complete list of objects. And be sure this list is to be complete - adequate measurements, category for its climatic requirements, status with regard to restoration needed (and when ready), and so on.

22.4. Crumple zone: a plan B for 5% & 25% less (or more)

It is quite uncommon to get more money than expected. On the contrary, we are all familiar with the situation when there is less budget than originally thought or promised. And as we know too, some cuts or shortages might turn up unexpectedly.

So, do have a plan B. Taken into account all discussions and processes, what is of lesser importance? Which modules can be skipped if the going gets tough? Which can be simplified? Make two demarcation lines: if you have 5% (a little) or 25% (a lot) less budget. The same holds true if it comes to gallery space. You want to be prepared when some spaces turn out not to be available. Or if at the last minute a mammoth has to be fitted in (a true story).

It is tempting to postpone preparatory work like this. Don't. Choosing is much easier when there is no stress or time pressure. And it does work out much easier when you incorporate it early on. And as you have followed the analysis grid way of working, part of the choice is already set.

However, there might unexpectedly be more money too, with or without additional requirements. When you have decided beforehand which opportunities are most promising, it is easier to adapt to changing circumstances and come up with suggestions to guide eventual additional requirements.

22.5. So think scenarios

Every museum professional will have its own list of sorrows and pains regarding delays. We do however assure you, stick to this methodology and it will ease it at least considerably. One last thing: the planning process itself cannot be taken lightly. Do invest time in building a detailed Gannt chart. And to conclude, as we described earlier, much delay can be planned for by having your slack time adjusted. See the chapter early on in our story. It is important for this way of working to have all your subphases and steps carefully monitored.

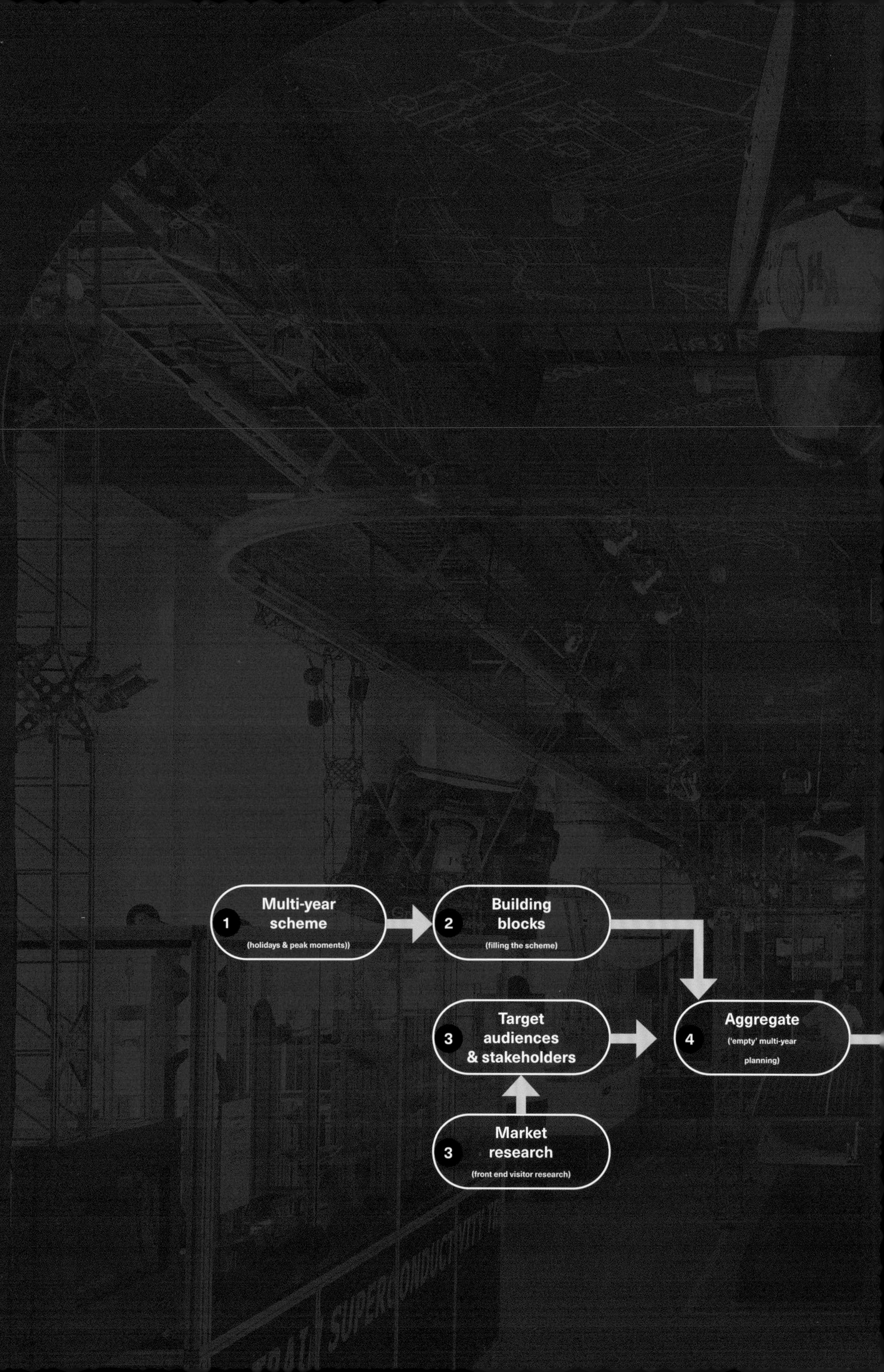

Science Centre Delft

Section 4

Plan ahead

Exhibition development can be done in sequence. One at a time. You develop one, have the opening, and start the procedure for the next one. When you have a larger museum and are used to have more overlapping exhibits, there is a need for a more thorough planning of several exhibits in parallel. However, also when you have a sequence of major exhibits, it is wise to think way ahead. It does not necessarily mean you work on them in parallel, but it does give you the opportunity to start some developments in time. Not in the least important, it does help the decision-making processes when there is a long-term programme.

With some repeats

This section describes the procedure to start a multi-annual planning. In the paragraph on choosing the subject matter there will be some repeating of what has been before.

This section outlines how to come to valued choices on exhibition themes – and develop a multi-annual scheme.

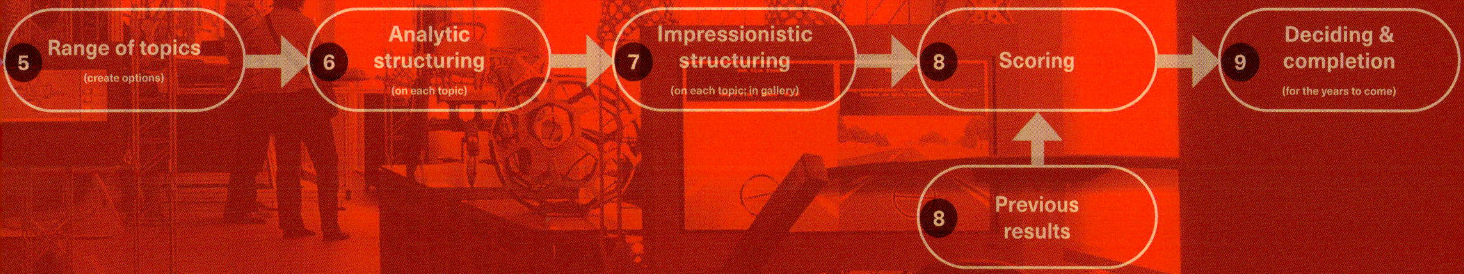

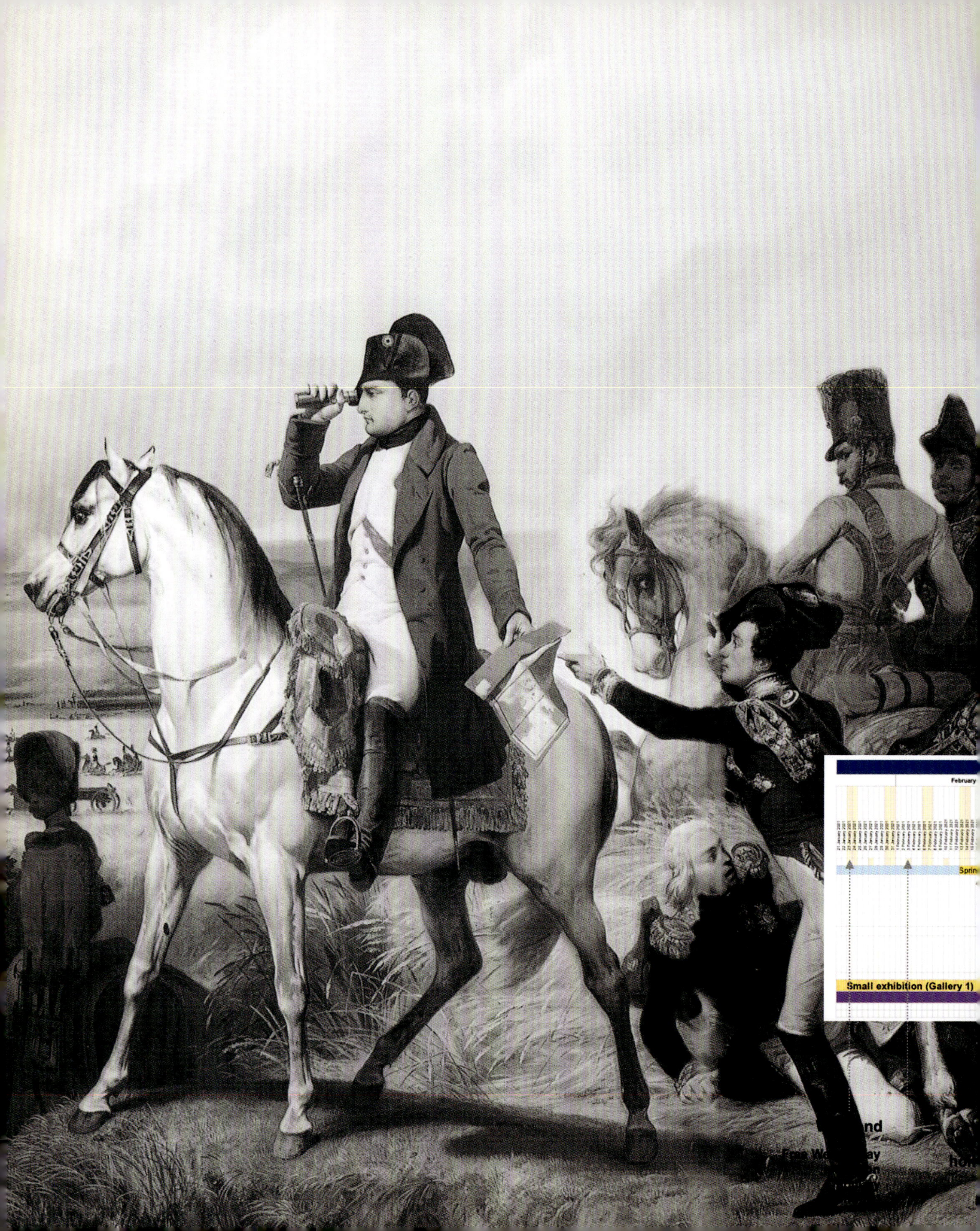
February
Small exhibition (Gallery 1)

23. An 'empty' multi-annual plan

Detail from the Battle of Wagram, 1835, Horace Vernet, Musée national des châteaux de Versailles et Trianon

23.1. Step 1: Establishing an empty scheme over the years to come

Time slots

Establishing a multi-annual planning – a plan for 2-3 years ahead - requires as a start an empty scheme, most easily made in a spreadsheet or in, more complicated, project software. There is a (small) column for each day, resulting in a several metres-long timesheet, which makes a plotter kind of handy (but not necessary).

Every national and/or religious holidays, all weekends, school seasonality, tourist peaks, all has to be 'coloured in'. The same has to be done for all known events related to the museum's topics, like remembrance days, periods of special excavations in the neighbourhood, festivities of related civil groups or colleagues which might compete or can be used for publicity. Take note of the relevant peak times for visitors – for your target groups separately if necessary, so 'colour in' when for example retirees might be 'on the road'.
Have for each category a different 'row' in the spreadsheet.

On another series of rows, you can 'colour in' the timeslots for temporary exhibitions and events. And yes, put in events to, because events and activities might be a strategic component of an exhibition, to position in time wisely.

It might look a little overdone. And it certainly is a lot of work. However, you won't regret it. The resulting 'empty' planning helps structuring your activities over the coming years.

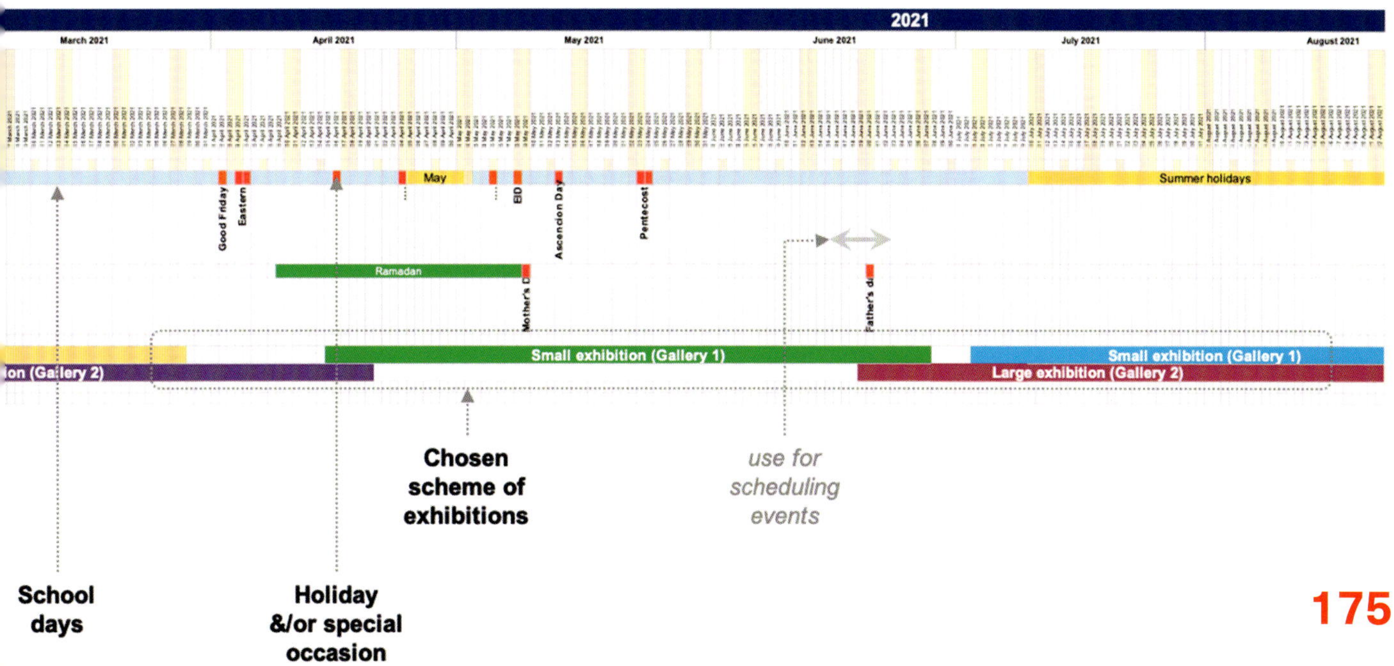

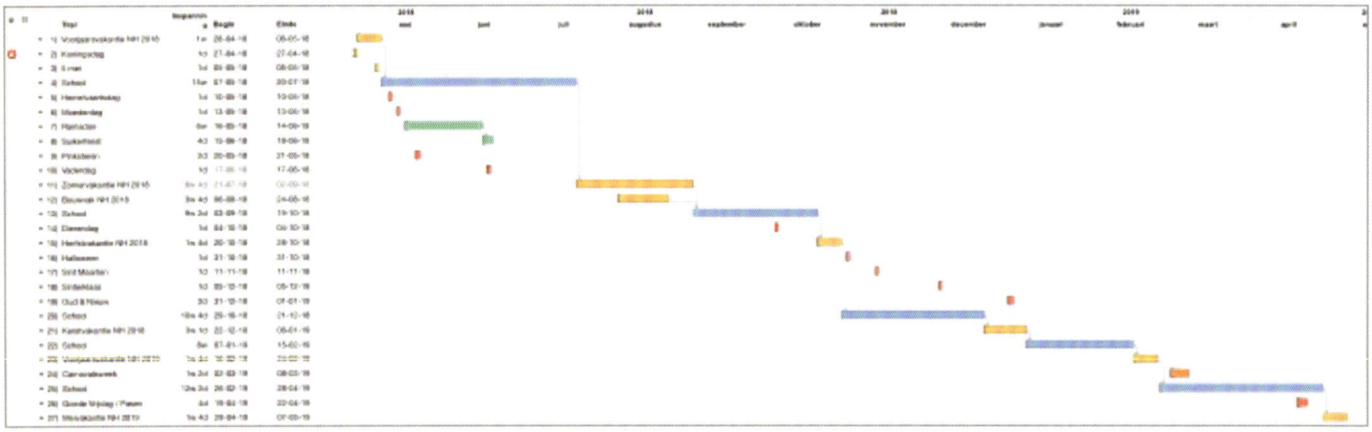

NB. A scheme in a spreadsheet and in project software, where 'blue' are the school periods, yellow the school holidays and red & green special (free) moments like Eastern, Ramadan and the adjacent festivities. A distinction can be made to the periods that schools come along for lessons - and when they focus on trips.

23.2. Step 2: Exhibitions and events: when to start, how long

In most museums temporary exhibitions are regarded the backbone of its public work, including additional activities in the widest sense of the word (events, happenings). We all have them. But the rotation, the synchronicity with holidays, the scheduling, this all differs for every museum.

So, start with filling in the empty schedule with exhibition time slots, again on different rows for each gallery. What duration? When do you want them to have publicity and thus open? Are they aligned with (school)holidays? Are you planning two or more exhibitions a year for each gallery (requires quite some capacity) or do you take cycles of a year or more for each exhibition (easier on work, but requires smarter planning the activities)?

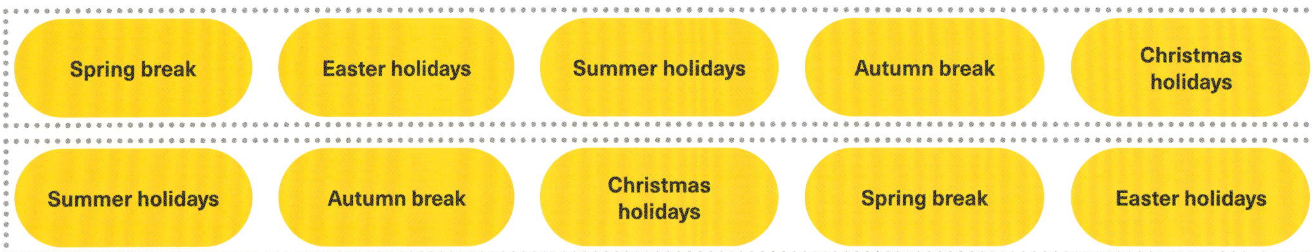

A scheme of one exhibition (per gallery) for each year, aligned with the five school holidays (in case of The Netherlands), but starting at different moments.

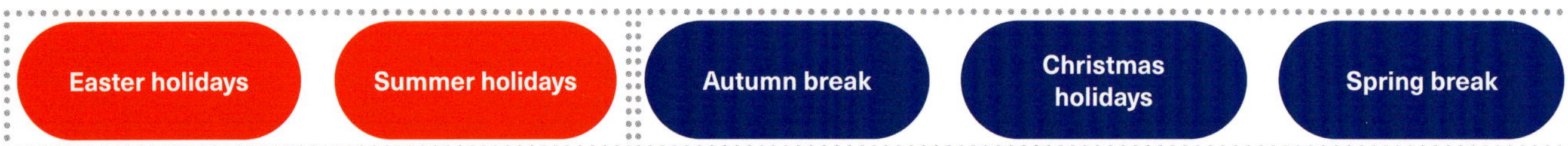

An alternative would be having temporary exhibitions twice a year, whether or not different in approach and style. The May holidays and summer holiday exhibition focuses on families and school outings. At the start of the summer holidays, there then could be an additional event to renew free publicity. The second series can, for example, focus more on school curricula and educational programmes.

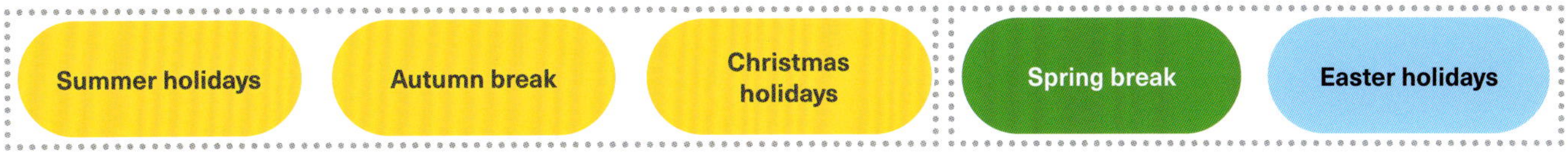

Another alternative might be having one temporary exhibition for half a year and two short exhibitions / events for the other holidays.

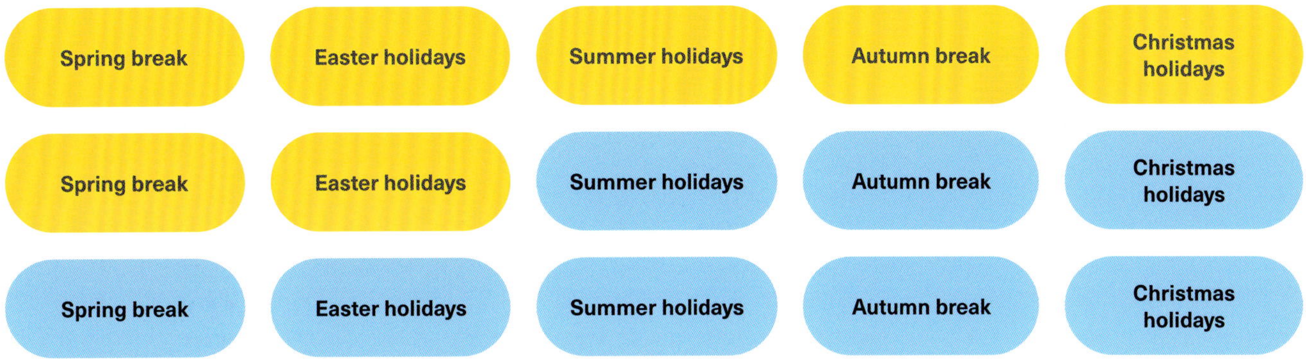

An alternate series for a longer timespan probably would ask for more endorsing events.

Events

The same line of thinking and 'colouring in' works for events as well. When do you want there to be events and programmes? And can you fill in series for a longer time-span, like a 'First Friday' series of music and lectures for example. Or a series of child matinees when schools are closed.

A series of activities in a coherent set works well, as the investment can be spread over time, and because repetition also means reinforcement and often generates a dedicated audience after a while. Series are also ideally suited for cooperation and connection to local and regional organizations.

Be sure to 'colour in' all remembrance days, religious and other national days, all types of special moments connected to the museum-topics, and so on.

Intermezzo

The events you choose will have to fit to the preferences of your audience, the target groups. Nevertheless, it too is determined by the experience and competencies within the museum.

Sometimes it is wise to experiment, to prototype, and once in a while leave the beaten track and actively try new combinations – in substance and in form. So, you could fill what type of events you want at certain moments in time, as we still work in empty moments.

23.3. Step 3: Personas as representatives of your (target) audiences?

Target groups

As each museum has its own specific group and/or type of visitors, you are familiar with your own audience. This existing audience can be split into various (sub-)target groups. And please do so. Take the top 3 (or top 5) in numbers or importance and define each in its interests, the timeslots it prefers, and suchlike.
They will each get their own line, their own row in the multi-annual planning, so you can visualize what offerings – exhibitions, events – are meant for whom. The differentiation is made visually clear.

Personas

You can add to each target (audience) group a hypothetical archetype member of the specific group. This 'person' represents behaviour patterns, goals, skills, attitudes, and the environment, with a few fictional personal details to make the persona a realistic character.

The technique is used more often in IT projects, but there are several advantages by doing so in exhibition development too. Most of all: it makes the group more 'alive' to many involved. It is a symbolic representative 'alive' and thus easier to discuss the worth of certain features in the design and content.

This methodology does not fit to every museum, as some think it childish, and others think it narrows down the characteristics too much. However, some do favour it quite enthusiastically. If you use them, do be sure you get them right. Use visitor surveys and interviews to see if the interviewed more or less match the general descriptions.

The general audience

Though we want to discourage the use of 'the general audience' as much as possible, we certainly do not throw away the idea as any museum counts on a core of visitors who cannot easily ascribed to a given category. Besides categories do frequently overlap. So, if you do not have the skills and tools (for example enough data) to distinguish, you might visualize and describe some key-figures in your audience that are relevant for developing an effective strategy in positioning our museum both in the public opinion and in the public 'imagination'.

Quantify

When determining target groups, be sure you can 'measure' them. They have to be addressed, quantified and counted within your audience. It is of no use to speak of 'the general audience'. In principle, each specific group can be described, though sometimes roughly, and quantified. It is better to have an incomplete and partly inaccurate picture at the start than none at all.

Suppose the main group of visitors in numbers consists of (grand)parents with children of which at least one is of a primary school age. They probably come from the immediate vicinity, within a radius of say 20 kilometres. From some specific cities or campsites (tourists) in the area? What potential numbers are we talking? And how many households with children of primary school age do you have in your area? How many tourists – family groups or adult couples - are there in the holiday months - and in what composition of the family?

This is not as hard as it seems. In many countries there are data available at agencies, and otherwise there is a lot to gather by just doing some real dedicated homework and asking around.

Then form your own data, partly also by asking and looking closely: what are the numbers in the various categories? Which part consists of repeat visits? Is this a substantial category? What did they come for?

Your offering

If you take in mind a specific group: which part of them is actually visiting the museum once in a while? Or willing to do so? What for? What is/appears to be an attractive offer? How they decide?

From your first quantitative (!) inventories and from own experiences, you might come up with a good range of options for what type of events and exhibition subject and 'form' to offer. You also know what time they spend on average and on which moments 'they have enough'. You know, for example, that in a family visit it often ends when one or two of the children get bored.

So, you can think of some major characteristics which should be there in your multi-annual scheme on certain timeslots.

When? = preferred moments in time (year, week, day)

For each of your audience groups there will be a different set of preferred timeslots. There will be shared moments – holidays, weekends when most families have time to kill – but there are some differences too.

Front end visitor research by yourself. Just do it. KISS

As said, having a picture, however rough, is always better than having none at all. And where there are no figures ready, you just start to collect them yourself. But keep it simple. Watching and asking often helps enormously. We will get back to this later in a separate chapter of this methodology.

So, what do you get?

	Group 1	Group 2a	Group 2b	Group 3	Reputation Group 1
Numbers					
Percent (%)					
Average time visited					
Preferences time					
Preferences 'form'					

The resulting table is there to guide you through deciding which type of exhibitions and events when.

23.4. Step 4: Blending it all into one scheme

It is time to blend it all into your spreadsheet for the years to come. You know what type of exhibitions and events you have to have, and when. It is the empty format for your portfolio.

You have:

- All holidays, festivities, remembrance days etcetera, all 'coloured in' in separate rows of your spreadsheet (or project scheme)
- A table with the major target groups and when you preferably need something (new) to attract them
- Type of exhibitions – in form, experiences, subjects

The result: a multi-annual plan which than can be filled with the actual themes

24. Choosing the subject matter

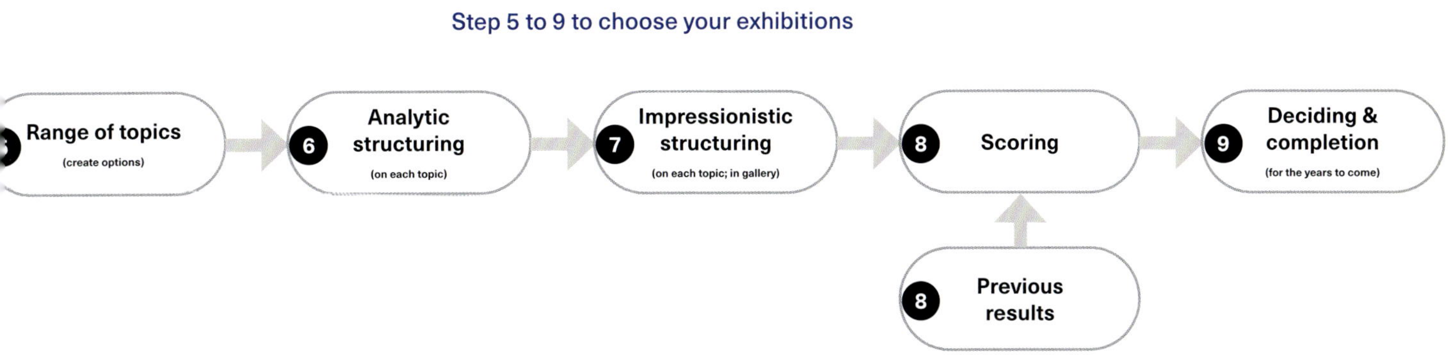

The next steps consider the choice of the subject matter, within the established pre-structured multiannual planning. This concerns the choice of the topics, the themes, with an indication of the approach to media and forms.

The classic method is discussing the potential topics amidst a group of decision-makers, often curators and staff. After the collection of ideas, by brainstorming and such, a number of options are on the table, discussed, and partly on the basis of most votes, choices are made. The voice / influence of the key decision-makers normally is quite large.

There is nothing wrong with this way of working. We think there are better ways though. More systematic too. Experience shows a higher acceptance when there is a more objective method, having each option accompanied with some drawings and an analysis and then having them scored and judged. Scoring (a marketing technique) in itself helps to get a better supported, more solid portfolio.

24.1. Step 5: Acquiring a range of options

Each museum has a range of interesting and / or 'usual suspect' topics on the shelf. They are a starting point, but no more than that. It needs expanding in a broader, systematic way by using suggestions by different groups and individuals. That can be very open, such as 'something with ....'. but it can also be more specific and outlined. Anyway, ask the different groups within the museums and certainly do not forget the attendants as they are the eyes and ears on the floor.

You can also question your museum audience. Make it easy and ask for three topics they think interesting if the museum would have exhibitions on them.

It is quite a job, so take your time and ask one or two participants to spend some days to find suggestions. And do it systematically.

School curricula and children's books

Place the school textbooks and curricula on the table. Have important and/or inspiring books around and do search for themes, historical developments or processes which are considered important. Select and scan series of children's books and illustrated encyclopedic works too.

Think series

Especially when there are more galleries, it is helpful to organize the options into series, which can also include photo exhibitions in your restaurant for example.

- Context exhibitions – aimed at larger thematic topics in which an innovation changed the world, or a theme which has connections to the world today (the discovery and innovations stemming from new materials, for example)
- Collection exhibitions – in which a group of objects is the starting point for a story
- Photo exhibitions and/or art exhibitions
- Processes from the work field - about techniques and working methods (excavating, amateurs in the field, dating back to)

Series are mainly used to systematize your thinking and get valuable new, innovative ideas. They are certainly do not exclude topics.

Analyse your strengths and market opportunities

In commercial settings it is common to start with a solid internal and external analysis. What are we good at? What do we have inhouse? In which subject matter do we have weaknesses? What are market opportunities? What is not (yet) offered by our con-colleagues? What are the current developments we could or should play a role in?

On the basis of these analyses the result should be a cross table made of strengths/ weaknesses versus opportunities/threats, the so-called SWOT analysis.

	Opportunities What is asked. What might be new chances.	**Threats** What would leave us behind. What are colleagues doing.
Strengths. What are we good at.	**Go ahead.**	**Do we have to react?**
Weaknesses. What do we lack. Where are we short on.	**Think. Look for partnerships.**	**Stop.**

OK, this might look a little too much to go into, but trying won't hurt either. It certainly sharpens your thinking and leads to looking at topics / subject matter from a different perspective.

The result: series of options which can be used for the choosing process.

24.2. Step 6: A baseline for every topic with a descriptive work title

Each potential topic has to have an interpretation in the form of a modular build analysis grid. It is not enough to have a description in one or two paragraphs. You deconstruct the content into modular build, Lego-wise, with a box-in-box building bricks. For each and every potential topic this modular 'analytic' is to be made. That means, the subject matter is divided into mutually excluding topics, with sometimes needs some deeper delving within modules.

In earlier paragraphs this way of working is discussed in-depth.

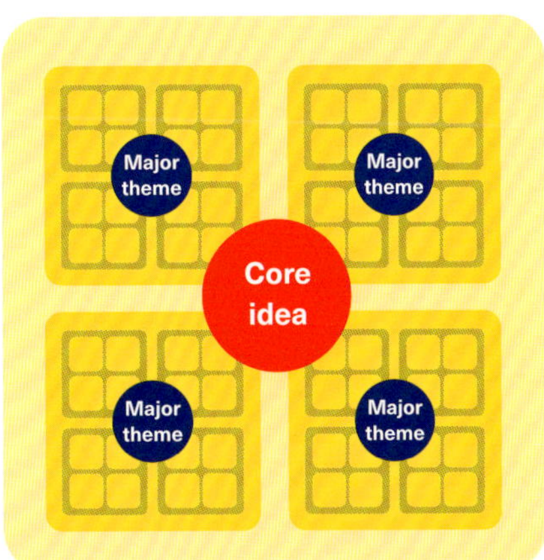

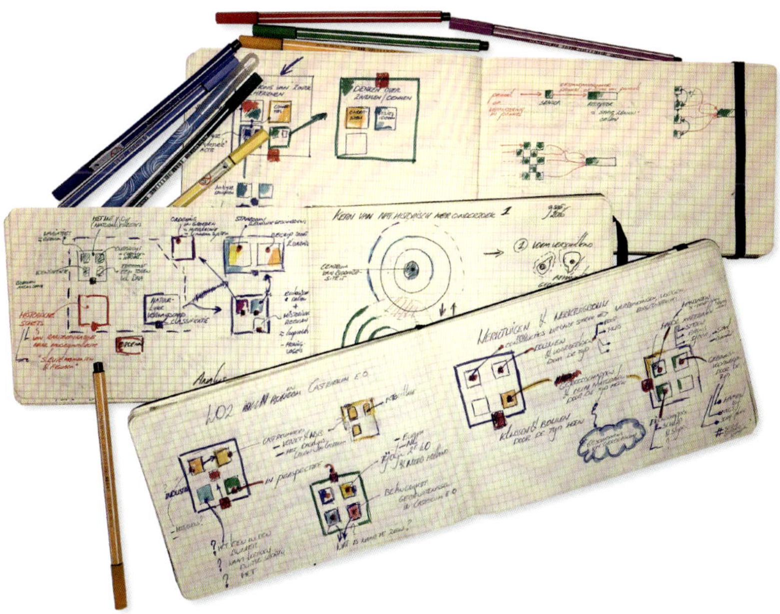

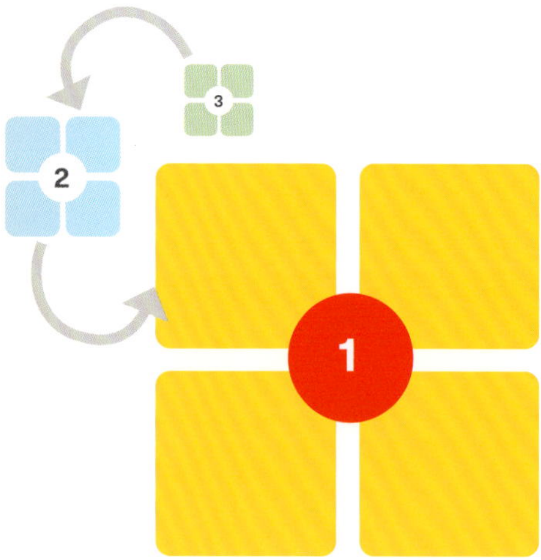

In the centre (see the coloured boxes in the diagram) the core-idea of each module is named. This core frames the content. It encompasses the baseline, the keyword or -sentence which signals this module.

It is necessary to dissect a subject matter precise and clear-cut. And each module has to exclude the other one(s). There is a clear reason why every box has the same form and size. It is important to keep this property. That is a visible 'token' to readers that one subject is not more important than the other one.

Take for example a rather small archeological museum preparing an exhibition on 'iron'. It is about the innovation itself and what it did in terms of economic and social changes and progress. But you might have one module to put 'iron' in context to other 'hardened' materials (stone, bronze) and how 'iron' would fit in. Then, within this module a (sub)module could get into its discovery. What (could have) led to its discovery? What was the existing technology on which the innovation was based? Another 'higher' module might go into its uses into the living households and what it did mean for food gathering, preparation – and even to a change in diet.

The result of this exercise will lead to a presentable structured content. And of course, you'll need a working title and a schematic sketch too.

24.3. Step 7: A schematic sketch

With the working title and the modular 'analytic' in hand you have to draw a sketch, a schematic sketch. That certainly is not a proposed layout or design for the gallery. It is first and foremost intended to paint a picture, an indicative first thought. It does 'push' the modular analytic into the gallery floor, though it is primarily meant to give the evaluators a shared image, a shared 'feeling' with the subject matter, so they can 'picture' it.

The imaginative schematic sketch is to be done for all themes on the table. This will be accompanied with a short description, a picture, an estimate of the cost and time involved, a note on the available objects, some advantages and disadvantages with the subject matter and suchlike.

To draw a schematic sketch

A sketch literally is a (abstract) sketch. If you feel uncomfortable doing it, don't make it too big and just give it a try. But true too, it is a subjective process. It can be directive.

Choose again for a standardized format. The format may resemble the (possible) gallery, but it is sensible not exactly to do so. Keep it somewhat abstract, to avoid it is taken too literally. It is first and foremost meant as an image.

The image is a fascinating picture with a number of possibilities and advantages and disadvantages.

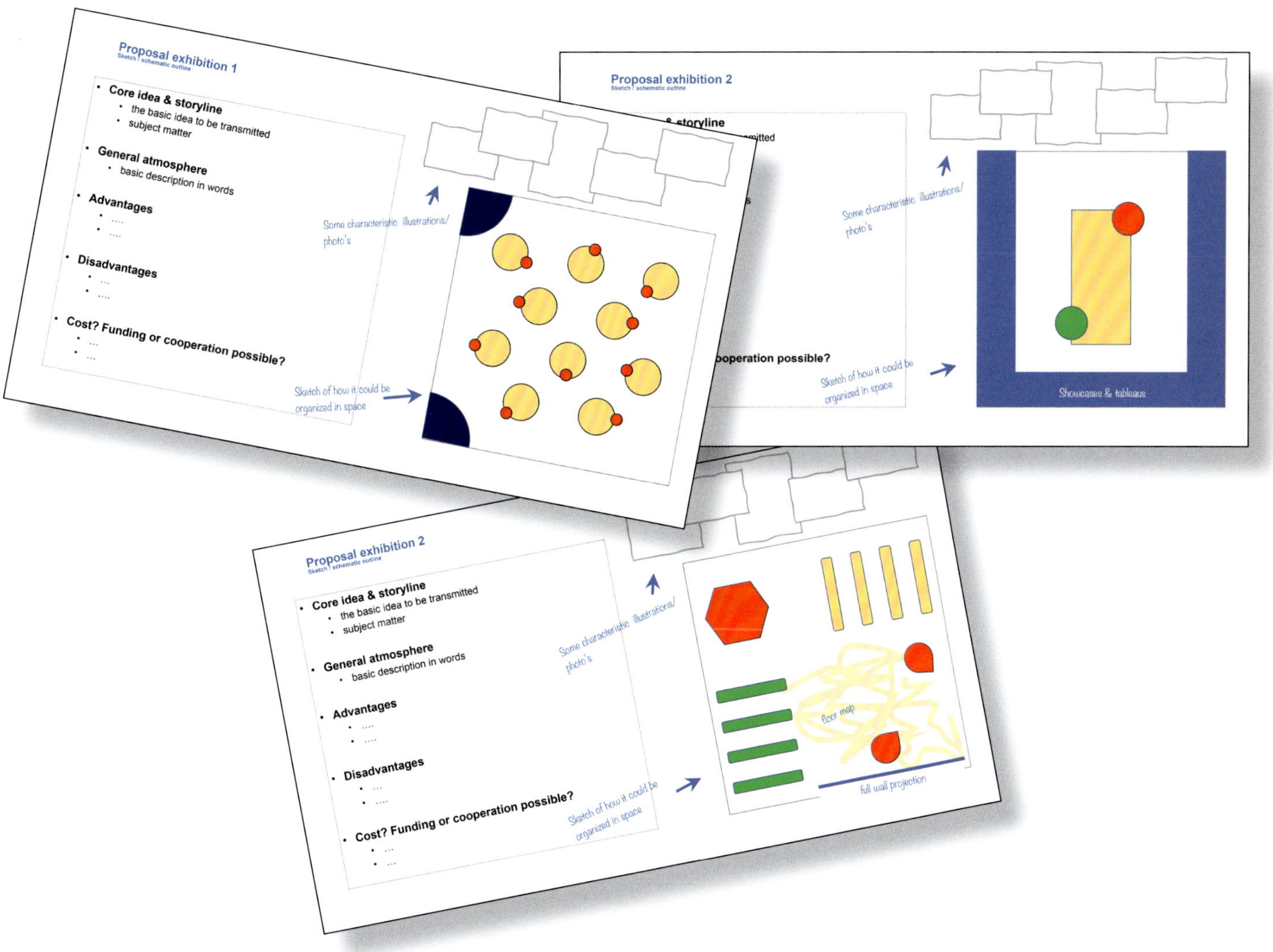

24.4. Step 8: Scoring options

Test with different stakeholders

The sketches – the portfolio of options you've made - is to be submitted to different groups. That applies, of course, to the exhibition team, but also to scientists / curators, the attendants, the educational service and the like. Whenever possible, depending on the size of the museum, each group has its own session, so there is a more distinctive judgement.

All options are briefly presented, titles with a sketchy drawing and description, in a slideshow, in two- three minutes per option maximum. They are subsequently scored by the participants, each on its own form. Questions are allowed, but no discussion. Try to get the mutual talking and influencing out. It is about each private, first primary feeling. So, each participant rates for himself, not consulting his neighbours.

Which parameters

The ones each evaluator has to score are:

- How attractive will it be to our audience? Does it have 'attracting power'?
- Does it fit our museum? Is the subject matter something which we feel natural and comfortable with?

Some other parameters might be, depending on the group:

- Would it be attractive to potential partners or civil organizations?
- Does it fit the school curricula?

Use a Likert scale

Scoring might best be done on a Likert scale, either a 5- or a 7-point one. The format of a typical five-level Likert item, for example, could be: (-2) Strongly disagree; (-1) Disagree; (0) Neither agree nor disagree, i.e. Neutral; (1) Agree; (2) Strongly agree,

The result

After the session all forms will be reworked into a spreadsheet and can be visualized in a graphic. This graphic is one of the most convincing tools for decisions.

-2 = not at all; -1 = no; 0 = neutral; 1 = yes; 2 = yes, very strongly so	**Will attract visitors**	**Fits our museum**	**.......**
Title 1			
2			
3			
4			
5			
6			
... etc			

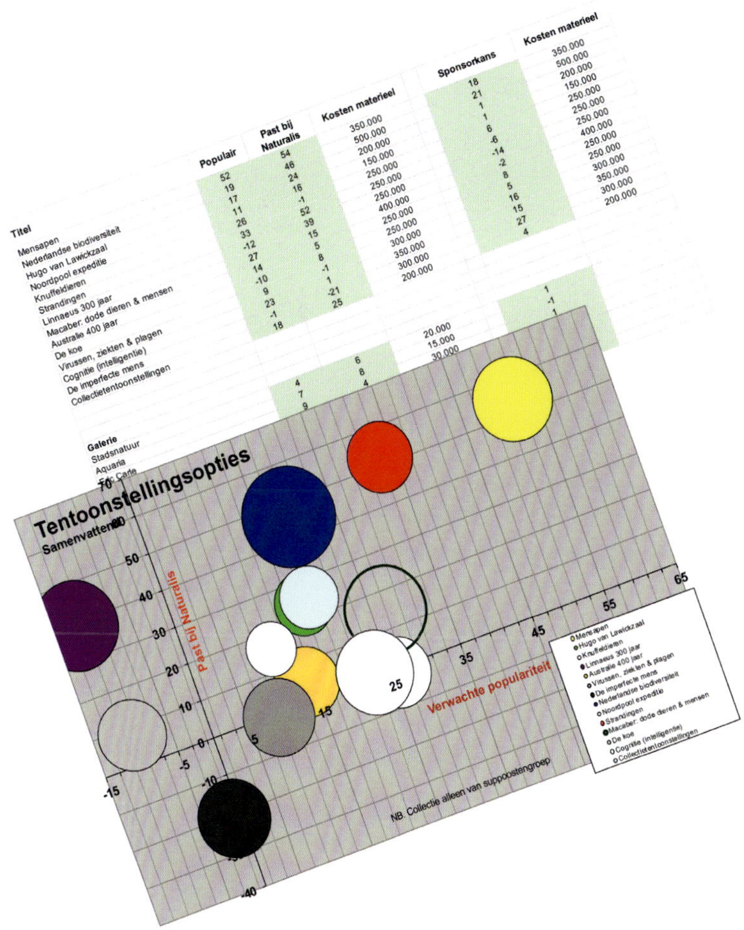

The graphic shown was the result of 2005 sessions. The x-axes is a (summoned) scale of the expected popularity. The y-axes the fit to the museum. The size of the circle indicates the expected cost.

The obvious choices – the yellow, red and blue – became the first exhibitions in the forthcoming years – each very successful too.

An interesting sideline: there were quite some differences in the evaluation by the different evaluation groups. We took special care evaluating those differences, and they were taken into account when the exhibitions went into development.

24.5 Step 8 addendum: Present previous results as a warm-up

It does help to present the results of the previous exhibitions before the assessment. Look at it this way. Almost all of the museum employees have an impression how successful a previous exhibition was. This often is a shared feeling within a group, not based on solid figures. It is not a sharp image. And it helps an evaluator, sometimes, to have these figures before judging the potentials of new titles.

What kind of figures you can present? There are the so-called 'hard' figures, which are visitor numbers and financial results.

The financials are the sum of income (number of visitors * average revenue per visitor entrance) versus costs, which are the material costs in the administration, including all the hiring. The costs of the private team are an estimation of the commitment * salary (including personnel costs). The result (blue in the tables) is the summation of costs and benefits.

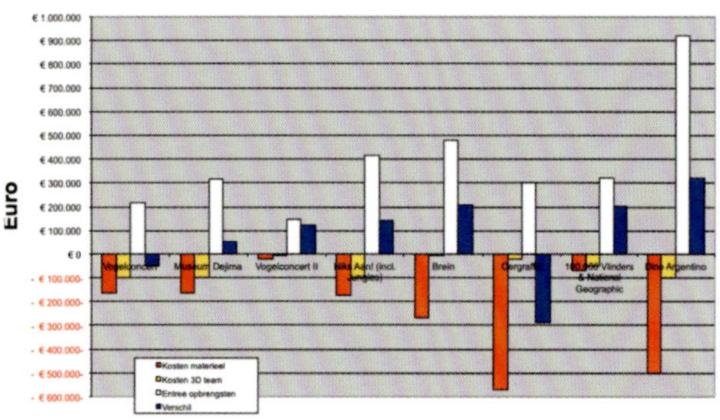

Of course, it is very rough and not entirely fair. There are no overheads taken into account, for example. And visitors come not only for a temporary exhibition. The weather conditions play a role. And an exhibition might be very successful in the visitors' appreciation, but do not score in the 'pull' to get them to the museum. The exhibition 'Bird Concert' in Naturalis for example, was very popular in its appreciation scores and visit duration but did not have much attracting power.

It is not exact. It comes down to getting a picture. The table from the early years of Naturalis was really an eye opener for all.

Exhibition	Material costs	Costs of the exhibition team	Income entrees	Financial result
1				
2				
3				
4				
5				
6				
7				
8				

24.6. Step 9: The final choices in the multi-annual planning

The final step is to choose the subject matters for the exhibitions and to fit them into the schedule, the empty multi-annual planning. Take into account the preparation time needed.

This final decision process is almost always done by the decisionmakers and the staff involved. This resulting final multi-annual planning then has to be shared with all.

The preparations for the first exhibition will then begin. The methodology to do so will be the subject of the next section.

Events

The choice of events could be done using this same toolset. You take into account how it would fit the exhibitions – or contrast it regarding other target groups.

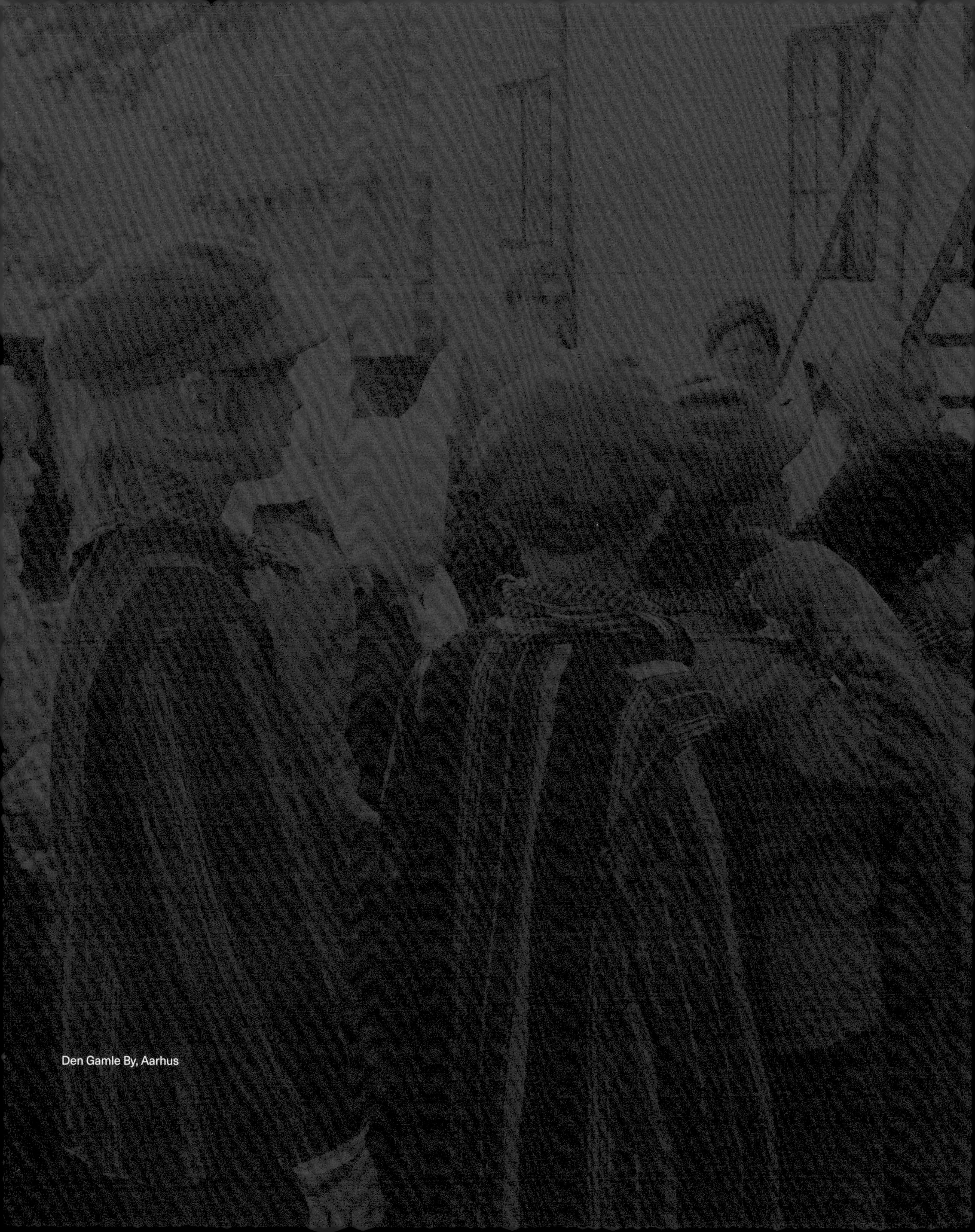

Den Gamle By, Aarhus

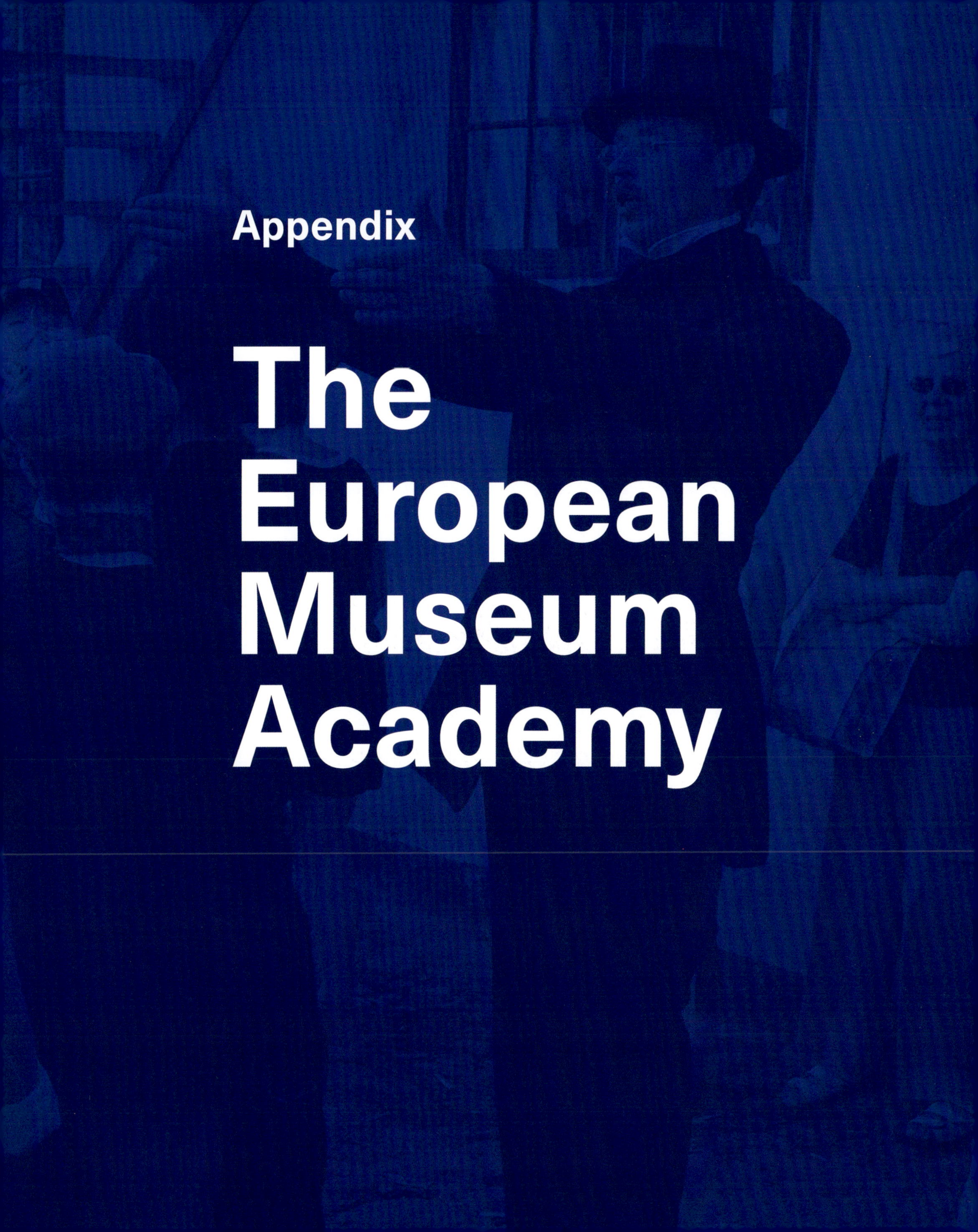

Appendix

The European Museum Academy

25. The European Museum Academy

http://europeanmuseumacademy.eu

25.1. The Academy

The Akademia historically was a school dedicated to Athena, the goddess of wisdom, outside the city walls of ancient Athens. Today an Academy is an institution of higher learning, research and honorary membership - where innovations are deeply discussed and widely validated.

We took it as an example. The European Museum Academy is an independent, international group of experienced European museum professionals since 2009. It is a large network, consisting of individual and organizational partners spread all over Europe and active in a variety of different areas of museum related issues.

As an academy it functions as a think-tank on the practice and future of museums. This is outlined in the European Museum Academy Awards and also in lectures and publications, some European projects, exchanges and teaching. As most of its members do work in museums and universities, its thinking is closely related to the practice and operations within the museological field.

As it is an European group – in the broadest sense, thus the Council of Europe states – it is meant to be inclusive to the diversity of European cultures. That alone is sufficient to realize that there is not such a thing as a single truth, working method or organizational setup. However, this cannot be an excuse for not taking the responsibility to formulate working hypotheses, to seek commonalities in thinking and working. That is what we do.

25.2. Some thoughts on networking the museum

As said, the context in which museums exist today is changing. And so, museums are too. That is nothing new in itself. Museums respond to the changing needs of society. That is: they change in their role, in their organizational setup, as well as in the techniques used to convey stories. This is true of all times, but there is no doubt however that we are now again amidst turbulent times. Everything changes with amazing speed. We don't live in an era of change, but in a change of era.[5] In every aspect of life there will be major changes, based on the globalized world with digital, sensor-based techniques. It is perfectly clear we are thus awaiting a revolution and upheaval in our museological world of storytelling and collecting too.

We do not think we exaggerate.

To be clear, we are not, by any means, pessimistic. Although these pandemic times shaked the world of museums to its foundations, the interest in museums and what they stand

Here are some more quotes from Kenneth Hudson

I have no general theories about how museums should be run, although I think I can observe certain changes and trends. Noticing these changes and developments certainly does not amount, for me, to acknowledging an academic subject called Museology, which I have defined as 'the science of museum organisation'. There is no such science, no set of rules by which museums operate and succeed, any more than there are rules for turning the English language into books that people want to read. People with flair and originality create good museums and good books. People without these qualities do not.
(Kenneth Hudson, 1997)

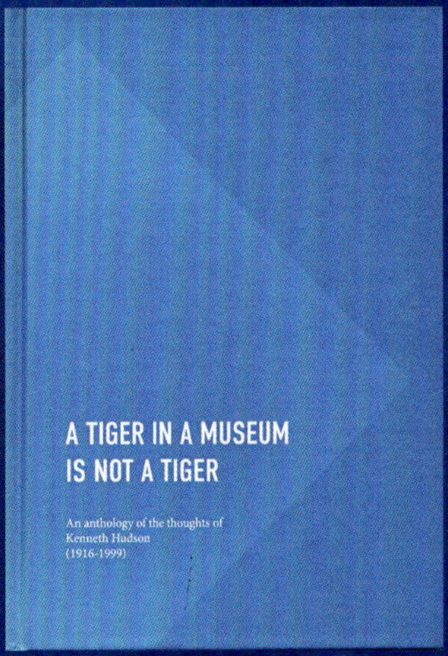

Kenneth Hudson (1916-1999) was a great museological thinker and the inspiration for founding EMA.

We are at last beginning to think of museums as centres of discussion and questions which help us to understand our lives and our environment, rather than as places where the past can be kept in safe storage and worshipped in prescribed ways.
(Kenneth Hudson, 1997)

You insist that museums must continue to be object-centred. This is my opinion, too. During the next twenty years there's going to be a great battle over the definition of a museum, between the object people and the computer enthusiastic. If the object people don't win, museums have no future.
(Kenneth Hudson, 1997)

You also mention 'charm and chairs' as essential characteristics of the successful museum, and very sensibly add 'children'. ... I understand that the museum has been a sensational failure, with plenty of chairs but no charm.
(Kenneth Hudson, 1997)

for – our common history and culture – is growing. The overall number of museums is still increasing, and though competition for visitors' leisure time is increasing – so many things to choose from – attendance numbers are actually sometimes quite staggering.
Then there is a growing awareness too in our local, regional and national history, with ever increasing numbers of groups researching their family and local history.
Museum life is not easy of course. Financial support often is really difficult. And due to the development of audio-visual and 3D-techniques, and the digital home-based experiences speed up by the lockdown, we have to find answers to the growing (visual and experience) story-telling expectations of society. There are also the ever-growing collections, mostly hidden in depots and it is too expensive to keep this accumulation going on in the same rate.

But all in all, as a branch, we do quite well. So where is the real challenge?
Well, we think for one that the growing sophistication of the visual and digital culture and digital 'life' in general, the public interest in historic events and 'cultural landscapes' as well as the enormous increase in the number of information sources, are impacting the museum's role in the cultural landscape. We will have to find answers to acquire real relevance.
And there is where a platform like the European Museum Academy steps in. To discuss, exchange and award good examples.

25.3. The Awards and its ceremonies as platforms for exchanging ideas

Awards do have a function. They are like 'signalling flags'. They put inspiring examples into the light. And that means different examples, from museums all over Europe. It is not so much about the winners, it is about seeing, discussing, thinking all kind of approaches and results. The more and the more diverse, the better. So, there are several awards, on different topics.

Luigi Micheletti Award

The Luigi Micheletti Award focus on innovative museums / exhibitions of 20th century history, of science, technology, industry, science centres, ecomuseums, or interpretation centres. There is a special interest in new museological ideas and/or practices and on the impact of a museum on the local, regional, national and international scene. The Award is supported by the Fondazione Luigi Micheletti, a research centre on contemporary history, and specialized on collecting and spreading material and immaterial heritage of the 20th and 21st centuries.

DASA Award

The basic criteria of this award are more educational: the quality of the storyline, the learning opportunities, the creativity of the exhibition design and the programming of educational activities. Specific attention is also given to personal mediation, the interactive participation of the public and an effective mix of education and entertainment. The DASA Award is supported by the DASA Museum in Dortmund.

EMA Prize

The EMA prize is a once-in-a-while prize and decided by the Board of the Academy when a museum, an individual or a cultural institution is of outstanding quality, impact or approach. It has been established with the aim of recognizing the outstanding results of organisations, researchers and cultural institutions in creating pioneering museums or producing studies and carrying on projects of European relevance which are destined to influence the development of museological discourse at the international level.

Children in Museums Award

The Children in Museums Award is a joint venture between Hands On! International and the European Museum Academy. The judges are on the look-out for creative and innovative exhibitions and programmes for the age group up to 14 years old. The judges not only value creativity and innovation, but also consider the ways in which an exhibition or programme can change the course of museum thinking or museum practice, nationally as well as internationally. How can elements of the winning exhibition or programme be incorporated into the museum field? That is why the judges pay special attention to interpretation and presentation.

Heritage in Motion Award

The Heritage in Motion Award was launched by Europa Nostra and the European Museum Academy to gather the best multimedia products and achievements. It is an annual competition for the creators of films, games, apps and websites on themes related to Europe's heritage, cultural and natural, tangible and intangible. Heritage in Motion grants awards and celebrates the best multimedia achievements and products, through varied, creative and innovative means, in order to draw attention to the value of Europe's cultural and natural heritage in all its facets.

Museums in Short Award

The Museums in Short awards recognize the value of short films in disseminating museums' contents in an engaging and direct way. The Award is promoted by the European Museum Academy (EMA), the Fondazione Brescia Musei and Cinema Nuovo Eden and Musil – Museum of Industry and Labour - in collaboration with ICOM Italia. The contest is open to all the different forms of videos produced by museums. In particular the Museums in Short awards will be delivered to the best short films (max. 10 min.) conceived to promote museums or their activities and films used in permanent or temporary exhibitions

Master Study of the Year Award

The European Museum Academy Master Study of the Year Award was launched by EMA in 2019. The aim is to promote high quality in research by master students in universities in Europe within relevant courses and subjects for museums.

Art Museum Award – New Ideas for the 21st Century

The Art Museum Award is dedicated to esteem groundbreaking projects that are dealing with art or art interventions in museums or galleries – inspirational projects that think and act outside the box and prove social relevance. The award seeks to enhance core values like dialogue, accessibility, participation, inclusion, openness and awareness.
The Art Museum Award is supported by and co-organised with the A.G. Leventis Foundation.

The Živa Award: an Award of the Forum of Slavic Culture

The Živa Award (from the Slavic goddess Živa representing life, fertility and such) has been established by the Forum of Slavic Culture member countries. The European Museum Academy is involved in the jury.
The Award is meant to recognize excellence in the sector of movable and immovable heritage in a special region in Europe, promote the best practices in the tangible cultural heritage and also to stimulate exchanges of knowledge and experience throughout the member countries and beyond.

25.4. Training programmes, projects and publications

As it is a crucial aspect of our mission to share knowledge and promote training in the museum field at the European level, EMA is actively involved since its inception in training programmes. At the moment three courses in Museology are developed under the auspices of EMA:

- the Executive Master Course in European Museology at International University of Languages and Media (IULM) of Milan.
- the Online Master Course in Museology New Media and Museums
- the International Summer School of Museology promoted by the Forum of Slavic Cultures at the Piranova Research Centre in Piran, Slovenia.

EMA supports also courses organized in Östersund (Sweden) by the Nordic Centre of Heritage Learning and Creativity (NCK) in collaboration with the Research Centre for Museums and Galleries (RCMG) at the University of Leicester's School of Museum Studies. And, it is partner of the State University of Padua for the Erasmus Mundus course 'Techniques Patrimoine Territoires de l'Industrie' (TPTI).

More and more the European Museum Academy is involved in European projects, mainly by adding the knowledge and experiences of its many members.

On the level of publications: there have been quite some articles by some of the EMA-group. And EMA was involved in publications by others. However, there has not been an EMA publication platform yet. This book might be a first step in organizing one.

26. Acknowledgements and authors

26.1. On this methodology and its history

As we said before, there is no such thing as a single truth, the best working method or one-and-only organizational setup. There are more ways to organize your process. However, taking into account differences across museums and cultures, including linguistic ones, there is much in common too. The methodology as described in this book, especially its backbone, will be recognized by many.

As stated in this book, this methodology has its own history. It is based on the work in the 1990s at Naturalis, the National Museum of Natural History in Leiden, The Netherlands. It had its starting point however in the work of the Chicago Field Museum (the late Janet Kamien, Geoffrey Grove and their team, Jeff Hayward) when they taught the Naturalis team 'how to organize the work'. And as important, there was the structured methodology developed by Han Meeter at the Reinwardt Academy (Museum Studies). In Naturalis they were combined and developed during the years, by the team at the time, most noticeable Wim Gertenaar, Peter Zuure, Wim Tamboer, Manon Laterveer-de Beer, HansJorg Ahrens, Floor Verbiest, Piet Staffeleu, René Malherbe, and Erik Jan Elderman.
The methodology served for building a completely new museum as well as many temporary exhibitions. An earlier version was described (2008) in Mastering a Museum Plan, complemented, honed by and co-written with Vanda Vitali of The Natural History Museum of Los Angeles County.

European Museum Academy

The methodology has since been elaborated further. The experiences in the Executive Master Course in European Museology at the IULM University of Milan were of great help, as they merged so to say into the core as described. Although the master course also has an academic and philosophical side to it, the practical experiences were quite similar, and so they fitted in easily. Then there were the experiences as well as the contributions by European Museum Academy members.

The experiences and exchanges in the European Museum Academy meetings made us aware that this methodology deserved to be shared and extended by sharing it in our community, practising as well as asking for new and improved tools and ideas. It does suit the purposes of the Academy perfectly, as we are a place of exchange, learning and sharing, awarding, researching and experimenting. So, we have invested a lot of time and money to have this book written and sent out into the museum world.

26.2. Acknowledgements

Yes, we did write the book as individuals within our European Museum Academy setting. But as we explained, there was a shared history, with earlier contributions by many others.

Then, some helped us enormously. Like **Frans Schouten**, a former museum academy director, a teacher, a visiting professor and above all an expert in the field where museums, heritage and tourism meet. He wrote a chapter on sites, extended the chapter on storylines and thoroughly helped us in the reasoning in the book. As did **Wim van der Weiden**, amidst several major directorships one of the founders of EMA, who meticulously helped us in the explanations and reasoning too. Wim was also a driving force as he truly believes in sharing experiences.

Then there are some supporting and critical co-readers, for which we have to name especially Manon Laterveer-de Beer, Elia Vlachou, René Capovin, Damiët Schneeweisz, Emek Yilmaz, Dick Heijdra, Han Meeter, Karl Murr, Henrik Zipsane and Johan Heeffer, who all contributed with suggestions, critical notes, and new ideas. And surely there is Ann Nicholls, who helped us keep our language understandable and battled 'Americanisms'.

26.3. The authors

Massimo Negri

Massimo decided the European Museum Academy should have a book on methodology. His extensive knowledge of the field, his experience in temporary exhibitions and in the set-up of some ten new museums - combined with the experiences of his post-graduate students - made him fully aware there was a critical lack of tools and methods, resulting in a lot of frustration, errors and energy leaks in many processes. And as the EMA strives to improve the quality of museums, the EMA should take the initiative. Being a practitioner, teacher and museologist, he turned to Dirk Houtgraaf for joining forces in doing so.

For the formal part: Massimo Negri, EMA Scientific Director. He is also the Scientific Director of the Executive Master in European Museology at the International University of Languages and Media (IULM) of Milan. He also teaches Museography at the Erasmus Mundus Course on Industrial Heritage within the Course of History, Faculty of Letters and Philosophy, of the State University of Padua. He was the former Director of the European Museum Forum (1999-2009) and one of the founders of the European Museum Academy. In 1993 he was awarded the Cross of Officer of the Orden de Isabel la Catòlica by the King of Spain.

Dirk Houtgraaf

Dirk thinks in building blocks, strategic perspectives and logical systems. His main goal is to understand and then to visualize systems and processes for educational purposes. Being a behavioural biologist and strategic marketing expert, he has made extensive educational exhibitions and used this type of thinking in books such as 'Business models' (Dutch) and 'Mastering a Museum Plan: Strategies for Exhibit Development' (English). So, Massimo's quest and broad perspective definitely touched a spot.

Dirk Houtgraaf worked for many years as leader of the exhibition development team of the new Naturalis museum at the time and became director of Public Services, Vice-President and interim President afterwards. He supervised the permanent exhibitions and something like 150 temporary exhibitions. He is currently working at the Cultural Heritage Agency of the Netherlands - an Agency of the Dutch Ministry of Culture, Education and Science - as strategic advisor and focused on information strategies and on positioning and branding in not-profit organizations. The Agency, an institute of knowledge workers, policy makers and administering subsidies, is focused on supporting the Dutch cultural heritage field.

27. Supporters of this publication

Cultural Heritage Agency of the Netherlands

The Cultural Heritage Agency is the Netherlands› centre of expertise for heritage. The motto is to give the future a – recognisable – past and the past a future.
The Agency is an executive body of the Ministry for Education, Culture and Science. It is a unique combination of expertise and information services, advisors and consultants, policy preparation, laboratory services and subsidy processes.

The Cultural Heritage Agency is to support the workers, organizations and policies in several domains of cultural heritage. Its tasks go beyond merely preserving and protecting historical buildings, sites and works of art. Culture and cultural heritage do have an important economic and societal impact. From that perspective, an open exchange of knowledge, methodologies and experiences is therefore exactly what the Agency stands for.

Reinwardt Academy / Applied Museum & Heritage Studies

The Reinwardt Academy, part of the Amsterdam University of the Arts, is an internationally renowned school of cultural heritage in the lively, historic and museum-rich centre of Amsterdam. The Academy offers a bachelor›s programme in Cultural Heritage (taught in Dutch) and an English-taught master›s programme in Applied Museum & Heritage Studies.

The Reinwardt Academy strives to be one of the foremost knowledge, research, and training centres in this domain, where established as well as future cultural heritage professionals, from all over the world, can exchange knowledge, share inspiring ideas and develop innovative professional products.

Forum of Slavic Cultures (FSC)

The Forum of Slavic Cultures is an international foundation which unites more than 300 million Slavs in 13 Slavic countries. In 15 years the Foundation has become a referential platform of intercultural dialogue as well as took over the role of a key hub of Slavic countries in the fields of art and culture, education and science and cultural tourism. FSC creates opportunities for presentation and promotion of Slavic heritage in the international arena and building an intercultural dialogue by seeking and involving like-minded partners. One of the most fruitful is the long-term cooperation with the EMA, reflected in many common projects and activities.

A. G. Leventis Foundation & Gallery

The A. G. Leventis Foundation is the outcome of the vision of the Cypriot entrepreneur Anastasios G. Leventis (1902-1978), who laid the bases of its focus on society, education and culture. Now in its fourth decade, the Foundation retains its adherence to these priorities, keenly supporting the dissemination of Greek and Cypriot cultural heritage, as well as extensive public benefits programs, pioneering environmental protection projects, and medical research worldwide.

An important aspect of the dynamic presence of the A. G. Leventis Foundation in cultural affairs is the Foundation's art collections: the Paris Collection of European Art, the Collection of Works by Greek Artists of the 19th and 20th Centuries, the Collection of Works by Cypriot Artists, and the Gold Coins Collection. These four collections, which afford a unique aesthetic and educational experience, are united and housed in the new A. G. Leventis Gallery in Nicosia, designed by Feilden Clegg Bradley Studios, Architects, which opened its doors to the public in 2014.

University of Padua / Master Course Erasmus Mundus TPTI

The Course of Museography of Industrial Heritage at the State University of Padua is developed in the context of the TPTI Master Course, one of the most prestigious and long-standing post graduate courses funded by the European Union. It is meant for heritage professionals from all over the world, to enhance their skills and focus on new concepts.
TPTI is carried on together with Paris 1 Panthéon-Sorbonne, Universidade de Evora, Universidad de Alicante, Polytechnic of Praga and other important academic institutions. The European Museum Academy Foundation is an associate partner since its inception.

28. References

1 See: http://www.platformexhibitions.org/?lang=en for an in-depth description of the exhibition planning process.
2 There are many books on organizing projects, building timelines and so on. Up to you if you like to go there. We think however reading some works of Eliyahu M. Goldratt will be of real help.
3 In describing this chapter, we acknowledge much of the do-it-yourself principles and structure we were taught by Jeff Hayward's company People, Places & Design Research.
4 See also the book '*Managing Indoor Climate Risks in Museums*' by Bart Ankersmit and Marc Stappers, both working at the Cultural Heritage Agency, Netherlands.
5 A fundamental look at change is Jan Rotmans: Change of Era, Uitgeverij Boom, November 2017

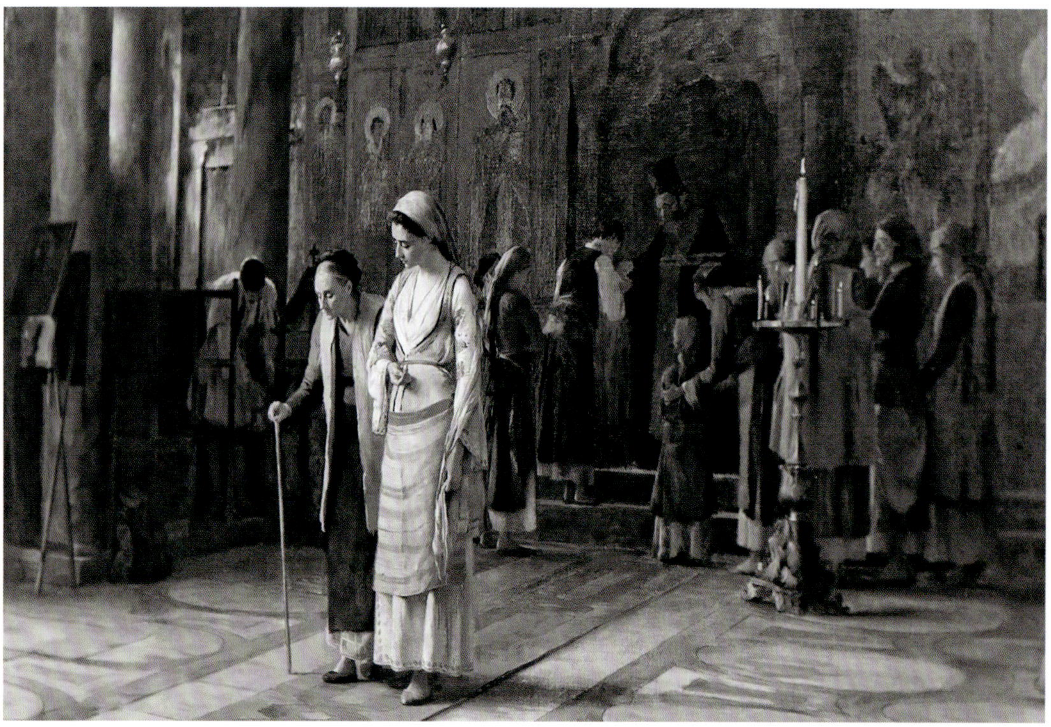

After The Service, Theodoros Rallis, A.G. Leventis Gallery, Nicosia

Addendum:
A case study of storyline development for a series of sites: The Roman Limes

Heritage sites are to be seen as places which have a lot in common with museums, especially in the way of interpreting and communicating to the public. The methodology can be applied to both. Where do we stand, however, when it comes to a series of sites? How to deal with them? An example.

Frans Schouten

Storylines can be developed diachronically, through time, on one location. It then describes *what happened here through time*. The emphasis will in those cases be on the different layers of habitation of a site, a biography of the landscape if you like. This is what you see most, at sites. The story unfolds at the spot and there often is no more than some modest notice on how it fits within a bigger story.

It becomes more difficult when a storyline encompasses one historical period in geographically different locations, and especially so when your site is one of many 'markers' in a bigger story, but as such is not a spectacular site in itself. In this appendix we discuss an example of the latter.

In this appendix we discuss a storyline developed for an archaeological-tourism project regarding The Limes, the frontier of the Roman Empire in The Netherlands, which followed the delta of the great West-European rivers, which constitute most of the Low Countries.

A frontier of military strongholds and centres of population

In The Netherlands this Roman frontier followed the ancient course of the river Rhine. On the European continent this frontier stretched from the North Sea through Germany, Austria and Hungary till Constanta in Romania to the shore of the Black Sea.
Across the North Sea The Limes continues in Hadrian's Wall at the border between England and Scotland.

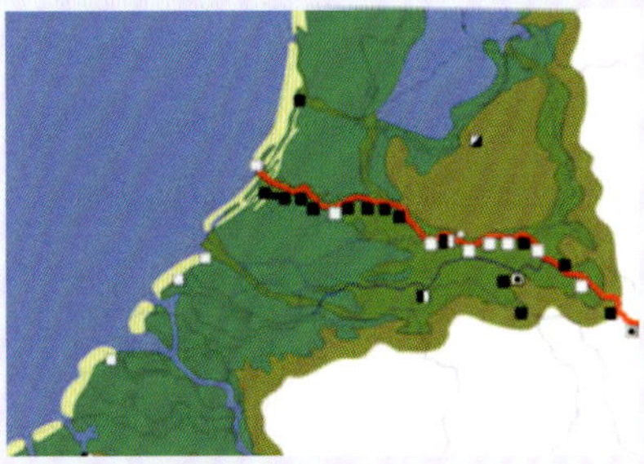

The Roman Limes is not a fixed and stable line. Particularly in The Netherlands the dynamics of the ever-changing flow of water in the delta makes it hard to pinpoint the geographical position of the Limes exactly.

Due to this ever-changing landscape The Limes in The Netherlands is, unlike Hadrian's Wall, not a dominant feature in the environment, but a feature hidden in the soil of which occasionally an aspect becomes visible.

We know most of its centres of population, military strongholds and parts of the connecting infrastructure through archaeological surveys. However big parts of the Limes are most literately "terra incognita".

Unknown to the public and thus to the local authorities

For the public at large The Limes is unknown due to the absence of physical remains of this period, which results in insufficient attention from the fragile remains that are still to be discovered in the soil. The challenge was to make the fragile remains of The Limes as visible as possible in order to raise the awareness of the public at large and of local authorities for the need to preserve this unique archaeological feature.

Three objectives were to be achieved by the State Archaeological Survey in cooperation with the provincial authorities:

- Coordinate the mapping of the area of The Limes
- Design an integrated land-use plan for The Limes
- Improve the public awareness of The Limes through interpretation and recreational and tourism initiatives – and have
- the Limes as a more 'visible' feature in the landscape.

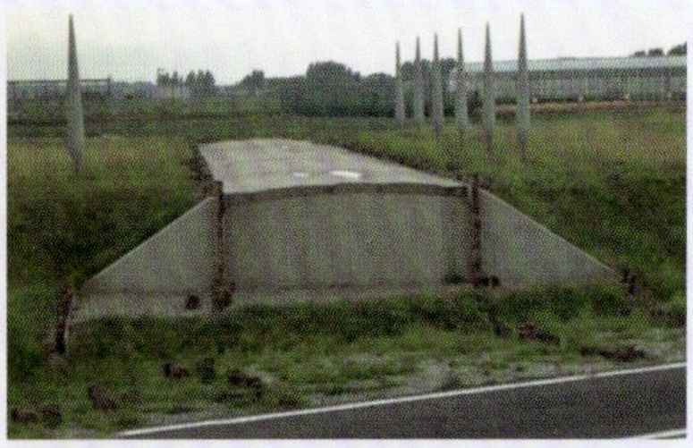

Reconstruction of Roman road in The Limes near the ancient course of the Rhine.

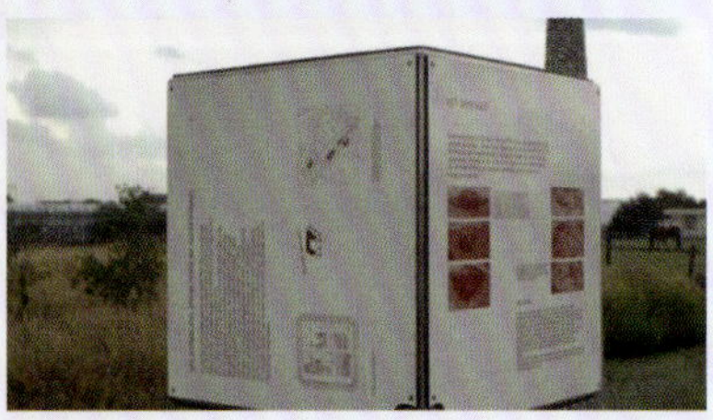

Information panel at the Roman road. Note that part of the text is turned, the cube can be turned around the pole.

Improve the public awareness

We present here an overview of the proposals developed for the interpretation of The Limes for the public, using the technique of storytelling in the product development.

As mentioned earlier there are virtually no remains of the Roman period preserved in the terrain, so we have to rely on secondary means like reconstructions and signing to visualise this part of history. Moreover, many of the indicated areas are almost identical with no distinctive features, at the sites there is a limited use of interpretative techniques possible, the accessibility is badly organised, as sign posting is either non-existent, inadequate, or inconsistent.

We decided on putting the focus on The Limes as a flexible border of the Roman Empire, consisting of:

1. Military strongholds;
2. Connecting infrastructures;
3. Population (and trading) centres.

The archaeological remains often could be addressed to one of those three components.

Given this baseline, the following limited amount of core themes about The Limes will be presented:

1. Defence and attack (connected to military strongholds);
2. Transport (infrastructure);
3. Living and working (population centres);
4. Government (population centres);
5. Believe systems (population centres).

Modular based developing

These five core themes, allied to the three site remains, made it possible to come up with one core story, and different underlying themes to be singled out at a certain site. The connecting line would be The Limes as a border, while having each specific site a small paragraph in the larger themes and story.

These themes offer some strategic advances:

- A flexible system for different sites to establish their own storyline. It stimulates relations between sites and themes, and makes them at the same time distinct from each other;
- A structure that connects the different sites;
- It provides directions for marketing and promotion efforts;
- It gives focus and inspiration to efforts of developing attractions along The Limes.

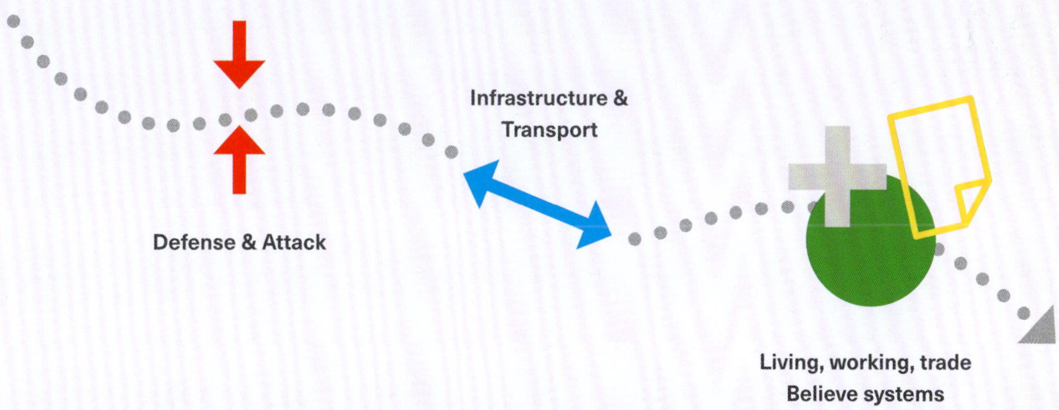

Overview of the themes and storylines for The Limes

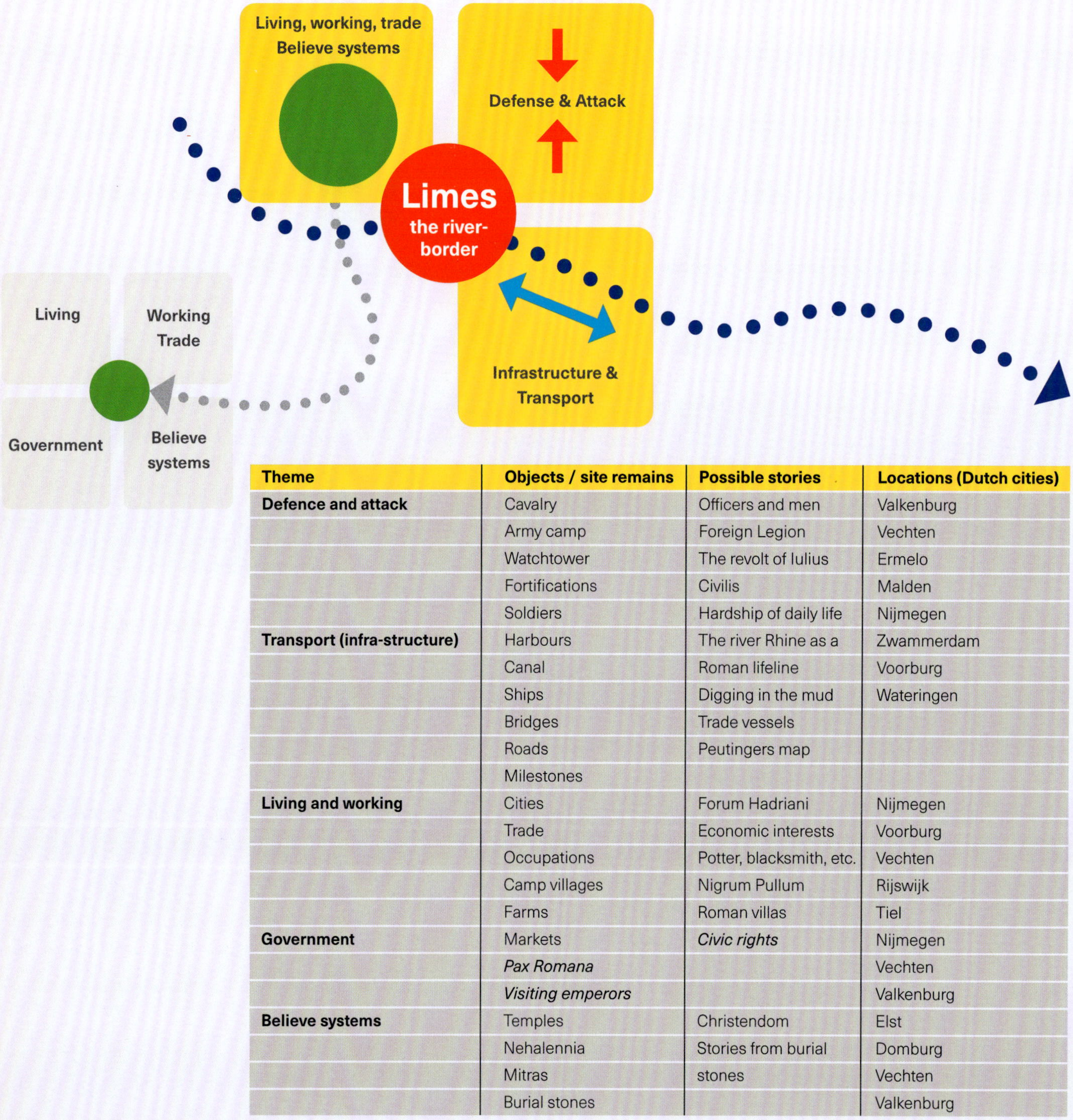

Theme	Objects / site remains	Possible stories	Locations (Dutch cities)
Defence and attack	Cavalry	Officers and men	Valkenburg
	Army camp	Foreign Legion	Vechten
	Watchtower	The revolt of Iulius	Ermelo
	Fortifications	Civilis	Malden
	Soldiers	Hardship of daily life	Nijmegen
Transport (infra-structure)	Harbours	The river Rhine as a	Zwammerdam
	Canal	Roman lifeline	Voorburg
	Ships	Digging in the mud	Wateringen
	Bridges	Trade vessels	
	Roads	Peutingers map	
	Milestones		
Living and working	Cities	Forum Hadriani	Nijmegen
	Trade	Economic interests	Voorburg
	Occupations	Potter, blacksmith, etc.	Vechten
	Camp villages	Nigrum Pullum	Rijswijk
	Farms	Roman villas	Tiel
Government	Markets	*Civic rights*	Nijmegen
	Pax Romana		Vechten
	Visiting emperors		Valkenburg
Believe systems	Temples	Christendom	Elst
	Nehalennia	Stories from burial	Domburg
	Mitras	stones	Vechten
	Burial stones		Valkenburg

It is important to emphasise that the themes and storylines are not a straitjacket but must be viewed as an assistant to bring cohesion into the information on offer at various locations. It is important for visitors to experience an integrated offer of provisions and experiences that make the fragile and rare remains of the past both physically and intellectually accessible.

Signs and signing at the different spots

There are several ways in which the storylines can be communicated to the visitors.

Information panels

On most archaeological sites information panels are available for visitors. The information is in most cases very factual. If graphics are used, it is in most cases for layout plans and maps instead of reconstruction drawings of impressions of the landscape in the past. Working with themes and storylines greatly enhances this well-tested method of information transmission.

Mile stones

Replicas of Roman milestones as signposts along cycling- and footpaths can enhance the visitor experience and will provide a sense of place. It could also be a connecting element along The Limes to link the different sites together in a pattern.

Reconstructions and virtual reconstructions

Reconstructions provide great interpretation resources for visitors. In an area of newly built houses, a sauna will be built on the site and in the style of a Roman bathhouse. Many archaeological discoveries have been made whilst digging for new building sites. Using the different layers of archaeological remains as orientation devices inside the parking lot provides both a better atmosphere as well as a quick insight into the past of the place. Modern technology gives us the opportunity for new interpretative media on historical sites. In Ename in Belgium reconstructions of the different periods of the archaeological site can be seen on location on demand on a computer screen.

Video

Recordings of archaeological digs can be built in as a permanent feature on the site, even in the pavement in a city centre. A variation on the video is the peeping window – a mini diorama – that everywhere can be built into a wall. Such a device can give the visitor an unexpected view into the past of a place.

Viewpoints

At many locations in the landscape it is possible to build viewpoints which enable the visitors to have an overview of the terrain. It is technically not too difficult to install telescopes, which instead of the actual image give an historical image of different periods on demand, also in a 360° perspective.

Colophon

Published by European Museum Academy &
Waanders Publishers, Zwolle

Distributed by Waanders Publishers

Authors:
Dirk Houtgraaf, Massimo Negri

Advisors:
Frans Schouten, Wim van der Weiden

Design:
Frank de Wit

Printing:
Wilco Art Books, Amersfoort

Developing exhibitions: There is a method in this madness / Dirk Houtgraaf and Massimo Negri

ISBN 978 94 6262 306 4
NUR 657